"Guterl focuses much of the story on himself and his closest siblings, Bear and Bug, and on the realities of growing up in a big family. But he is clear-eyed about his privilege, even within his family, and about his parents who, with the best of intentions, have the whiff of white saviors."   —*Booklist*

"Guterl, professor of Africana studies and American studies at Brown University and author of *Seeing Race in America*, fashions a moving, elegant memoir of his childhood within the 'idealized experiment' of multiracialism. . . . An earnestly felt, beautifully wrought story of an American family in all its complexity."

—*Kirkus Reviews*, starred review

"With precision and unwavering care, Guterl explores the ethics involved in his parents' endeavor and confronts the consequences of even the best intentions. The result is an eye-opening, instructional, and necessary take on race in America."   —*Publishers Weekly*

Also by Matthew Pratt Guterl

Josephine Baker and the Rainbow Tribe

Seeing Race in Modern America

Skinfolk

A MEMOIR

Matthew Pratt Guterl

LIVERIGHT PUBLISHING CORPORATION

A Division of W. W. Norton & Company

Independent Publishers Since 1923

For information about permission to reproduce selections from this book,
write to Permissions, Liveright Publishing Corporation, a division of
W. W. Norton & Company, Inc., 500 Fifth Avenue, New York, NY 10110

For information about special discounts for bulk purchases, please contact
W. W. Norton Special Sales at specialsales@wwnorton.com or 800-233-4830

Manufacturing by Lakeside Book Company
Book design by Marysarah Quinn
Production manager: Anna Oler

ISBN 978-1-324-09449-4 pbk.

Liveright Publishing Corporation, 500 Fifth Avenue, New York, N.Y. 10110
www.wwnorton.com

W. W. Norton & Company Ltd., 15 Carlisle Street, London W1D 3BS

1 2 3 4 5 6 7 8 9 0

For Sandi, for our children,
for my siblings, and for Mom.
For all found family. For Bob.

All my skinfolk ain't kinfolk.

—ZORA NEALE HURSTON

Note to readers

Naming one's siblings in a memoir is a fraught enterprise. There is also a certain delicacy of naming in any account of an adoptive family, where assigned birth names were erased (but not forgotten), and where new names and new subject positions were conjured out of thin air to manufacture a sense of family. Names also change as people grow up, as we take on new identities, as we are reborn or remade. In this work, then, I have proceeded carefully. I use a mix of birth names, nicknames, and adoptive names, depending on sibling preference and history.

"Memories," Joan Didion once wrote, "are what you no longer want to remember." These are my memories. Even where I quote my siblings or my mother, the story is mine alone. They would each tell it differently, asking their own questions and seeking other conclusions. That is to be expected and welcomed, for they surely have other things they wish to forget.

Preface

A young white couple sit patiently in two mid-century chairs, waiting for their chance to make history. The man is lean, tall, and dark haired, with a slight, expectant smile on his face. The woman is blonde with blue eyes, her hair swept back over her shoulders in a late 1960s sort of way. They are in a crowded, dimly lit waiting area, surrounded by strangers, some of whom are seated in a long row of those same chairs while others mill about. The young couple cling to each other nervously, making small talk. An hour builds, and they watch as anonymous strangers pass them by or swirl around them. Like everyone else in the space, they are anticipating something remarkable, something life changing, something wild and radical. The man leans forward, his hands clenched in his lap. He absentmindedly twists his wedding ring. Her eyes focus on a doorway, on a door, and on a doorknob, watching for even the slightest turn or a rattle, for some sign that the gray metal portal is about to sweep open and reveal their destiny.

It is 1972. The scene is JFK International Airport, a place famous for arrivals and departures. They had each been to Queens when they were younger. Independently and with their parents, and only a few years before that night at the airport—before, as well, they meet, date, and get married—they are among the millions standing before the Unisphere at the 1964 World's Fair. Like many, they are awed by the massive, 140-foot-tall sculpture of the planet, and are beguiled by the fair's catchy slogan, "Peace through Understanding," suggesting that as the world gets smaller, it might also grow more collegial. There is a striking Disney exhibit at the fair, later turned into the centerpiece of Disneyworld, into a soft-drink slogan, into a national wish. "It's a Small World, After All" features a boat tour around the globe, an introduction to children on every continent, singing together about the dazzling interconnections of a planet, and celebrating the idea that, under the technicolored skin tones and beneath the ethnic dress, everyone is the same. The Unisphere and the Disney exhibit are inspiring, but the two young white people both leave troubled. Change, they know, isn't merely an advertising catchphrase; it demands planning, intention, and action. The World's Fair sticks with them. When they meet for the first time a few years later as young adults, they bond over their global concerns and discover a common desire to build a better world.

At the airport, the couple turn their attention to the small group of adults circling them. Most are pacing, a reflection of their anxiety, which seems to course through the space. The strangers are all paired off, sharing a common role as prospective parents, which is what brings them to this lonely side of the airport. Some are older and some are younger, but all are coupled. No one is here alone. No one has brought a grandparent or another child. All are white.

The doorknob finally turns. In a burst of activity, the Jetway doors swing open and a gaggle of children enter the terminal. Some walk hand in hand with smiling stewardesses, those recognizable icons of the decade. The tiny fingers of the children are curled inside the older hand of their minder. Some are infants, half asleep or with their eyes wide open, and are swaddled and carried by stern and serious adoption agents, who survey the prospective parents with a judging eye. Some walk on their own, old enough to be independent. These older children seem afraid, or nervous, or excited, or all of these things at once. None of the children are white. All come from Korea. For a moment, the flood of children pauses. The two groups face each other. The adults in the waiting room crane their necks, clasping their hands together in anticipation. And then, one by one, with patience and attention to detail, the line breaks. The stewardesses and agents hustle here and there, clipboards in hand, to ensure that every Asian child is delivered to

Sheryl holding our brother Bug at JFK airport in 1972.

their new white parents. Identification is checked and double-checked. Papers are signed. Handshakes are offered and accepted.

The young woman with the blonde hair finds herself cradling an infant wearing a red, white, and blue jumper. She gazes with wonderment in her eyes. The young man bends down, laughs, and wags a finger playfully in front of the child. Suddenly and happily, they are oblivious to everyone else and awestruck.

The emotions of the couple echo widely in the room. The quiet nervousness in the space has been replaced by animated conversation, punctuated by gestures that are meant to bridge a stark language gap. Tears run down faces. In almost every case, this is the very first meeting of child and parents, and there is a shock of the embrace, of the tactile memory that is created when you physically hold on to a person for the first time, when you first touch their skin. As the chorus of introductions crests, a photographer bobs and weaves through the crowd, the shutter on his camera clicking audibly and the flash blooming repeatedly. And then, suddenly and all at once, each of these newly expanded families departs for the exits, leaving the antiseptic space of the airport, that row of plastic chairs, and the metal door to the Jetway. In groups of three, they make their way out into the night, toward some version of home.

It is late at night, and this is just the beginning. In two dozen homes in the tri-state region, there are other family members waiting for a grander embrace. There are banners hung over fireplaces, reading "Welcome!" There are casseroles and potato chips out for everyone. There are aunts and uncles pulling back the curtain, watching for the family car to pull up the driveway, readying for another round of embraces, of tears, of animated gestures, anticipating the haptic souvenirs forged when skin meets skin. It will be a long while before everyone—children included—is asleep.

The tall, dark-haired man and the blonde, blue-eyed woman and their infant son from Korea head for the parking lot. They have many hours of driving ahead of them. It is almost morning when they pull up to the white house with the white picket fence where they have made a home.

This is their story—our story, the story of a large, multiracial adopted family assembled in suburban New Jersey in the middle of the Cold War. It is a story that begins with the conception of a beneficent idea by an idealistic young couple. The two handsome young people are Bob and Sheryl, our parents. And the child in their arms is Bug, our brother, whose life began in Korea. They bring Bug home that night, driving for hours along the Belt Parkway, through Staten Island—back to me, into New Jersey. There are many origin points in our story, but that endless, white-knuckled car ride home from the airport is a clear one, a foundational moment that hews closely to the prevailing narrative of adoption, where generous white parents open their hearts and their homes to less fortunate children of color, orphaned by war, famine, or some combination of disastrous circumstances, and draw them into the American way.

Our story upends the conventions of that narrative. In the end, there are six of us, a live cliché. I am born in the summer of 1970, the white "first child" with blond hair and blue eyes. Bug—a nickname so old that it has no genesis that we can recall—is our first adoptive addition, but not our last. Mark, another biological white son, is born in 1973. Two years later, we adopt Bear, a mixed-race, Black-Asian child brought out of Saigon. He is days older than me, and just barely five years old when he arrives, having celebrated his birthday in the bowels of a military transport plane. Anna, our older adopted sister, arrives from Seoul in 1977 when she is thirteen, a beautiful Asian-and-white child, a proto-adult and a surrogate mother to us all. Our youngest sibling, Eddie, adorable, Black, and with a quick smile, is our last adoption, arriving at six years old in 1983 from the South Bronx. The cycle of acquisition and incorporation stops there. Yet our story continues.

From the moment of our creation, we are an arcadian experiment: a varied ensemble of kids of different races raised together by a visionary couple in a white clapboard house with a white picket fence in a town so small and so quaint that it might have been a movie set. Our father, Bob, is a prominent man in the county, and our generous creation is a part of his reputation. Sheryl, our mother, is an even-keeled idealist, committed to making a better world possible, an effort that begins, she insists, in the home. Our place in their experiment is clear. Clear because we discuss it at the breakfast table, a big, broad, heavy thing, which our parents have purchased to ensure that we all have room, with extra leaves that allow for a dozen. Clear because it is inscribed in our public persona as political objects, in our clothing, our assemblage as a platoon, our orchestration for photographs. Clear because other people comment on us, or ask about us, or express incomprehension about us. Even as we expand from two to four to six, we understand that our multiracial composition is a critique of the present, our color-blind consanguinity an omen of the future. We are the mechanical dolls of the subterranean Disney exhibit at the World's Fair brought to life, singing of tears, and hopes, and fears, imploring our public to wake up and recognize the chaos humans have wrought. We are a reminder of the good and the bad, of the consequences of war and violence, of the end-time that is coming.

We have a good, if somewhat peculiar, life. We are not poor. We are not physically abused. We do not suffer from physical violence at the hands of cruel parents. We are adored. We are supported at home. We have everything we need, insofar as we (or anyone) understands what is needed for a family like ours. Everything we need except, of course, for a popular template. There is almost nothing on television, in books, or on film that matches our experience. Just about every family we see on-screen is impossibly white. The Partridges of California. The Ingalls family of Minnesota. The Waltons of Virginia. The Cunninghams of Milwaukee. Even the large blended families we encounter on *The Brady Bunch* or *Eight Is Enough* are unfailingly, unquestionably white.

The Bible is a more useful guide. Early on, I am taught to see the house with the white picket fence as a biblical ark for the age of the nuclear bomb, of race riots, of war. Presiding at the kitchen table, Bob butters his bread at the start of dinner and recalls the lessons of the Old Testament. Noah, "a righteous man, blameless in his generation," has been forewarned that the grotesqueries of the vice-ridden human world will soon be wiped clean. God has decided to "make an end of all flesh, for the earth is filled with violence," and chooses Noah and his family alone to survive. So, following God's instructions, Noah gathers up the species of the earth by twos, and brings them aboard a magnificent vessel of his own making, to ensure that all of the innocent creations will survive. "Two of every kind shall come into you, to keep them alive," Bob notes. Noah keeps these creatures alive while the floodwaters rise, tending to them while the rest of humankind drowns in God's vengeance, and sets them loose upon a replenished planet in the wake of this cleansing devastation. As a sign of fealty to his God, though, he selects a few of the animals he has saved, and burns them on an altar. For this effort, Noah is rewarded, striking a new covenant with God.

"Two of every race," Bob says with a wink and a smile, pushing backward in his oak chair, writing us into scripture, turning it into a joke. "Two of every race," he repeats, as if that simple phrase is a shorthand that everyone can understand, as if it explains everything. As he says this, the radiator pipes that run against the wall—wrapped in blue-and-yellow wallpaper decorated with pineapples—clang and shudder. The great big oil burner in the basement has kicked into action, and the sound is a terrifying confirmation of the seriousness of the ark our parents have built. As a young child, I hear the fanatical, messianic tones in his sermon. And I believe. It takes me years—or decades—to understand the importance of the wink and the smile, the warm sense of humor that undercuts the Holy Writ.

"Two of every race."

Saying it this way, Bob twists the lines of race and family, of skin and kin.

We nod, understanding the Old Testament reference, acknowledging the sins of the world. The environment is collapsing, Bob continues. The planet cannot sustain life. He will build something, he tells us, to keep us safe. We are innocents, meant to survive an apocalypse, and meant, as well, to remake the earth in its wake. We are also a sacrifice. "Which of us," I wonder to myself, looking around, "will die?" While he speaks, my fingertips cling tightly to the edge of the table, and my flesh commits to memory the slickness of the varnished surface, the rustle of the newspaper, the timbre of his voice, the shared fear that the world is coming to an end. At night, assuming the worst, I lie in bed and design bomb shelters with modernist furniture, pocket rooms, and underground swimming pools, a fit home for the bunch of us during a long nuclear winter. Sheryl turns the light out. Alone, with fingers curled around my blankets in bed, I anticipate the early tremble of an earthquake, the roar of an oncoming tidal wave, the slow-rising hiss of the flood that comes with an endless downpour. My eyelids grow heavy. When I finally give in and fall asleep, I am at least comforted that we, together, are meaningful, that we have a wondrous purpose, that a vengeful God will find in our assembly a reason to pass over the white house with the picket fence.

Again, it is important that you understand that we are well tended, loved, and celebrated. That you don't expect a dystopian narrative from this memoir, one that is full of reality-television drunks with their crashed cars, messy divorces, and catastrophic affairs, their self-loathing and violence, their habitual confinement in reform schools and prison. Even if some of those things, by the end of it, are a part of the story; even if, indeed, some of those things wreck us. It is important, also, that you acknowledge the depth of the care in this house for one another, for our parents, and for the very concept of "us." Even if later, despite that same ethos, we sometimes make decisions that hurt one another, that hurt ourselves, that hurt all of us at once. Even if bad things seep in. Even if we sometimes encourage that seepage. It is important because we all survive. And it is important because while rains definitely come, and we are all tossed and turned and some of us are heaved overboard, the world does not end.

Skinfolk

1

A few years after they get married—in 1968, to be specific—Bob and Sheryl set out to find a house. They want something big enough to match their ambitions. They are renting a tidy, claustrophobic apartment in the central New Jersey city of Raritan, the very last stop on one of the state's commuter-railroad spurs. Bob works in Somerville, the next city over. They dream of having children. At night, they lie awake in bed envisioning a big family, troubleshooting all the hurdles in the way. They wonder if they will make good parents. They worry about money, about careers, and about the necessity of more space. With only a general sense of what they need, they seek a home, something roomier, something more private, something more cinematic. They drive all around the state on the weekends, hunting and hoping.

One Sunday morning, an advertisement for an enticing prospect appears in the local newspaper. A spacious farmhouse is being sold at the edge of another, much smaller town a little farther out, beyond the railroads and the interstates. Eager and unafraid, they head out to see it. The roads narrow and twist. The fringe remnants of the city are replaced by bright red barns, and woodlands give way to pasture and farmland. They cross rivers and railroad tracks. They drive until they come across an old crossroads and happen upon a house with a hand-painted "For Sale" sign out front. A row of maples borders the front of the property, with branches reaching up to the sky, arching across the street. They laugh at each other. This isn't the farmhouse from the newspaper. They are lost. But luck has brought them to an intriguing alternate possibility.

Standing in the street, they survey a tall white house, its outline marked by angles and bump-outs, a mishmash of architectural styles. The lot is large, and the house clings to one side of it. Sheryl calls it "cute." She animatedly points to its oversize windows and its bright exterior. Bob shakes his head in mild disagreement. He sees it as majestic, not cute. Gesturing broadly, he enthuses over the wooded side yard, the small front porch, the detached garage, and the prominent

The white house with the picket fence in winter. We used to hide behind the hedges to watch visitors to the general store across the street.

prow of the house, jutting out toward the street. After venturing to the porch, they are drawn inside by the current owners, a polite older couple. Bob whispers commentary behind his hand to Sheryl. A smile crosses her face. The older couple is a peculiar, mismatched pair, and a source of some amusement. Sheryl turns it into a private joke. She finds the inside of the house drab and dreary. They can both see past that, though. They love its simple interior lines, its refusal of right angles, its tall ceilings, and its considerable distance from the street. The house is elevated—on a high lot, with a tall foundation—and this, Sheryl notes to herself, permits a sense of polite discretion. She values privacy. The tour continues. The kitchen is an antique. They smile at the doorway to each of the three bedrooms. Sheryl takes stock of the secluded backyard. The basement is terrifyingly dark and cluttered, with a big, lumbering oil tank in one corner, but also dry and spacious.

It is all just perfect.

The drive back to Raritan seems to take forever, their impatience warping the distance. They talk about the white house the entire time, repairing and remodeling it together in their minds. Back in the apartment, they do some math, call their bank, and scrape together as much cash as they can. It takes them just a few days. And then, impulsively, Bob and Sheryl buy the white house they have found by luck in a town they know almost nothing about.

Moving day comes quickly. Determined to make the house their own, Bob and Sheryl hastily remove its dusty old curtains. They repaint the interior in lighter colors, and hang new, more contemporary wallpaper. They want the house to reflect their youth, even though they are way out in the countryside, in a part of the state neither of them really knows well. Working together on the weekends, they dedicate themselves to the effort, to the careful retrofitting of the interior living spaces of the old home to support the world to come.

There is more work to do outside. The street front is the biggest challenge. A simple wire fence, providing enclosure but no real seclusion, was strung years earlier inside a row of beautiful street trees. A big white house needs something impressive, they agree, something that catches the eye and conceals what is within. A nearby lumberyard provides posts and pickets for a proper fence, the sort of decorative border that has been conventionally understood as an emblem of middle-class prosperity but that has its origins in the violence of colonialism. Two centuries earlier, those pickets would have been sharpened pikes. And the fence itself would have been a deterrent. Knowing nothing of this ancient history, they install the fence themselves over the first summer, and paint it a bright, glossy white to match the house. When the town's small Fourth of July parade marches past, the fence is half complete. By Labor Day, it is finished.

This is another moment where our story might begin: in the sun-dappled street, as these two young people stand in front of that house, pondering their new fence, their new house, and their good fortune.

What comes next will take some time to unfold. Within a year, Sheryl is pregnant. Within three, they'll have adopted my brother Bug. A year later, Sheryl is pregnant again, with Mark. Then, quite consciously, and through the conspicuous display of our cosmopolitan details, Bob and Sheryl slowly create a utopian family representing, as Bob repeatedly puts it, the three great racial divisions of humankind. By 1973, there are three of us. By 1977, we are five. By 1983, our number is fixed at six. As members of this family, this monument to radical futurity, we live in a house that is both private and public, in a small town that is picture-perfect, in the middle of nowhere. There, we are science fiction brought to life. And we are biblical, a living reminder of the world's failures.

In all of this work, the white house is our setting, our theatrical stage, our fortress, our ark. It is our everything. It has its own pedagogy, too. Before we get to "us," I have to explain the importance of the house.

Those gleaming white pickets are both defensive and decorative.

Welcoming home Mark in the driveway in the summer of 1973. Bug and I cling to each other, reaching behind Sheryl. Someone has given us lollipops as a distraction. A family picnic followed in the private backyard, with a table full of cold cuts and cupcakes.

Growing up within the fence walls, we learn a lot about race. The reasons for this are obvious: as a polyglot, multiracial unit in post-civil-rights-era America, we are objects of intensely felt rituals of display and performance. We bring together visions of domestic normalcy with those of an exotic foreign diaspora to challenge conventional understandings of race and family. To challenge them and, of course, occasionally to embody them.

We learn that our family is rare—but not truly unique. We seek out exceptions to the white nuclear family in mass culture. When a parallel creation is discovered, Bob and Sheryl foster conversation and community. On a handful of precious nights, we huddle under blankets and watch the DeBolts on television. We watch in amazement as nineteen children are bivouacked in a California bungalow, parented by superconfident white people, and learn to do laundry and cook and clean together, despite missing limbs or sight, or despite the internal scars of war. Or we watch *Diff'rent Strokes*, where the rich white parent, Phillip Drummond, with a single white daughter, adopts two streetwise Black brothers. High jinks ensue, of course. We get the fish-out-of-water jokes and we laugh. We learn about Pearl Buck, the activist and humanitarian who founded Welcome House. And Jim Jones, the megalomaniacal preacher with his expansive family and his multiracial flock and his suicidal tendencies. And Josephine Baker, the superstar performer with a vast rainbow tribe and astonishing stage presence. From these lessons, we understand that families like ours are precious, and have a glamour to them.

We learn to see through that glamour, finding the dirty underside of the nation's troublesome fixation on mixture. We track the obsession with integration to the movie theater. We find variants of ourselves in military platoons, in baseball teams, in buddy-cop pairings, in diverse classrooms, in mixed-up gangs. There, in the glow of the projector, some of that dark cinematic magic rubs off onto all of us, soaks into our skin, and stays with us in our day-to-day lives. Some of it disturbs us. We get drunk on it. Our fairy-tale mythos, we learn, can be an intoxicant. We are, in a word, momentous. We are stars.

We receive an uncommon education, but we are also shielded from many things. The lessons came at us sideways, out of alignment with what we see on the nightly news. Ensconced in the Jersey countryside, barricaded behind that fence, we learn comparatively little about the bloody grit of residential segregation, violence and crime, and the political economy of oppression. Except, that is, for what we glean from one another, and especially from the shared stories of the past lives of our adopted siblings. Their stories are distant and unimaginable, though, off-loading the worst of racism to everything outside the picket fence, and onto the faraway landscapes of the American empire. Inside the ark, the time and space of racism are confusing.

Bigots with nooses and pickup trucks and southern drawls. Bullets on the riverbank under tropical foliage. Pagodas full of supposedly abandoned children. Sex work and the occupying army. Prejudice against mixed-race kids so severe that they are warehoused near an American embassy. When we are young, if you ask us where to find racism, we gesture across the street as if it were the other side of the world. Outside of the picket fence, there is only faraway time and faraway space. I look between the pickets and see Vietnam. Or Mississippi. Or Chicago. Saigon feels as close as Birmingham, Alabama, where the bloodiest civil rights struggles were staged. Inside the fence, the future feels closer than the past.

We are all there because of Bob, who was born and raised in Jersey City, on a dead-end, cobblestone street lined with brownstone apartment buildings and row houses. Bob has always wanted to live in the country. As a child, I fantasize about this origin point. Not knowing the story of how he and Sheryl found the house together, I imagine that Bob takes the railroad to its terminus when he finishes law school, gets a job, and then drives until he is out of gas and can go no farther. Having gone to the end of the map of the known world, I imagine, he settles in the sort of place that one might find in fictional 1950s Iowa, a single loop of sturdy, respectable homes built on the remains of an old nineteenth-century orchard, with no other people of color for miles. After acquiring the house and shoring up its defenses, he plants a reminder of his reputation at the entrance. Not an American flag, but a metal sign made for the end of the driveway, one with his name in big bold letters, and type underneath that reads, "Attorney at Law." This pennant hangs on a white wooden post just inside the fence line. For years, whenever we are tasked with repainting the fence, we are charged with doing the same with the sign, to ensure that everyone who passes by knows the ruler of this well-marked American domain.

Bob is a big, bold figure: tall, lean, outsize, grandiose, and theatrical, with a quick wit and enormous compassion for us and the world.

Bob and Sheryl, at the start of it all, in 1968.

Lording over breakfast, with the *Star-Ledger* unfolded on the table, he delivers impromptu lectures on the globe's impending overpopulation, and on the need for reorienting, world-shaking corrections. He reads deeply in the biographies of great white men who made what he sees as a critical difference in the racialized world: men like Abraham Lincoln and John Brown. Our rooms overflow with bookshelves, and our bookshelves are filled with the biographies of these men. Principled and unafraid, Bob is not the sort of person to sit by and watch something terrible happen. He is a man of action. His response to human tragedy, though, is inventive, not operational. He lives in the imaginative world of the fantastic. His solutions to global crises are manifested in the house, not on the street or in social movements. He will not stockpile weapons, or soak the ground with blood.

At an early age, we come to believe that only someone like Bob— only a charismatic figure of extraordinary sincerity—can bind six strangers together, turn them on an anvil until they are hammered into the shape of a family, and then put them on a pedestal for the world to admire. He elicits a mix of adoration and respect and awe from us all.

A lifelong lover of cinema and Broadway musicals, Bob sees that isolated hamlet with a keen eye for the picturesque. This is true inside the fence and out. Our plot of land has a bright and sunny front yard, which serves as a stage for us to play upon. And there is vast shrubbery running along the base of the house grown so large that it conceals the foundation. Bob nourishes the hedges and shrubs on the property's sidelines, but he keeps the front yard clear. The lot is divided in half by a long driveway that runs past the house to the ancient garage. The seclusion of the backyard is ensured by the garage and a neighbor's red barn, which runs along the back fence line, and by the heavily wooded edges of the property, reflecting Bob's commitment to tree planting. He shows a childish delight at the discovery of volunteer maple saplings, which he transplants around the backyard to further guarantee privacy and shade and offers up to neighbors for their own properties. When Bob says that he wants a house that looks as pretty as a movie set, he means that the entire street needs to be tree lined so that one can walk to the end of the driveway, turn to look down the block, and be stunned by the extraordinary natural latticework that forms in the sky, high above the pavement. He keeps our property as well groomed as a public park.

If Bob is the wild-eyed dreamer, Sheryl is the practical one. A single child raised in a family that moved around a lot—her father, Tom, works in the pharmaceutical industry—she wants to settle in one place for a long while. For her, the old white house has an aura of permanence about it. Even while she strips the old wallpaper and paints the trim, she finds a job as an elementary school teacher nearby and commits herself to the work, which she loves immediately. She has, like Bob, a fantasist's eye. But she also prefers simple solutions, plain speech, and the shortest distance between two points. A few years later, when the house is filled with children, she will be the one responsible for cooking most of the meals, and she devises a straightforward routine that saves time and energy and expense. Macaroni and chopped meat one night and fish cakes the next, pizza followed by pork chops, green bean casserole alongside baked potatoes, the same thing on the same night almost every week. She values privacy in a way that Bob does not. In the first few years, his parents often drop in without warning. They are charming people—fast talkers with wry wits—but she does not appreciate their spontaneous appearance in the driveway. Her first big fight with Bob is about his parents showing up without an invitation.

She may seem the quieter one, at first glance. Bob is the bold visionary with the big personality. He is flashy and dynamic, tragically tilting at windmills. Still, her fingerprints are all over this experiment. Indeed, her willingness to look back on our story with a gimlet eye—many years after it all happened—suggests a courage that runs astonishingly deep. Courage and, of course, an intense commitment to realpolitik, a balance to his frenetic romanticism. Bob envisions "us" as something to be seen in real time, as if we were actors on the stage in a live performance; Sheryl believes that ours is a story meant to be told after years of careful reflection. In the moment of our composition, she prudently grounds his lighter-than-air improvisations.

The town they settle in is timeless. Small and isolated, it consists of a wobbly oval full of big old homes, with a few dead-ends and a single "new" development extending off one side. There are signs of modest prosperity through the 1920s, when the railroad was replaced by the highway and this region was cut off from growth. Across the street from the white house there is an electrician's shop, owned by a very kind man named Casey, with curly brown hair. And next to that shop is a general store, a high-traffic location for anyone looking for a sandwich, for groceries, for cigarettes, or for anything else. The general store changes hands many times—most famously, in our youth it is owned by a wild-eyed Federalist candidate for governor named Charlie, a tall, stooped man who wears a pacifier around his neck "for his back" and who mounts an ancient WWII cannon on his front lawn and ties up a pet goat next to it. When he sells the store, Charlie drags the cannon away even though its rubber tires have disintegrated, and leaves deep grooves in the road, grooves that run straight from the store to his house on top of a hill about a half mile away. Every owner of the general store is a character like Charlie. But the store never changes its function or its look. The specials are always the same. The menu for the kitchen in the back is fixed. The same customers come and go, day in and day out.

The traffic drawn to our otherwise residential block makes it seem as if these three adjoined plots—the electrical shop, the general store, and the front lawn of our house—are a commercial strip. We are the entertainment for those who pause across the street for lunch, who park in front of the house, and then stare, sometimes with disbelief, at the racial spectacle in our yard. That is by design. The visual provocation of a multiracial family is the point of this decorative white picket fence, this almost comically earnest American front yard. To emphasize the point, Bob hangs the stars and stripes from the front of the house. It flaps in the breeze while we play kickball.

In a way, then, we are homesteaders from the future, meant to establish a settler outpost among those who are suspicious, if not fearful, of what we represent. The overall effect is to create a sense of distance between "us" and "them," between the diverse ensemble within the picket-fenced yard and the uniformly white town on the other side. The fence is the edge of our stage, the border of our territory, the end of our time, all at once.

The experiment transforms "outsiders" into "insiders," settling global sojourners in a locale that is quintessentially "American," so that no one can ever question our commitment to the nation. The white picket fence isn't merely a border; it signifies American-made cars, apple pie, baseball, and churchgoing. It is a frame, like the curtains and gilded scrollwork that border the stage at a dance hall, establishing a sight line. Look here, it calls: this is America. Even our endless maintenance of the fence—the annual painting and repair of the pickets, all conducted in full view of our public—is an homage to Tom Sawyer, a performance of folksy Americanism that reassures and inspires. The whole enterprise, in accordance with Bob's wishes, is meant to be seen.

We are seen, and we see things. At age five, dark-skinned Bear joins us. I begin to note a troubling public surveillance of our whole ensemble, our various skin tones on display. I watch as cars drive by, and see how quickly the heads turn to see the wide world of rainbow at play in our picket-fenced front yard. A game of catch. A throw of the football. Choosing up teams for Wiffle ball. With Blackness added, our performed comity means something more.

We learn how to be racial objects. We learn to play with stereotype, to embody or transgress the essence of difference; to study those who watch us, catching the moment when they assess our bodies, scrutinize our features, measure the dissonance of our skin tones. We also learn where to unwind so that no one can watch us and learn how to get along when we are, in turn, being admired (or condemned) by our publics. The backyard is private; the sun-stroked front yard is not. A tall, leafy maple tree inside the fence line is easily climbed. From a perch in the sky, the tree offers an elevated, forward position from which to study the cyclists, tourists, and power drinkers who stare into our yard. The arborvitae hedge that runs along the front of the house gives us a different vantage point. We find warrens in its interior; hollow it out and hide inside, watching the streetscape. We turn the anthropological gaze back on them. We play our role when we want to, laughing in the grass. We surveil when we want to, from the top of the tree or the bowels of the hedge. We retreat to the backyard when we wish to do neither.

The three of us—me, Bear, and Bug, white, Black, and Asian—on the lawn in the summer of 1975.

It is hard, even now, to put into words the weight we carry, the burden of representing so many things at once when we are together, and the way we grow up so keenly aware of that same burden.

Years later, when I am writing a book about Josephine Baker's family, I ask one of her adopted sons, Jari, how it felt to be on display so often, to be drawn out into the front-facing public gardens at Les Milandes to enthrall the audiences with the vision of interracial play. Jari hesitates, because he doesn't want to speak ill of Josephine. And then, with a slight smile, he turns to tell me about the secret tree house the children built by the river, where they amuse themselves out of the spotlight. I can imagine the ubiquitous presence of cameras, capturing the private lives of these much more famous children. I recognize their awareness of the paparazzi, which echoes our sense of watchfulness. I respect the needs, once more, for privacy and publicity in equal measure.

All large adoptive families, Jari reminds me, are public properties. They belong to the nation-state. They are engagements with the nation's future, heralds of what is to come as the country's demographics are transformed by the simplest and most powerful force in the world's history: human movement. International and multiracial adoptive families, he knows, are also powerful reminders of empire's sharp edge, of the desolation left behind after wars, natural disasters, and failed public policies. Jari's family was globally famous, but the lessons are the same for me, for us, for the six children raised together by Bob and Sheryl. Our bodies are mysterious and often threatening objects of speculation. They do not always belong to us.

The residents of our small town are good people. We learn this tentatively. The first adoptions are shocking—a white couple new to the territory accumulates a dazzling array of children. As our family grows, the town is modestly supportive. People ask fewer and fewer questions. We never hear any racial epithets within earshot. No one makes an unsettling remark. The surveillance changes, suspicion is replaced by half-hearted admiration. We become, rather quickly, not a threat but a quirky oddity, an extension of our liberal outsider parents, especially Bob, who is increasingly ensconced as a respected local attorney and later a judge. He routinely holds court at the edge of the fence, leaning against it and making small talk with neighbors out for a walk. Behind him, Bear and I play catch, throwing a baseball back and forth for hours, decorative examples of the good intentions of integration. The town watches over us and changes, and that air of watchfulness is now protective. We learn all of this slowly, and embrace it cautiously.

Outside of our town, though, our arrival can be greeted with angry confrontation. We learn quickly not to vacation in strange places. When Bear and I are seven, the family takes a chance on the upper south, staying at a local campground on the Chesapeake Bay. My memories of that trip center around a mosquito-fumigation truck that trundles through the campground at night and how all of the children follow it, laughing and running through the smoke. We think this is magical, this dense fog that clings to us and makes it possible to play hide-and-seek in the twilight. I remember a T-shirt given to me with the state's catchy slogan: "Virginia Is for Lovers." Mom remembers the trip differently. Going south, she tells me, was a terrible mistake. With a deep inhale, she recalls that the Black campers were segregated into a corner of the campground. As she and Bob set up the tent in a small shady grove of scrubby pines along the edge of the ocean—far from the inland sites reserved for Black families—we set out to visit the camp's playground, a rusting collection of swings and seesaws. There, the local boys, with unfamiliar accents and thick drawls, call Bear "boy." We make repeated efforts to fix his real name in their minds, with no luck. They continue until we leave. We have unwittingly integrated the white part of the campground, and these boys are self-deputized to intimidate us.

Mom vows to make sure that never happens again. After that incident, we go north for vacations, with mixed results.

Bear is fifty now, and he has spent a lifetime in North Carolina, where he works as a mechanical engineer. His beard is flecked with gray. His shoulders are still broad and powerful. He has a sixth sense about racism. When I ask him what he remembers of our small town, he invokes "the dome of protection Dad put around me." "When Dad was near," he continues, his gravelly baritone adding a contemplative lilt, "I pretty much ignored the looks and feelings of strangers."

Ignored them, perhaps, but I'm sure they were still felt. For Bear, the house was safe, but so was anywhere near Bob.

I'm intrigued by his emphasis on sight, on watchfulness, on the gaze of strangers. I wait for a second, hoping he'll say more. "I was very aware of how people looked at me," he continues. That awareness was something he had learned in Vietnam, where he stood out as a visual reminder of the ongoing war, of race-mixing, of Blackness. "There were many people there who wanted me dead," he remembers, "and anyone who has eyes can see that. It was an unpleasant experience to have someone look at me that way. Compared to death looks in Vietnam, the hate stares in America made me feel like it was their problem and not mine." As long as our father was around, he felt protected. As long as he felt safe, he "could go back to having fun."

There is nowhere safer than the white house, where we live behind the barricades. Bob's name is on prominent display at the end of the driveway, reminding any passersby—or anyone sitting outside that general store, who might respond angrily to the provocation of us—that an "Attorney at Law" dwells within. That extraordinary feeling of safety burns the place into our memories. Over fifty years later, I can still recall the texture of the paint on the pickets, still hear the sound of that sign swinging in the breeze, still feel the bark of the tree we climb to survey the neighborhood, the texture of the arborvitae hedge on the back of my neck when I hide within it. I can draw the entire yard precisely, down to the slope and grade of the earth. I can tell you where the grass doesn't grow—and where it does. I can draw every flower and every leaf. All because it marked as safe.

We think of the proverbial white picket fence as a sign of welcome, of assimilation, or of middle-class achievement. I now know the ancient meaning of those pickets, and I wonder if, for Bob, some of that older history lingers deep in his memory. If he understands that a fence isn't just ornamental, that it can also be a deterrent. He has something precious that needs protecting. Maybe he reaches back in time for a sharp and dangerous warning. At some point, that local hardware store stops selling those premade pickets because safety concerns have encouraged alternative shapes. The new fashion for these fences is a simple plank, with a squared-off top. Bob looks at these and shakes his head in disgust. When our older pickets need to be replaced, he buys longer boards and cuts and reshapes them into those forbidding, sharpened tips. He cuts out the right shape with his jigsaw, and painstakingly planes down the edges by hand, making them wicked looking. The process takes some time, and it would be easy to skip it, to just adopt the new standard. He doesn't. As he works to maintain the fence on his terms, he teaches us to do the same. Early every summer, we sit with him in the driveway, cutting and sanding new pickets until they seem deadly serious. And then, once they are attached to the fence, we paint them with the same bright white as all the rest, so that they can be seen up and down the block.

We are brought together from around the world for a purpose. Those who bring us together are big hearted and have, as they see it, the very best of intentions. They are not fools about the way that the world works. They trust that picket fence, which we regularly repair and so routinely repaint, to protect us, to wrap us in an All-American mythology. And they sharpen the pickets.

2

There is a photo album on the table. After the first few well-organized pages, full of carefully tabulated statistical details, immunization dates, and developmental charts, there is a photograph. Like everything else in those first few pages, the photograph is located precisely where it should be. Sheryl has written "Easter, 1971" at the bottom.

Bob has his left hand on the stroller, signaling executive power and fiduciary responsibility. His right hand is on the small of Sheryl's back, a gesture that shows the intimacy of the moment. Dressed smartly in a slim, close-fitting brown suit with sunglasses, he gives a wry, perfunctory smile. He is pleased with himself because he has set up a timer to take the picture. Sheryl looks down at me, a bemused expression on her face, as if she is still struck with wonderment, still unable to comprehend the actual presence of this child in her life. They look fresh and handsome, so completely in control: a young couple in love, out for a holiday with their first child.

Always ready with a big laugh, our maternal grandfather—Tom—has a cocksure grin on his face. His head tilts to one side, as if a joke has just been shared. He is still laughing at it. He is amazed by the

A cold Easter in 1971, with Sheryl's parents, Tom and Jeanne.

camera's timer, by Bob's proficient use of it. Jeanne, our grandmother, looks down, showing no eagerness to pick me up, and no inclination to do anything beyond noting me as a new fact in her life. Aloof and at odds, Jeanne's reserve, her arch posture, is a contrary position, reflecting her commitment to life as a zero-sum game.

It is a bright and sunny day, though the clothing suggests cool weather. I am the infant, the one with white skin, clad in white, and settled unhappily on a white blanket, buckled into a chrome stroller.

Three generations appear in a single photograph taken on Easter Sunday. You have seen an image like this one, representing middle-class

America in the late Cold War. It conjures up a visualization of inheritance, generational solidarity, and class position. It frames the idea of "normal" as explicitly white, middle class, and suburban.

This picture is taped into the first few pages of my baby book, long ago purchased from *Better Homes and Gardens*. A volume like this— supplanted now by newer and increasingly digital mediums and online collections—is a product of its time, rooted in one place, one moment, celebrating a small town or a single family. Its circulation relies on proximity, on the afternoon visitor sitting on the couch in the living room and thumbing through the pages. This particular book is, by the close, different, containing the difficult intimacies of centuries and continents. It yearns for a broader, more wide-ranging distribution. Held open on a coffee table, passed back and forth between visiting aunts and uncles and cousins, it raises questions and gives no easy answers. It challenges the certainties and convictions of that first photograph.

A white vinyl cover mimics the look and feel of wood grain. The words "Our Baby" appear on the cover in oversize cursive script. The book arrived on my desk a few years back, along with a collection of photo albums and slides, material that Mom was eager to jettison, making space for her new life.

Inside the album, you will find a collection of photographs taken at the start of the experiment, from 1970 through 1975. In the opening few pages, you will learn that I love to travel, and that Sheryl and Bob take me camping to state forests across the mid-Atlantic. Sheryl reports in her enviably precise handwriting that I was born preemptively in the hospital bathroom, and was so eager to join the world of the living that the whole thing took just a few minutes. As verification, a "certificate of truth" is affixed to the inside front cover, and is signed by three attending nurses. In these early pages, which span a year or two, there are numerous snapshots of me alone—running, sitting, staring back at the camera. There is a family tree, going back at least three generations, listing me as the inheritor of a long history. There is a list

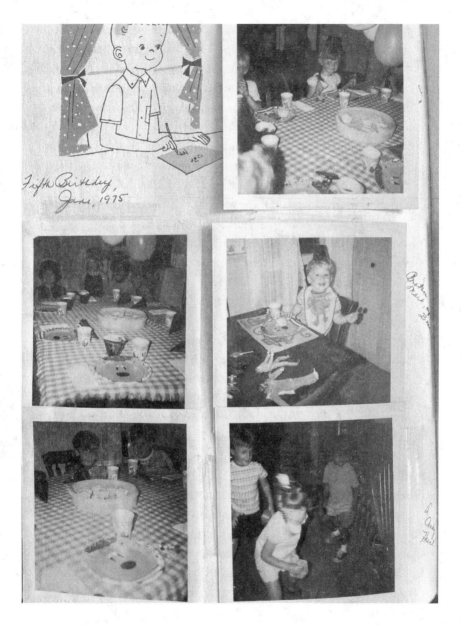

A page from my birth book, Our Baby. *We celebrated Bear's fifth birthday with mine.*

of gifts, of cards, of visitors to the house, a lock of my hair—trimmed and sequestered in a small envelope—and an elaborate chart of my daily activities, my height and weight, my dietary preferences. The book is meant to document several years of my life, and for the first of these years it is scrupulously neat, focused, and detailed, with every image taped down in the appropriate spot and labeled in crisp script.

The volume swells after that first year, though, becoming rapidly wilder, until it is chaos itself. The handwritten text recedes on every page, as the number of images increases. The adoptions go without written comment, while the photographs tell another, different story. The visual plotlines are increasingly complicated, as Bug and Mark and Bear, my first few siblings, arrive and join up together. As the photos crowd out the text, details get lost. The Scotch tape no longer holds. The ensemble takes pride of place. *Our Baby* becomes an accidental chronicle of the experiment, as the family expands beyond the capacity of cultural conventions and material artifacts meant for new mothers and fathers. There is nothing too unusual about this, perhaps, but I have been taught to think otherwise.

Big changes are already being plotted and measured and sketched out. Even as he grips the handle of my stroller, Bob has already begun to draw up his fantasies of a big, variegated family, and has begun to look for a way to bring them to life. That picture from Easter 1971 holds a thousand histories. I see our young parents, so strong and confident, standing next to their stroller. I see the ebb and flow of history behind them, the diverse family trees that bring them to that point, the long march of whiteness that makes it easy for them to stand there with such confidence, such authority, to try to slip out of the comfortable, familiar groove that history has created for them in the American landscape. Their whiteness empowers them to act, authorizes them to do whatever they feel is urgent or necessary, no matter the cost. I see in their faces a forceful resolution: they want to change the world. Whiteness gives them permission to dream that big.

I am the white child. I, too, am a race concept. I am the fixed type. That is my function in the family—a referent, an anchor, a "first born" symbol. I am unalloyed whiteness in the flesh, weaponized on behalf of this American ensemble. As such, I have one foot planted in this place and this time. Right there in New Jersey, on Easter Sunday 1971. Then and there, I am the flesh and blood materialization of a historical racial endowment.

The rest of me is with my brothers and sister, in the slipstream, drawn forward into the future, out of pace with everything else. There is a peculiar strangeness to this sense of time. Time is the building block of the nation—and the family. And, in any account of us, our story breaks free of the regular habits of record keeping, or ordinary linear constructs of the American family. Bear is born before me, but is not yet here. He is a month and a half older than me. "I only remember one birthday," he says now, "and it is yours." At the moment of my own birth—when the composition of *Our Baby* is still neat and orderly and white—I am not actually alone. In that stroller, I am already the middle child. Anna is in Korea, dancing onstage in a school play. Bear is also on the other side of the world, an outcast because his father is Black. He plays with bullet shells, building castles out of them along the banks of a river. Bob and Sheryl have already put in motion the plans to bring us together. Within a year of that photo, Bug is in an orphanage, lying alone in a bed. The paperwork for his adoption is filled out. Bear arrives in the summer of 1975, before my fifth birthday. By then, the singular narrative of the early pages of *Our Baby* has been displaced, and the album that is meant as an index of my own experiences reflects all of us in real life, as we come together, are shaped by each other, and grow to embody the plan.

The last photograph in the book is from my sixth birthday party. It clings to the bottom of the page, a final, desperate addition to an already overstuffed album. A group of children is in the backyard, gathered around an old red picnic table, decorated by half-eaten slices of chocolate cake. Our cousins are there—five wonderfully rowdy boys who live just up the road. Bug, Bear, and Mark are there, along with me. The scene is intimate, a tangle of arms and grins, an emotional knot. Bear is laughing wildly with the cousins, already integrated and adored. The interplay between Bear and the cousins is the central drama of the image. I, in the foreground, am at the margins of the group and out of focus. I look right at the camera, but Bob's cinematic eye sees only our aggregate splendor.

Another birthday party with cousins in the backyard grotto, from the back pages of Our Baby. *The backyard was where we felt safe, unwatched, and free to be ourselves.*

3

The first photograph of my brother Bug is not in a baby book. It is in a green legal folder that Bob keeps in his desk.

It is a spare, artless thing, about two inches by three inches with a plain white border. There's a stone wall in the background. A child carrier or car seat is in the foreground, draped with a bright, clean, white blanket. Nestled into the folds, a small infant—a few weeks old, perhaps, and clad in a white jumper—stares out at the camera. A shock of black hair shoots off in all directions. My brother's eyes are reflective. Look closely at them and you can see the outline of a figure bending down, some agent of the orphanage, silhouetted against the sky, leaning in to take an official portrait.

The image is a study in contrasts—dark skin on white cotton against gray stone. The archival object is just as interesting. Wrapped in a plastic sheath, bordered with yellowed Scotch tape, it is a purely utilitarian object, meant to enable the physical identification of a child, not to capture some moment of joy, or some milestone or achievement.

On the back, there is a single line of text: KW-1175, a case number. A Korean name. Another number is handwritten in red: 2267.

The picture travels. This is how the state, the orphanage, and the

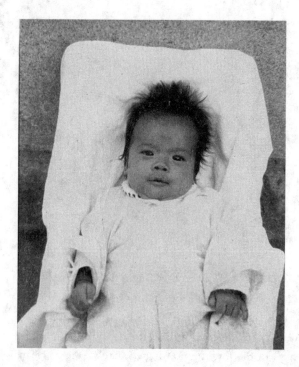

*The small photo of
Bug taken by the
state orphanage in
Seoul in 1971.*

adoption agency present him to our parents, in an image that is, at once, inaccurate and dehumanizing, enthralling and revelatory. That tiny photo in the plastic sleeve arrives in New Jersey and is passed around the dinner table. It is shared with friends and family. Despite its documentary-like staging, this representation is used by two white people on the opposite side of the world to write this infant, marked in every document as "full blooded Korean," into their family. Into "us." The cold spareness of the photo authorizes capture—or rescue, as they see it. It is a key piece in the story of how we are joined, how the plan is hatched.

I have no memory of life before Bug, the name I have always had for my brother. There is always Bug, always us, sharing a bedroom, sharing toys, growing up together. And the cultivation of that sense of *always* is, really, the story. This, I tell myself, is why this small, detailed image isn't fastened inside of some family album. It is a reminder of *before*.

At the time of their application to adopt, Mom and Dad have been married for just over three years. They pay $153 a month in mortgage fees and taxes against a debt of $14,000 for the white house with the picket fence. Bob works at a law firm in nearby Somerville. Mom has walked away from teaching to raise a family, and lists herself on the form as "Homemaker, mother." They are, once more, young and idealistic, and grounded in the middle-class ethos of mid-century America. If you tried to place them in history, you wouldn't call them radicals, even if they seem buoyed by the rising currents of the civil rights movement, by the sense that the future will be different. In their own way, they want to be a part of that effort—and of those imminent possibilities. And they see the family they are building as the key to that radical future.

In late July of 1971, they contact an agency: Welcome House, famously liberal and nondenominational, with celebrity supporters like musical-theater composer Oscar Hammerstein and Nobel Prize–winning novelist Pearl Buck. They are interested in adoption, Bob explains. The agency replies to the inquiry with a request for more information—"your ages, birth places, size of your home, education, income, racial strains, physical conditions"—and they both respond quickly, sharing as many of these details as they can.

Their eagerness compels another enticement from the agency. "If you are willing to consider a child of full Korean or full Indian heritage of the age range up to two years," Mary Graves, the executive director, responds, "we would be willing to go ahead with your application." She adds that the child would likely come from outside of the United States, either from Korea or northwest Canada. Korea seems more likely. "At the present time," she explains, "Canada has informed us that all their extremely young boys have been placed for adoption."

This, of course, is what they have been hoping to hear. They have wanted all along to adopt a boy of less than three years, preferably from India or Korea. These two places loom large in their minds, if for different reasons. Korea is a touchstone for international adoptions, home to the sympathetic icon of the mixed-race child, a consequence of war and empire. India they understand—primarily through the medium of television news—as an overpopulated hellscape. When asked about a "coloring preference," they respond: "None." Not once, in any of this correspondence—or any subsequent exchanges or acquisitions—will they think about finding a white child, domestically or internationally. They jump immediately to adopt a child of color.

The form requires more information. "What medical opinion," a prompt reads, "have you had about the possibility of parenthood for yourselves?" The question prompts some soul-searching. Sheryl is a private person, not keen to disclose more than necessary. The answer they give is curt and clinical: "The probability of our conceiving another child is slim." Bob fills out the form, typing out the answers one letter at a time. Sheryl's handwriting is impeccable. She would never use a typewriter for such a personal document.

A vital expression of liberal sentiment, Welcome House is the first international and interracial adoption agency, and it retains a progressive luster into the 1970s, when it continues an expanded mission, placing older children, children with disabilities, and "part Negro and full Negro children" in suburban white middle-class homes. Its political reputation is what draws Bob and Sheryl to it. Founded by Pearl Buck in 1949, the organization is headquartered in Doylestown, Pennsylvania, not far from where they live. They know the history, as well. It was launched in the early Cold War as a radical alternative to the traditional race-matching programs of the past, which had joined white orphans with white parents in "the best interest" of the child. Buck, a well-connected and much-admired novelist and cultural critic, was the child of white missionaries and the author of the 1931 middlebrow sensation *The Good Earth*, which purported to offer a more sympathetic portrait of everyday Chinese life, emphasizing the universal values of hard work, family, and closeness to the land. She founded her organization with considerable international experience, hoping to connect white middle-class families with Asian and "mixed" adoptees, many of them the children of US servicemen sent abroad during the 1940s and 1950s. The agency was renowned for its color-blind offer of "adoptive homes of varying racial extraction to children of different races." Hammerstein, famous for his interracial love stories onstage and on-screen, was on the board of directors. Black sociologist and Nobel Peace Prize winner Ralph Bunche was, too.

Growing up, I understand Welcome House as a civil rights organization, akin to the Southern Christian Leadership Conference or the Congress of Racial Equality. We return each summer to Doylestown for the Welcome House family picnic. Occasionally, we invite these families out to New Jersey for dinner. On those weekends, every table

A casual snapshot of a Welcome House picnic in the early 1970s.

is overflowing with Afros, every paper plate filled with ribs and collard greens, or kimchi and *japchae*, or *cha gio*. Even today, the mention of Buck's organization always resurrects a cognitive collage in my mind, a clutch of sensory memories about a moment in time when other vast assemblages gather together regularly, and where I feel—we feel—surrounded by others like us. An open field of people from around the world. A disorganized chorus of accents, grammars, and vocabularies. The contradictory smells of great food from five continents. Laughter. Black and brown and white skin. It feels dangerous and provocative. Attending Welcome House picnics, we are surrounded by other parallel orchestrations. At one event, it feels like an entire field is filled with families just like ours. We float together. As an extended and integrated family, we talk about other versions of us.

As a part of its vetting process, the agency requires the authorship of an autobiography from each parent. It must be typed, without any error or strikethrough. A carbon insert produces an onionskin copy, which you keep for yourself, while the original gets sent off for consideration.

Bob's autobiography is a narrative of triumphant accomplishment. He begins with a brief reference to his father—"a college professor at St. Peter's College and also principal of Snyder High School in Jersey City"—before listing out his own accomplishments in the past tense. He received a Jesuit education from birth through college, and then went to Rutgers Law, joined the national guard, and was commissioned as a lieutenant, JG, in the Navy Judge Advocate General Corps. Desiring to leave Jersey City, he set out, with great intention, to find "employment in a small law firm in a rural community." Ending up in central New Jersey, Bob represented municipalities and townships in the courts, and then glided into Republican politics, becoming a district committeeman and a campaign manager for the party in Branchburg, the rural township where he settled. He describes himself as athletic, active outdoors, and having a love of sailing, rejecting his childhood in the city. He has abundant family nearby, including a brother who lives two miles away with his wife and four boys, and a sister in Jersey City who will soon join them in the same community. His mother, now widowed and living in a brownstone on Virginia Terrace in the city, is still close to them all. "My background," he asserts, "is that of strong family ties and close family relationships." As final proof, he notes that his father "came from a family of nine boys, all of whom have remained very close."

Those "nine boys" are his model. "With the family background I have," he admits, "it has always been my hope to have a family of at least four children. Prior to our marriage Sheryl and I had agreed to have two adopted children in a planned family of four, since we do share a mutual concern about the problems of population growth." (Two internationally adopted children, he fails to add, was the federal maximum until the mid-1970s.) "It is our wish," he continues, "that we could adopt a boy of somewhat similar age not necessarily as a companion to our son Matthew, but rather because in my own family experience I have found that a close relationship between brothers is fostered by a small difference in ages." There is the germ of a big idea here, in this notion of an intimacy that is greater—more intensive, more meaningful—than companionship. He wants, I know, to recast the oversize, big-hearted Irish Catholic family of his youth into a modern, multiracial phenomenon, something bolder and more powerful than the small-scale nuclear families that are currently center stage.

Bob's prose is syntactically wild, full of run-ons and structural improvisations. Sheryl writes like a dutiful English major, with precision and perfect grammar, every thought diagrammed appropriately. As a consequence, her autobiography is leaner, less emotional, and more direct. The daughter of a pharmaceutical executive and a petrochemical secretarial worker, she was repeatedly moved around the country. Her high school years were peripatetic, as she drifted from Iowa to Illinois to New Jersey. As a result, she hated transience. She was a rising junior at a small college in Minnesota when she took up a summer position at a family friend's law firm in central New Jersey. That is where she met Bob, an aspiring attorney only recently out of law school. They dated while she attended college and got married after she'd completed the bachelor's degree. She moved back east, seeking a grounded stability with her new husband. She wanted to be in one place, she explains, to settle in, to grow roots. Reflecting on the extraordinary transformations of the past few years, she tells the agency that she finds teaching fulfilling, and she pointedly collapses the gap between elementary and domestic pedagogies. She will be a good mother, her brief memoir insists, because she is a good teacher. In her closing lines, she echoes Bob, putting stress on health and vigor, and on the love of the outdoors, on the thrill of sailing, camping, and hiking. "Being outdoors makes one conservation-conscious," she explains, adding that she is "the current chairman of the Branchburg Township Recycling Committee."

In the last few lines of her narrative, she dwells on her childhood seclusion as the only child of two rootless parents. "Bob and I have found parenthood even better than we imagined. We are enthused about expanding our responsibilities. There are many reasons why we want to adopt a child, but one very personal reason is that I was an only child. Knowing the loneliness an only child can feel, I have always wanted a family of more than one." "Adoption," she closes, "is a family plan we talked about even before we were married."

If there is a constant throughline in this material, it is the parallelism of adoption and environmental sustainability, the idea that recycling and adoption are methods of global repair. Overpopulation has become the subject of considerable debate; the very first Earth Day is in April of 1970. The world is just filled with too much of everything, they both stress, and we all need to be more mindful of how to safeguard and budget our resources, whether material or biological. In saying this, Bob and Sheryl are typical of their generation. Their drive to adopt reflects, in part, the astonishing population growth of the previous twenty years and their consequent worries that the natural environment is buckling under the strain and will soon break.

"Some things have to change," Dad says at the breakfast table, where he often shares the day's bad news. He wrinkles his brow and shakes out the newspaper. "There are too many people!" The family is one of those things, he suggests, casually affiliating orphaned children with excess material waste. A family can be as big as anyone wants, so long as it reflects a better organization of humankind's surplus.

Asked about this now, Mom is quick to reference Paul and Anne Ehrlich's 1968 barn burner, *The Population Bomb*. Paul Ehrlich was a professor of biology at Stanford, whose dark musings on the fate of the world caught the attention of David Brower, the head of the Sierra Club. Brower, sensing the importance of the topic, encouraged a book, and *The Population Bomb*, a wily bit of pop-science scaremongering coauthored by husband and wife, was the result. The Ehrlichs proposed that the human population of the world was soon doomed to exceed the capacity of the planet to provide enough food, water, and outdoor spaces. They envisioned massive famines, wars from food insecurity, state-mandated population controls, and the rationing of the future. And they were particularly concerned about India, which was verging on another doubling of its population, and which historically had witnessed a plague of malnutrition, with terrible human consequences. "Population control or race to oblivion?" the Ehrlichs ask on the cover of the book. To underscore the point, in the bottom right corner of the paperback, there is a tiny bomb. And next to it, the terrifying statement in boldfaced typewriter font: "While you are reading these words four people will have died from starvation. Most of them children."

"That was our motivation," Mom remembers now: "zero population growth (ZPG) was a hot topic at the time, and it made sense."

I'm a little surprised by this, of course. So many adoptive families in the United States have a missionary origin point—and there surely is some old-fashioned missionary zeal in ours—but this endorsement of a political philosophy rooted in an impending apocalypse and endorsing dramatic, global social engineering catches my breath. It also clicks audibly in my mind, drawing together so many aspects of our assemblage and our story. I can see what they see: the link between recycling and adoption, and their love of a supposedly pure and unpopulated outdoor world they sincerely fear will vanish by the end of their lives. They want a large family, including biological children of their own. They take overpopulation seriously, and do not want to be wasteful. They also want to make a political statement about the coming decimation. International, multiracial adoption is the solution.

This ideology stands in sharp contrast, I know, to other abstract solutions to the problems of poverty and overpopulation, which argue for a fairer, more judicious reallocation of resources—instead of people. Those hotly contested, policy-based alternatives seem beyond the

Bob and Sheryl, at home in the woods, in the late 1960s. Bob used a tripod and a timer to take this casual photo, which was a part of a series of wilderness-themed images he staged.

reach of our parents, though, and the crisis in front of them—the photographs presented by adoption agents, the sympathetic biographies
revealed over the phone to prospective parents—seem too urgent to
wait for movements or political parties. Ideologies of salvage and rescue require a strong sense of immediate, unyielding crisis, and valorize
the lonely actor who bucks the trends. They depend on the belief in
world-ending dystopias, and on the creation of structures that enable
survival in the face of terrible odds. They require righteousness, or so
Bob and Sheryl believe.

"Two of every race."

The white picket fence.

The Korean Ministry of Foreign Affairs extracts one last promise
before Bug is transferred from the Asian periphery to the imperial
American center: "I am willing and able," the last line of Form 101
reads, "to adopt, love, maintain, support, and educate the prospective immigrant(s) listed above." Dad signs boldly for both himself and
Mom, his signature having his characteristic sweep and flair.

Often, the official narrative makes adoptions easier, assuaging any
bothersome feelings of guilt. Wrapped up tightly in a blanket, the
story goes, Bug is dropped off in front of the Korean Social Services
(KSS) orphanage building in Seoul. Mountains loom in the distance.
A miniature playground has been set up outside. Small brick buildings communicate officiousness. A slip of paper has been pinned to his
clothing, with a notation that "indicated briefly the mother's wish for
adoptive placement." The note includes the child's Korean name and
his birth date. The dramatic abandonment, whether fictional or otherwise, serves as a kind of severance, cutting Bug off from his homeland
and trimming off any domestic complications.

He is presumed to be a Korean of full Korean background, though
an agent guesses that "the child was born out of wedlock." The "Adoptive Child Study Summary," a formal document composed by the
KSS, emphasizes the purity of a racial type, describing Bug as "a cute

looking baby . . . who has average complexion as a full Korean with dark hair and dark-brown eyes, and can be easily identified as a full Korean baby because of their physical colouring and appearance." The child is "alert and quite well matured," the report continues, before running through a set of physiological milestones that would resonate with any new mother on the other side of the world, any mother, that is, who is dutifully noting every inch of growth and every new skill acquired by the children already in her own house. "Beginning to lift [his] head and chest lying on [his] stomach. . . . Beginning to recognize familiar faces and to smile in response to others . . . to turn [his] head to sounds." There are echoes of the first few pages of *Our Baby*, echoes I am certain Sheryl does not miss. The caseworker concludes with a single, strong recommendation: the child "is in need of any adoptive placement," including "overseas adoptive placement."

Decades later, after the whole endeavor begins to unravel, Dad searches for some way to blame the agency. He tells us that Bug lay in the crib for so long, abandoned for hours without human touch, that the back of his head flattened before his arrival at JFK. Bob's expression turns morose when he remembers running his fingers along the back of Bug's skull. For Bob, it all comes back to that silhouette in Bug's eye, and to the stony edifice of the orphanage in the backdrop. They are responsible. Not us. Not this place. Not what has happened at our home.

To prepare white, middle-class families, the agents at Welcome House helpfully provide a handy, three-page typescript on the care and feeding of adopted children from "the Orient," which looms in all of this literature as a cruel and strange place. "We urge," it reads, "as few tears (even tears of joy) as possible." Parents are encouraged to keep friends and family away, so that the new arrival can imprint upon— "belong" and "identify" are the active verbs—their new family. In the pamphlet, Korea seems like Mars. "The children are exhausted, confused, and upset," the guide documents, "by strange people, the strange sights, sounds, and odors and the strange language." Better,

then, that parents swiftly get them out of the airport without delay—
"transfer the child from the plane to your automobile as quietly, effi-
ciently and speedily as possible." Importantly, mothers should wear
dresses and not pants. "This is the way you are pictured when we send
pictures to Korea . . . [where] slacks and pants worn by women are
associated with very heavy outside work on non-festive occasions."
On the subject of discipline, Welcome House recommends tough-
ness. Korean children, the document explains, "have known consis-
tent, firm discipline," and they habitually "associate firm handling of
discipline with security. They appreciate knowing what is expected of
them and enjoy high standards of behavior."

Stamped at the bottom of the form sent to our parents is another
addition, a reminder of the stigma attached to immigrant bodies:
"Recommend treatment for head lice."

"We urge as few tears (even tears of joy) as possible."

That line sticks with me. And I wonder whether it stuck with
them, with our parents. So much of what is on this list is "Oriental-
ist" fantasy—the supposed pleasure that comes from strict discipline,
from a clean gender divide, from impossibly high standards. This is the
myth of the model minority turned into a list of parenting tips.

The flight to JFK takes almost twenty-four hours. Bug—still an
infant—is too young to notice such things, but the trip must still have
been stressful. On March 29, 1972, Northwest flight number 4 lands
at Kennedy Airport in the early evening. Armed with a clutch of official papers, Mom and Dad meet an agent at the arrivals gate, sweep
up Bug, and bring him home. Mary Graves meets them at the Jetway
door. There are many other parents there that night, each taking home
their own new, adopted child. I wonder how many of them have read
through that Welcome House list, how many of them envision their
new arrivals through that prescriptive pamphlet, hungering for discipline rather than tears, yearning for high standards instead of affection
and tenderness. The wondering leaves me shaken.

4

Mom and Dad heard about Welcome House, they claim in one of their letters to the agency, by reading "the exciting article by Jim Bouton" in the May 1971 issue of *Family Circle*. Bouton, a recently retired New York Yankees pitcher famous for writing the witty and scandalously candid memoir *Ball Four*, adopted a young Korean boy with his first wife, Bobbie. Together with two previous children, the Boutons settled into a suburban life in Teaneck, New Jersey, just about an hour from us.

There is reason to be suspicious of this convenient origin story: buried in Bob's personal papers there is an adoptive parents' newsletter— *The Welcomer*—from the spring and summer of 1970. Months before I am born and long before Bouton's essay appears, Bob is thinking of the next step. It is telling, to me, that he holds on to this newsletter, squirreling it away in his desk as a souvenir. Sheryl, too, reveals elsewhere in her application that they were planning to adopt long before I was born. This makes that story about Jim Bouton impossible. Perhaps, given everything, they find it easier to point to a popular celebrity, in much the same way that Bob later censures the orphanage for denying his son the gentleness of human contact. Maybe, in hindsight, the experiment feels too reckless, too ambitious, for them to own alone. Bouton's fame gives them cover.

I ask Mom again, in the midst of writing about Bug's arrival, where they first heard of the idea of a grandiose racial mélange. I have assumed that the root of this creation is somewhere in their own childhoods—in other extravagantly outsize families. Like the one imagined by Bertha and Harry Holt, who needed an act of Congress to adopt eight children from Korea, offering them safety—and religious salvation in a white Christian nation. Or the technicolored "Family Nobody Wanted," created by Helen and Carl Doss, who were profiled in a best-selling book in 1954—and in a film twenty years later. Or perhaps, more radically, they have been inspired by Josephine Baker in France, with her ensemble of a dozen kids brought together from around the world in the 1950s and raised in a castle. Mom proves me wrong, though. These earlier ensembles seem, to her, dated and quite different from what she and Bob are trying to accomplish. By 1970, these other famous parents all have grown children and—in the case of Baker—fraying celebrity. I am surprised, once more, to hear Mom cite Bouton, the oddball journeyman pitcher with a legendary candor.

"At first I thought I had wrecked our lives." That is Bouton's opening gambit, in the story of his family's adoption of a young boy named Kyong Jo from Korea. "Why We Adopted an Interracial Child," the article that appears in *Family Circle*, is written from a defensive crouch, as if the shock of interracial adoption can be studied only while squinting under the brightest spotlight. Throughout, Bouton describes the arrival of Kyong Jo—later renamed David—as an earthquake, tearing the family down to its foundations, emphasizing throughout what he sees as the extraordinary challenges of racial difference, and using language that would surely scare off the faint of heart. Even now, Bouton's honesty about the obstacles faced by adoptees and their parents is refreshing, as is his confessional tone, his willingness to admit his own mistakes.

The story is buried in the back of the magazine. Mom does not remember how the article came to her. I try to imagine her flipping through *Family Circle* in the grocery store checkout line, moving past the dress patterns and the quirky Jell-O recipes. Once you have found it, the single image on the story's first page will compel you to buy the magazine. There is the whole family—Jim and his wife, Bobbie, their children, Michael and Laurie and David. The kids are all squeezed into an oversize kitchen chair, the three of them laughing, touching, physically intimate in the way that children—brothers and sisters—often are. David's big smile is infectious. The picture is the proof: if you get through the rough spots, the family you create will be just fine and normal. Or perhaps even much better than that.

Bouton is a big man—blond, thick necked, with a cleft chin. His personality is huge. He is opinionated and confident, even when his opinions and confidences are daring and wild. His honesty is a kind of improvisation, spinning away from anything predictable or doctrinaire. And, in plain language and with great conviction, he presents international, multiracial adoption as a rational, radical political commitment, rooted in progressive concerns about surging global population and the attendant consequences for the natural world. He argues for a reduction of the federal child tax credit for families where the parents have more than "two of their own"; adopt children, he proposes, and you might get a subsidy. He argues that "vasectomies should be free" and that there should be tax incentives to encourage them. "If we're going to save the world from strangling itself," he opines, "we ought to be willing to pay for a program to do it." He characterizes the drive to "have" more than two children as entirely ego driven. The "Zero Population Growth people have the right idea," he writes; "I don't think we have the right to litter up the world with our offspring."

This is Bob's ideology of personal restraint and global redistribution, too—I recognize the strident language of the pragmatic social engineer who understands the dilemma and believes that human beings can be led to do the right thing if we just pitch the argument, and tilt the landscape, in the right way. Someone just needs to take the lead and create the right symbol. Dad says eerily similar things at breakfast. I wonder, more than once, whether Bob knew Jim Bouton somehow, whether they played basketball against each other in some North Jersey Catholic Youth Organization league.

These similarities have limits. There is something in Bouton's discussion of race, for instance, that seems off, even dissonant. "His skin color really is beautiful," he writes of David, using language I have never heard from Bob or Sheryl. It strikes me, reading the piece, that this language of fetish—the pleasing aesthetics of round eyes or olive skin—is entirely absent from our house. Indeed, that is the sort of thinking we relentlessly mock, at least in private. Beyond the skin, Bouton goes on to describe the rest of David's Korean past as a difficult problem, or as something to be solved. The food, he argues, is strange and hard to reproduce. Only in moments of extreme crisis, when David is absolutely inconsolable, will Bobbie attempt to make it. Asian culture—Bouton routinely aggregates all of Asia—is stiff, formal, and incompatible with the casual cultural landscape of New Jersey. The solution is a swift, complete incorporation into the American "normal," a jarring, dislocating process that draws Kyong Jo into the family and that excises everything seemingly foreign or alien.

Blackness is a different matter. Bouton and his wife "seriously thought about adopting a black child," but concluded that "we just didn't have the courage." They worry about a child caught between two worlds, and worry that "the Negro community" would look strangely upon them for "taking one of their kids and raising a Black Anglo-Saxon Protestant." They fret that, when older, the child would reject them, insisting that "I'd have been better off in the ghetto." "How," Bouton asks, "do you raise a black kid in a suburban home and still have him grow up with some feeling of identity?"

Reading this passage, I pause. I am puzzling through Bouton's strange notion that adopting a Black child requires a unique sort of "courage," which he confesses he lacks; the equally perverse idea that Black culture is so impossibly distant, so unreachable, that any attempt to provide it will fail; and the sense that these two things—the "courage" supposedly required to adopt across the white-Black color line and the capacity to link an adopted child to the culture of their homeland—simply aren't relevant when it comes to the adoption of East Asian children like Kyong Jo/David. As Bouton describes it, David's relocation from the other side of the world frees his new parents from caring about his cultural heritage. The global span of the American empire makes it easier. Adopting a Black child would be different, he assumes, both because Black culture is a ubiquitous feature of American culture—and because Bouton cannot imagine having any kind of meaningful access to it. Blackness is, for him, intimately familiar—and yet impossible to understand.

"So many overlapping, intertwining, and knotted threads in this strange, moving essay," I think to myself.

Another passage catches my eye. "He's my friend," young Michael says at one point, introducing David to a stranger, who is confused by the presentation of difference, by the mismatch of skin, hair, and eyes. And "he's my brother, too." I recognize that confusion—that gap between "friend" and "brother." And I recognize, too, the need to explain, or introduce, the mystery of a multiracial family to a white stranger.

Bouton's focus on what he calls "Oriental stoicism" is typical of the times. David, Bouton notes, suffers pain without complaint, drawing on a common stereotype to explain why the young boy, far from home, has kept something that hurts a secret. Bouton goes on to declare that the key to David's incorporation is the realization that the child responds best to strength and authority, suggesting that this positive response is rooted in Asian culture, where strict discipline is preferred. Meeting David at the airport, Bouton's first impulse is to speak in reassuring, soft tones, to sweep the four-year-old child up, and to squeeze him tight. That would be wrong. Noting David's eyes—"big and round and black"—and unnerved by the "terror" he finds in the boy's gaze, Bouton realizes that what is needed is a firmer hand. "I stood up," he recalls, "straightened to my full height, and said in my best Prussian manner, 'Stand up, Kyong Jo, and come with us.'" Only then, he reports, does David rise and hold Bouton's hand "obediently." "And off we went," Bouton closes, "into adventure."

Reading this, I recall the final scene of John Wayne's 1968 film, *The Green Berets*, which closes with Wayne, a soldier in uniform, walking toward the sunset hand in hand with the young Ham Chuck, whose future is uncertain. "What will happen to me now?" Ham Chuck asks, a tear rolling down his cheek. Wayne's Colonel Kirby, on his knees and in camo fatigues, places an army beret on the child's head. "You let me worry about that," he says to Ham Chuck, the orphan he has come to accept as a ward. Authority. Strength. Confidence. Paternalism. Racial geopolitics that become parenting tips.

I call Mom. I want to know what she did when Bug came off the plane, whether she retreated to a cool distance when confronted with a confused young child. Did she draw herself up high, and mobilize an imperial stance to provide reassurance? I ask if Bug came off the plane in a carrier. "Did you take him home that way?" I wonder aloud. To myself, I ask: Did you get down on one knee, brush the tears away, and provide stoic reassurance?

"Oh no," she says right away. There is an urgency in her voice. She has no idea why I am asking, but she wants me to know the truth and to never doubt it. "He was in my arms. He sat in my arms the whole time. We got lost heading home because we were so focused on looking at him that we missed a turn and ended up at the Yonkers raceway." Bug slept the whole time. Asked about *The Green Berets*, her voice turns sour. She has never seen the movie. "I don't like John Wayne," she offers as an explanation.

I am less than a year old when my parents read that piece in *Family Circle*, and less than two that night in late March of 1972, when they head out to what is then JFK's Northwest Orient terminal. I have no memories of their return from the airport, of any adjustments made to life in the house. I cannot tell you if our diet changes, or if structures of discipline are altered. My earliest recollections are of togetherness, of sharing a room—and bunk beds—with Bug. To me, there is no gap of any kind. I don't even remember thinking that Bug is younger, even much later, when I go to kindergarten and he doesn't. And that separation—a grade between the two of us—always feels strange and unnatural, all the way through high school. There is only the plural pronoun, the exquisite alignments of "us" and "we."

Such memories are confirmed by the archive. Family photo albums show us adjoined and aligned, almost from the moment of his arrival.

Bug and me on a sailboat on Haunted Lake in New Hampshire.

Two kids sailing. Two kids opening presents on Christmas. Two kids sitting on Great-Grandma's lap while she reads to them. (She wears horn-rimmed glasses, and a comfortable blue sweater, looking quintessentially midwestern.) Two kids on the beach, building sandcastles. Two kids on the deck of a sailboat. Two kids playing in the dirt. Two kids sound asleep on top of each other. When we are shown apart, we are usually doing the same things—reading a book with a parent, playing with a particular toy—and the photos appear to have been self-consciously taken in sequence, as if to demonstrate parity for the historical record. Our intimacy is camera ready, then, a gamble that has paid off. Bug's arrival is not an earthquake.

Great-Grandpa Everett and Bug at Bever Park in Cedar Rapids.

Of all of these images that showcase our connection, the most mov-ing set is taken on a crisp spring day in Bever Park in Cedar Rapids, Iowa. We have traveled out to the Midwest to visit great-grandparents and longtime family friends. The park has a small petting zoo, and is a favorite of ours for years. In one image, Bug and I are side by side in a pair of swings. We're alone. No adult is pushing us. We're both looking off to the left, at something on the ground. The second fea-tures Bug in the same swing. I've left the frame. Great-Grandpa Ever-ett is standing behind him, with a slightly pleased look on his face. The swing is drawn back and Everett holds the frame, preparing to let it go. Bug looks nervous and expectant, wary of that exhilarat-ing feeling that attends the release, anticipating the physical sensation that comes with it as your body follows with the earth's pull. Caught in the moment before something magical happens, there is a radical notion of a new kind of family in Everett's tensed muscles and in Bug's excited look, one that is confidently moving into the future, one that is a monument to organization, to engineering, to social science, to "bleeding heart" liberalism. The image freezes all of us. Makes us hold our breath with Bug. At any minute, Everett will let go.

5

Bear comes next. He joins us in the late spring of 1975, just as the maple trees leaf out in the yard. We play together hesitantly while whirligig seedpods twirl to the ground from high above. The grass is awake and green again, and as we run and laugh Sheryl plants a few small flowers along the edge of the driveway. Impatiens, with soft pink and red and white petals.

His arrival is as sudden, as shocking, and as thrilling as a rabbit pulled from a magician's hat. One day he isn't there—I'm not even aware of his existence—and the next day he is sleeping in the top bunk (vacant since Bug has gotten his own room) and wearing my pajamas. There is no preparation or fanfare. No search for additional supplies or clothes. No family meeting. Just a single moment of improvisation, a daring, impulsive commitment to the power of "yes." One day, after a series of hasty phone calls, we take a drive to nearby Doylestown, and suddenly there are four of us.

Bear is a refugee, a word I learn the day he arrives.

He was evacuated from Saigon with terrible suddenness. With his dark skin—his birth father is an African American enlisted man—he is an outcast in the city in the final weeks and months of the American presence in Vietnam. Viewed with suspicion and anger, Bear has been placed in a residential school attached to the US embassy by his mother, who has desperately signed away her legal parental responsibilities in order to keep him safe. Then, in April of 1975, with the American occupation of the city coming to a rapid close, the school is no longer safe. One day, suddenly, it is time to leave. Along with a few dozen other children at the same school—mixed-race children with American servicemen as fathers—he is hustled into the back of an army-green C-130 transport. A machine gunner is positioned at the cargo bay entrance, his eyes scanning the horizon. The plane is fueled up and ready to go, and with engines running. Four massive propellers make the body of the plane throb with urgency. The vibrations, the guns, and the helter-skelter rush to the runway add to the children's feelings of confusion and fear. There are no seats in the cavernous transport, and the children are entangled in the cargo nets, their fingers curled around the threads and bands of the netting for something like safety. Bear's two older half siblings—Peter and Amy—join him on the plane, and the three of them hang together; their mother, Mae, stays behind. Almost as soon as they are onboard, the plane surges forward and accelerates, racing to the end of the runway, just as the North Vietnamese army enters the embassy compound.

This wild-eyed flight out of Saigon is less famous than the much-publicized "rescue" of Vietnamese orphans known as "Operation Babylift." That other export of several thousand "orphaned" children was a part of the organized withdrawal of US personnel from Vietnam earlier that spring. "Babylift" brings a great deal of public attention to the plight of the mixed-race "war orphan," a sympathetic figure in the minds of liberal white families, but that attention comes with a steep price tag, as when the first military transport to leave Saigon, carrying dozens of red-eyed children strapped in two to a seat, crashes in dramatic fashion just after takeoff. Seventy-eight children are killed, along with dozens of military and State Department personnel. After the crash, the mainstream press more dutifully covers the exodus, circulating glossy photos of military and commercial planes filled with children, baby boxes filled with infants strapped in while stylized, 1970s-era stewardesses and State Department officials watch over them with scrupulous mindfulness.

Bear's removal, on the other hand, is a part of "Operation Frequent Wind," a name that implies an organizational strategy for what is clearly a slapdash, white-knuckled effort to just get as much stuff— people, matériel, whatever—out of Saigon, on the precipice of the American rout. There are no comfortable seats. No pretty stewardesses. No photographers. No time for a scene like the one at the end of *The Green Berets*, where Colonel Kirby and Ham Chuck walk slowly along the sand. Just a grim hustle to grab everything and go. And to abandon everything left behind. As French and American empires fall around Saigon, there is a small miracle buried in the mere fact of our brother's survival.

The surprising agent of Bear's remarkable deliverance isn't the United States Air Force. It is a man named Victor Srinivasan, a Zelig-like character with a fascinating backstory. Born an untouchable in caste-ridden India, Victor survived a life on the streets of Madras to join the British Royal Air Force and then, after independence in 1947, the Indian Air Force. At the end of his military service, he and his younger wife, Malini, volunteered to rescue war orphans. Victor runs Hope, one of the residential schools near the embassy for the mixed-race children of US servicemen, and has become a bit of a celebrity. He is profiled in an award-winning documentary, *The Sins of the Fathers*, produced by NBC, and is featured in a *New York Times* piece about the school. On April 29—the "day that Saigon fell"—he takes a phone call from the US embassy and is given fifteen minutes to grab as many children and school staff as possible. He proceeds to the airport, where a Magic Marker is used to hastily label each kid's belongings before they are stuffed into whatever bags are available. Once onboard, the

Saigon, 1974–75. The children of the school called Hope. Bear is on the far right, wearing pajamas and holding a coloring book.

adults throw the bags down and grab hold of the heavy cargo netting on the walls of the plane, and make sure that the children do the same, patiently explaining everything in reassuring tones. Then they wait, their hearts pounding, for the plane to lunge forward, to rumble along the pockmarked runway, to lift them into the sky.

This, at least, is how Victor tells the story. It is how his obituary frames it when he passes away in 1990. And it is how he tells it to us, whenever he visits the white house with the white picket fence in the late 1970s. He and Malini come often—Bob drives to nearby Pennsylvania to pick them up. It seems completely ordinary to us that a pair of Indian activists should come by for lunch. They are, as a couple, a study in contrasts. Victor, a small, wiry man with a full head of bushy hair, wears plain slacks and a white dress shirt with the sleeves rolled up. Malini, younger and less theatrical, is also rounder, with a softer voice, and favors a *salwar kameez* in bright colors. Once, Victor shows up with a copy of *Sins of the Fathers* on an old film reel. He encourages a showing in the family room, and Bob brings out the projector and the portable screen and sets it all up. "Bring your friends! Bring your family!" Victor implores. We watch the short film, beguiled by him, by the ongoing commentary of a man we understand to be an internationally famous human rights hero. As the projector rolls through the film with a humming noise and a regular clickety-clack, Bob stands at the ready with his hands on the controls, knowing that Victor likes to punctuate the viewings. "Can you stop it here?" the elder man often shouts in a thick British Indian accent. "I want to say something!"

A habitual smoker, Victor will always take a break after the showing ends, stepping out alone into our private backyard, a place where only family and the closest of friends are allowed. That, I remember, is unusual. Others smoke in the house. He, seeking the quiet contemplation of the garden, does not.

The *New York Times* story in which Victor is profiled—titled "War Children," and published in August of 1974—provides additional insight and some suggestive details, all in the eventual service of a subtle pro-American pitch for adoption. The school named Hope, the *Times* emphasizes, is a refuge from hate, from the "death stares" that Bear has always talked about. We are told this by one representative woman—identified as Tran Thi Thung—who has three kids at the school. "Three half black children by three different GIs," the *Times* describes. One of the children quoted in the piece is the age of Bear's older sister, Amy, and when I read the story for the first time, I ask myself if Tran Thi Thung is actually Mae, Bear's birth mother, who, like Bear, has been a part of our story for almost as long as I can remember. I know her as Mae, but she signs letters as Tran Thi Thoung, and the loss of that letter *o* in the *Times* piece seems like a simple error of reporting in the midst of war.

The four of them pose for a black-and-white photograph at some point before late April of 1975. Bear is the youngest and the smallest and the darkest of the three children. He wears a small bow tie and a short-sleeved shirt. He looks suspicious, or wary, of something just out of our view. Peter, his older brother, has his hand protectively around Bear's shoulder. Mae is seated next to Bear, a slight smile on her face. Her hair is parted in the middle and swept behind her. She has a striking confidence in her eyes. Years before I actually meet her, when all I have is this picture, I assume that she is strong willed and tough—a survivor who has seen a lot. Amy, the sister, stands on the end, looking directly at the camera. To me, it has always looked like Bear's left hand is reaching out to Amy beyond the frame of the photograph. I imagine that she is holding his hand with the same tenderness shown by Peter. That photograph comes with Bear to our house. I grow up with it, with his memories of these extraordinary people, and with this vision of care and protection and love, and with the great sorrow that he has

Mae's photo of her family. Peter has his arm around Bear, who is wearing a bow tie.

been ripped from that set of relations with such tremendous and severing force.

Racism and poverty and war are what drive Tran Thi Thung to place her three children in what is described by the *Times*, without irony, as an orphanage, as if Blackness were social death and as if any mother can truly live only if she warehouses her children where no one can find them. "No Vietnamese man," she explains, "will take three black kids." Victor, quoted in the middle of the piece, blames the necessity of Hope on "family pressure," on the desire of the Vietnamese to off-load the children as the byproduct of a rapacious war and then to "completely forget them." "Some adoption officials," the *Times* concludes, "believe that even with American society's own prejudices there is still more room for difference in the United States than in Vietnam." Adoption, the reporter editorializes, is the answer. Once more, I hear the all-powerful official narrative, authorizing the rescue of children incorrectly described as forsaken.

"That was their specialty," Bear remembers now, thinking of Hope. "They had a whole lot of us there." I share the *Times* piece with him. He doubts that the woman quoted is Mae, but he also can't explain the eerie parallels and the spectral possibilities. A single mother with three children, each of them fathered by a different Black soldier. "They had a whole lot of us," he repeats without any more detail. He remembers Hope as a refuge for the racially mixed and the marginalized. He reminds me of the dangerous world beyond the embassy compound, where his skin marked him for violence, and of the penumbra of security assured by the school, the embassy, the American military.

On the other side of the world in April of 1975, Bob and Sheryl sit in the kitchen, watching the local news coverage of that last flight out of Saigon—the plane that carries Bear. They know the folks at Welcome House, because they are model adoptive parents, and have led parent workshops on international adoption. They know that Mary Graves, the director of Welcome House, has been in Saigon, working behind the scenes, laying the groundwork for the final operation. They know what happens after takeoff, know that the children will wend their way to the United States and then, by way of a red-eye from Seattle, to a familiar white farmhouse in Pennsylvania, owned by a well-meaning woman, a patron of the agency.

"I don't think you should name her." Mom says this to me over the phone. We are talking, presently, about the woman who owned the farmhouse. I've been asking for more details from that day. "This was a very fly-by-night thing," she elaborates, choosing her words carefully, "and I'm not sure that the State Department was totally aware of everything that was happening." She wants me to be careful, even now.

That night in 1975, when the news coverage of the flight ends, the broadcast moves on but our parents' thoughts do not. Bob picks up the phone and calls the farmhouse in Doylestown. He asks for information about any infants on the flight who might not have been adopted. Sheryl watches him across the kitchen table, trying to read his face. The cradle for the phone is attached to the kitchen wall and he twirls the long cord of the receiver absentmindedly. Their empty dinner plates are still out. The local news is now focused on the minutiae of tri-state traffic and sports. Twilight spills gently into the room. A tray of flowers is on the picnic table outside, ready to be planted. Every minute or so, maple seeds pirouette to the ground, lazily drifting past the window.

Bob hangs up the phone. There are no infants, he tells her. "But they mentioned that they have a five-year-old without a family." His voice has a sad, resigned tone. His body sags.

Sheryl doesn't understand his melancholy. "Well," she replies, "did you tell them that we want him?"

Bob is looking for—hoping for—an infant. Again, he has a vision of what this will all look like when it is done. And she, unsurprisingly, is more practical. She is willing to adjust and improvise. The dream can change.

"We have a five-year-old already," she adds. "We know what that is like. We can do this."

It is the weekend. Bob calls back, rings up the farmhouse, where the folks from Welcome House have gathered waiting for children to arrive from the West Coast. Sheryl is on the edge of her seat, leaning forward, tugging on the edge of a blue-and-white-checked placemat. The woman's voice on the other end of the line is tired. It has been a long day at the farmhouse. She muffles the receiver. After a brief consultation with someone else, she comes back to the line and says: "If you can get here on Monday, he is yours."

On Monday, then, we all head out to Bucks County, Pennsylvania, in Big Red, the Chevy Suburban Bob has bought as a family transport. Big Red is overwhelmingly, comically big, with three rows of bench seats and a vast space behind that we call the back-back. On the way out to Doylestown, the three kids take up the middle bench seat. Bob and Sheryl, Bug and me, and our younger brother, Mark, joins us, too. He is two years old, a blond-haired, blue-eyed toddler. Still the baby of the family. Sheryl twists in the front seat, and does her best to explain what is about to happen. She tells us about refugees and the war, the plane and the long flight across the Pacific.

We arrive at the vast old farmhouse and discover that we are not alone. The place is a hive of activity. The driveway is filled with cars, their doors wide open, their trunk hatches lifted up. Voices shout across the yard, some in English and some in Vietnamese and some in French. Children play while parents stuff their cars with the same bags that were hastily labeled back at the embassy compound in Saigon. The bags are small. The children have little in the way of possessions. They watch nervously from the lawn, from the porch, from the windows. The driveway functions as a roulette wheel, and with each twist, each departing car, a child leaves, spun off into a back seat and written into a new life with a new identity. There are no clipboards, no official gate agents, and no photographer. The wild recklessness of the scene echoes the larger chaos of the last day of the American with-drawal. Many of the children airlifted out of Saigon have not yet been matched with parents. They have a few more days to wait. And some of them have been matched just as Bear is, long after that final plane took off, when someone purposefully picks up the phone to ask a frank question, and then just as purposefully gets into a car and heads out to the Pennsylvania countryside.

At the farmhouse, Bob and Sheryl present themselves as prospective parents of the unmatched five-year-old on-site. Bear, they learn, has a half sister, Amy, who has already been dispatched with her new mother, and a half brother, Peter, who is waiting for his new parents to arrive. Bob keeps Bug, Mark, and me busy with a game while Sheryl leads Peter and Bear into a large room filled with small beds. Peter walks over to a closet in the far corner and opens it. Sheryl peers inside, seeing a messy, tangled pile of personal belongings, stacked high with clothes jammed into bags of all sorts. Peter reaches into the pile and withdraws a small, brown vinyl duffel bag with three names on it. His name, Bear's, and Amy's—their Vietnamese names. He takes Bear by the hand and sits down on the floor to go through the bag, making sure that his brother has what he needs to survive. They discuss the items in turn, and create two piles, one for each of them. Peter packs everything that will belong to Bear into the brown bag, so that his little brother has something to carry his clothes in, so that he doesn't have to hold them loosely in his arms. Among the items he places in the bag is the black-and-white pho-tograph of the four of them. Sheryl takes Bear by the hand and walks them both outside, where Bob has already gotten the rest of us into Big Red. Standing by the idling car, the two brothers embrace. And then, slowly, we drive away while Peter watches and waves.

"The two boys were sad," Mom recalls now. I'm not sure that "sadness" can capture what they are feeling. After a wrenching inter-national relocation, they are being divvied up, sent away from each other, they imagine, forever. I interpret the deliberateness with which they debate the provenance of their shared material history and assume it is meant to slow down their last few minutes together. Mom is telling me this story over the phone almost fifty years later. I have to ask her a question. "Did you think about taking Peter, too?" I am imagining Dad out in the hallway managing three children, making small talk with the lady who owned the farmhouse. I am thinking of Mom's earlier impetuousness—"We have a five-year-old. We can do this!" And I am taking note of the presence of acutely felt, vivid detail in her account of the farmhouse, the bedroom, and the closet, an indication of the shock of that moment for her, for Bear and Peter, for all of us, as they all struggle—standing within feet of each other—with those powerful discourses of rescue and salvation that demand separation and alienation as a condition of incorporation. The closet. The tangle of bags. The actuarial precision of Peter's disposition of their remnants of a life in Vietnam. The names scribbled on the bag. The photograph, tucked inside. The goodbye at the edge of the driveway. The pull away from the curb. The tumultuous end to a dizzying tragedy that began with a phone call placed to the Hope school only a few days earlier. The emotional weight of these experiences has burned these details into her memory.

"It was all so rushed and so dramatic," she responds wistfully. "Peter's new parents were already on their way, and it was all described to us as a done deal." There is the suggestion of a wish in her voice, a breathlessness that dates back to that Monday in the driveway of the farmhouse. This moment, I realized, has been among the most difficult in her life. I know that she can still see Peter standing at the edge of the driveway while the car pulls away. And I regret, perhaps, that I have even asked the question.

All told, she reminds me, we are in and out of the farmhouse in less than an hour.

I remember none of this. Memories of the hour spent in Doylestown and the car ride there and back are lost. I have not a single second of it.

Not a smell or a sound or a frozen image. Except for the duffel bag. I remember the pebbled texture of the vinyl, the chocolate-brown sides, the black handles, and the scribbles on the side, the birth names written hastily in block letters, scribbled in the precious minutes before Bear, Peter, Amy, and too many others are hastily swept up into the belly of a cargo aircraft and exported to American soil.

For years, the bag sits empty in the back of a bedroom closet in our house, a trace of Bear's past and a reminder of that forced separation. I open it, explore it, obsess over it. Years later, moving away from the white house, we lose it.

After the flight from Vietnam and the long drive from Doylestown, Bear's arrival is rapturous. We get home late, and yet he races around the house, touching every surface, opening every door, looking out every window, gesturing excitedly to us, speaking only rapid Vietnamese. There is a small plastic slide in the house in the second-floor hallway. He discovers it quickly—gleefully. He goes up and down, up and down, over and over. All the while, he speaks to us animatedly, urgently, pointing and gesturing to explain how he is feeling and what he is seeing. His excitement is reassuring to Bob and Sheryl, in a way, even if no one can understand what he is saying. He is happy. After everything he has been through, his happiness is a gift.

" 'They have a slide!' " Bear recalls thinking now. "I remember that I went down it backwards, climbing the smooth part and going down the steps."

There were three of us when I woke up that morning. By the time I fall asleep, we are four.

As the days go by, we learn that Bear is a charming, happy, and easygoing child. He is an uncomplicated incorporation, as I remember it, and instantly the best athlete in the family. He climbs trees effortlessly, rides his bicycle with grace, picks up baseball as if he has been playing it all his life. In extended-family games that summer and beyond, he is a clear favorite—a sunny child with a great sense of humor and extraordinary skills on the ballfield. At summer camp, he is the first person picked when we choose up sides. On our Little League baseball team, he is the star, a talented pitcher and hitter. On the soccer field, he is unstoppable, an astonishingly fast and agile player, capable of ranging the full field without tiring. Bob and Sheryl drop him into our lives without any guardrails—in the manner of Jim Bouton—so he learns English swiftly.

In every single way, he is physically superior to me. And he is handsome and gregarious, a chatterbox with dimples. For the first few years, we play on the same teams, as you'd expect siblings of the same age to do. And then, rather quickly, the coaches elevate Bear to the so-called traveling baseball teams, which compete statewide. I stop playing sports soon after. I remember no real resentment, just resignation and sadness that I lack his skills. That I can't throw the ball with as much accuracy and force, can't range to my left and right, scooping up groundballs, can't play so recklessly. I watch from the sidelines as he wins trophies.

Mom says that I revert to baby talk when Bear arrives. That I am so completely flummoxed by his stardom that I freeze. Or that I simply stop speaking. For weeks, I remain mute. "We were so scared," she remembers: "What have we done?" So reminiscent, I think when she tells me this, of Jim Bouton, who worried about breaking his family.

I tell myself a different story. Self-servingly, I recall a single grand act of diplomacy in the driveway at the moment of Bear's arrival: the gift of my bicycle, a generous tribute to the new family member. I remember the two of us playing on the plastic slide inside the house, a seamless integration. In the small stack of photographs taken at my fifth birthday, Bear is right there next to me, with a big smile on his face and an enormous slice of cake in front of him. His birthday passes without notice, as he moves against the flow of time in the belly of that transport plane.

There are a dozen photographs from this extraordinary period of time—between May and Halloween of 1975. In one, we are both at the top of an outdoor slide, attached to a metal playset Bob has assembled

Bear and me, in 1976, with complementary red, white, and blue outfits and lunchboxes. We are waiting for the school bus.

for us. I'm poised to descend, a big smile on my face, my arms relaxed. Bear is right behind me, ready to push—or to follow. His smile is just as big, just as earnest.

We start twinning—in jest—when we meet for the very first time, a practice we continue through high school. We are just a month and a half apart in age, and roughly the same size, so it makes sense that Mom will match our clothing on some days, or heighten the contrast on others. So it comes to be that Bear will get the brown turtleneck and I will get the blue; he will be Batman and I will be Spiderman. We share a paper route, share a love of BMX bikes, which we build and rebuild and scrupulously maintain. We read the same kind of books—keeping a shared library in the house—play the same kind of sports, though Bear, again, is always so much better at them.

We turn the twinning into a joke, a routine that is meant to disarm and confuse. Our small town is, for many years, subject to visitations from religious missionaries—Jehovah's Witnesses. Some summers, these earnest types will knock on our door maybe three or four times, looking for someone to talk to. These are trim, clean-cut white men in earnest white shirts and khakis, holding a bundle of handouts, questing for someone to listen to them. Bear and I are home a lot and will alternate answering the door. Sometimes they will remember, with a start, the last time they were there. They will remember a different skin color.

Often, they frame this wonderment as a question. "Was there a white child here last time?" "We spoke with a young Black boy a few weeks back."

They look closer, attempting a discerning gaze. While one of us hides inside, the other offers a quick response and a deadpan look: "Oh, that was my twin brother." We let their memories of our skins twist. We give no explanation. They are always so serious, and there is little sense of irony or humor in the conversation. And we are very good at deadpan. I cannot remember answering a question about "us" straightforwardly. There is always a dissembling quality, always a kind of playful refusal. Our legend precedes us. By the rules of sight, it is obvious that we are different. We try to rewrite our narrative to get around those rules.

Our twinning means that when Peter comes it is hard.

Their reconnection comes courtesy of Malini, the wife of Victor, the man who hustled Bear and his siblings onboard that C-130. A talented social worker in her own right, she knows the kids from the Hope school, and knows how close they are. After everyone is airlifted to the United States, Malini is still living in Pennsylvania. She is the one who follows up with the parents to make sure that the kids are

Malini and Victor and the rest of us in the secluded backyard on a sunny fall day.

safe, and happy, and taken care of. She contacts Sheryl and asks if she might help bring Mae's children—Bear, Peter, and Amy—back together. At Malini's suggestion, Bob and Sheryl stage these reunions and reconnections regularly at our house, tucked behind that white picket fence, on the back patio where we can all be safe.

When I ask Mom about all of this now, she remembers Malini with keen fondness, seeing her as a kind social worker with the ambition to keep families intact against the interests of the American empire, which authorizes dispersal and diffusion as the means of assimilation. For Mom, the story of us in those earlier years hinges on Malini, not Victor, who did what he thought was right, enacting the rescue and salvation of children caught up in a global war. Malini, who seeks to ensure that those same children will never forget where they come from, is the one she celebrates.

A few years after enabling this reconnection, Malini and Victor leave for Florida, planning to resume their refugee-resettlement work in warmer climes. They fade from our memory even if, without them, "we" can never have been. Amy has moved farther away, and we see her rarely, if at all. We keep in closer touch with Peter, though. He is a familiar presence in our house, with a quick smile and so much love for his little brother. After Bear completes college, he moves into an apartment with Peter in Washington, DC. I stay down there with them for a few months, sleeping on the floor. It feels, in a word, natural—even though I know that is the wrong word. Natural and comfortable, familiar and easy.

Soon after Bear and Peter move in together, they bring their birth mother, Mae, over to the United States from Vietnam, restoring a connection among four people that the war almost severed over twenty years earlier. I remember, again, that photograph of the four of them. I think of what might have ended forever in that Pennsylvania farmhouse, with the division of their belongings, and the lurching reassignment to a new set of relations. I imagine the crunch of the gravel as Big Red pulls away, leaving Peter to wave goodbye. They are given new kin with a different skin, that skin representing the nation-state and global superpower that has torn their homeland into pieces. They have new fictions of relation. But the boys remember. Malini does, too. And Sheryl remembers Peter, sitting patiently, and slipping that photograph into that brown duffel bag.

6

A few days before that military transport rumbles down the runway and leaves Saigon, Mae is compelled to make a series of declarations, legal predicates for the eventual adoption of her three mixed-race children. In the first of these declarations, she names the African American soldier with whom she lived until 1971, establishing something like a common-law relationship, and then names the child—Bear—she bore him. She declares "honorably" that the same soldier acknowledged the child as his own, too, but adds that he abandoned her after Bear's birth. She has received no support since. "I am poor, have no occupation, and cannot support my child," she writes. She is willingly giving him up to the Vietnamese-American Children's Fund "to care for and seek adoptive parents for my child." The purpose is to testify to Bear's American parentage and to show that Mae has been effectively widowed by the war. This gives Bear an improvised special status and makes it possible, in those final minutes, to airlift him to an Air Force base on the West Coast.

The second document is substantially more sweeping. This "Release Certificate" gives total and everlasting control over his future to the

Fund. The form emphasizes Mae's "voluntary" signature, the Fund's "complete authority" to make decisions, including those related to travel, health care, and family assignment, and even the transfer of these absolute controls to another adoption organization. "Because of my situation," the form reads, "(husband returned to his country, poverty, many children, death, unemployment) I want to give my child a better future but I have not enough strength to raise them until they are grown up. I promise that from the day I sign this release," it closes, "I have no further authority regarding my child." And at the very bottom, she has signed her name over a single line of text: "I agree to give up my child forever."

As it turns out, Mae *is* the woman quoted in the *New York Times* in 1974. When she speaks to the *Times* reporter, her three children are nearby. Bear. Peter. Amy. I envision her words circulating in the printed edition of the *Times*, carried into the shared time and space of the United States, into the orbit of New York City. I wonder whether our parents buy a copy, how close they come to reading that story. Does it remind them of the Jim Bouton piece in *Family Circle*? Does Victor ever tell my parents about the story? Does he carry a printed copy around with him? I share the *New York Times* piece with Mom, who has no memory of ever seeing it. Bob, she corrects, was a loyal reader of the *Newark Star-Ledger*.

Something bothers me, though. A simple thing. That one word: *forever*. As in: *I voluntarily sign this paper to give up my child forever.* As in: *I agree to give up my child forever.*

The word is repeated several times in the English-language version of the letter that Mae signs in 1975. It is aggressively inserted in print and woven into the texture of the paper.

Mae signs only the Vietnamese version of the letter. And the question I need to ask—the obvious question that anyone would or should ask—isn't one I can put to Bear. It is too searing. It names, in a single query, the vastness of inequity, disadvantage, and abjection that confronts Mae in that moment, when the pen presses against her fingers, and her eyes absorb the words. Does that word—*forever*—appear in the actual letter she signs, the letter written in her own tongue?

If the word is missing, it would mean that Bear was stolen away, his mother assuming some return, his body and his future redistributed by the national security state, until it is well beyond her reach. It would mean that someone, somewhere along the way, realized just how much easier it would be to take this child—to place this child in a white suburban home—with just a little misdirection. A missing word is deceptive, suggesting a kind of violence of the shadows, of the dark, where lurching, wounded America—and all that it stood for—could find some final, cauterizing advantage. It would mean that Bear was repurposed to serve a postwar narrative of reconciliation, and that his mother never understood what was happening.

If the word is there, though, it would be a reminder of the nation-state's raw, naked power, its capacity to put its absolute authority, even in the twilight of its Far East empire, right on the page, in black and white, for everyone and all of human history to see. It would mean that someone in Saigon looked Mae in the eye and, without hesitation or embarrassment, thrice cut her loose.

Forever. A word that cuts through all entanglements. A word that ends. *Forever.*

A word that rings confidently, that confirms with a wax seal, that closes and locks the door, that enables the permanent, absolute incorporation. A word that makes adoption easier.

A friend agrees to translate for me. We share a cocktail, a necessary fortification. An old-fashioned at a local bar. As a welcome distraction, he gently shares with me his own story—born in 1975 in Vietnam, leaving for Hong Kong in 1980, arriving in the United States shortly after that. The biography is meant to be reassuring. He knows something of my concern. He gets it. He also understands the stakes—the larger, existential stakes—of the question.

"Let me take a look." He reads carefully. His finger points to a pair of words on the page.

vĩnh viễn

These words repeat, too.

vĩnh viễn

"forever"

He sighs. "Vietnamese words are precise," he says; "American English is vague." This distinction is important, he wants me to know. I can hear it in his voice. Very important. There are a few ways to say something like "forever," he wants me to know. "This word"—he presses his fingertip into the page, right below *vĩnh viễn*—"is bigger." "It signifies," he tells me, "the eternal, the never-ending, an epic sweep of the universe, an abandonment for all of time."

"I wonder," he continues, "what she was thinking when she signed it. When she saw that word, knowing its infinite meaning."

7

I am on a business trip, stuck in the Salt Lake City airport, when a young couple catch my eye. In a room of tired travelers, they are exceptional, laughing and bright eyed, tending to the excited five-year-old child in front of them. The child is hungry—pointing and talking—and they are rooting around in a backpack for some snacks.

They are white. A handsome couple, young and lean, with the rangy, tanned look of veteran travelers who love the outdoors, awakening my memories of Bob and Sheryl in the late 1960s. He is Black. A beautiful child, with a big, ready smile. He has on a yellow T-shirt with a smiley face on it and a pair of cargo pants with one knee worn out. His hair has grown out a little, I notice, and it is knotty and lumpy. His skin is ashen and cracked. It is clear that the three of them love one another; and it is obvious—I think, in my sojourning misery—that the parents need to learn a little more about how to take care of Black hair and Black skin.

Lazily surveilling this trio from my slumped-over position in a corner, I think of Bear right away. I might call him, explain the situation, ask him whether it would be worth my while to say a few words to the parents. Bear, the family philosopher, will know what to say. Or what not to say.

"Drop it," he will probably say. "Not your family; not your journey. They'll figure it out."

Bear has no cell phone at the time, so I sit there, fingers splayed on the cool terrazzo floor, for a little while longer, doing nothing. I have known many white parents who've adopted one or two Black children, and I've seen some of them struggle on this exact same cultural front. It is easier, I know, to diversify a bookshelf or a playlist, or a set of dolls, and a lot harder to know what you don't know, or to see your blind spots. Black skin and Black hair lie outside of what most white people understand, or what they can discern.

And I think of Bear, of course, because to some extent that is his story, too. Marched off to the shower every night, his skin dries out afterward. In his case, Sheryl and Bob pay attention. "It wasn't a Black or white issue," Mom tells me plainly now. "We could just see that he needed moisturizer." They buy big pump dispensers of it and leave them out in the bathroom. Their instant materialization and general ubiquity catches my eye. We are all encouraged to apply the stuff, but I hate the gummy, sticky feel of it, the way it makes me feel like I am covered in glue.

Bob and Sheryl have studied up—and then, as they often do, universalize the response. "I do remember having to ask a doctor," she continues, "whether Black skin could sunburn. Of course, the answer was yes. I don't remember sunscreen being the big thing it is today back in the 1970s but there was suntan lotion which offered some protection and kept skin moist. So we applied that to Bear."

"And to you," she adds, pointedly.

Bear's natural hair has a looser, more forgiving curl than some, but it still requires regular attention. Adopting older children, though, means that the children themselves come knowing things, which makes for fewer miscues and mistakes. Bear brings a plastic hair pick when he arrives that night in 1975, and he comes knowing how to use it. Later, he will leave his Afro comb stuck in the back of his hair as a stylistic marker, a fashionable complement to the red leather parachute pants and ripped T-shirts he is prone to wearing.

It must be Mae, his birth mother, who gets him that pick, and who ensures that it travels with him on that plane out of Saigon. Mae, one of the unsung heroes of our story, who entrusts her child to another mother she will not meet for decades. Mae, who tucks the pick into that small brown duffel bag he shares with Peter and Amy, provisioning her son with a basic tool for self-care. I wonder, thinking of that terrible moment when they divide up their things before separating, if Peter gives the pick to his younger brother. If Peter teaches Bear to use that pick, and if someone taught Peter, too—some Black GI lost to history, someone at the school or in Mae's life.

I remember trying Bear's pick once and enjoying the light scalp massage it provides. It doesn't work for my hair, of course, except as a comb. I have seen a pick before, and not just on television. I see them at those vast Welcome House picnics, and at our house, where other big families come for dinner or lunch.

We have all seen healthy Black skin before, and well-tended Black hair. We note their presence and their absence.

"Your flight is still delayed," the speaker barks, taking me away from the past. "We thank you for your patience while we wait for the storm to pass." The mom walks off with the child to check out a nearby display. I walk up to the dad. The boy, it turns out, was adopted from Haiti as a toddler, and is their only child, with no memories of home. Or none that they know.

I don't mention the hair. Or the skin.

"Not your family," Bear says in my mind; "not your journey."

"Maybe not, maybe so," I say quietly in response.

8

Years after Bob's death, Mom gives me a few disorganized bins of random ephemera. She is moving and needs to divest herself of artifacts from our past. Bear gets the rolltop desk. Mark gets the oversize dining table, the one that Bob made specially for us. I get the historical stuff kept belowground in the white house.

The material from the basement is a random accumulation. Most of it fits in a pair of plastic bins with blue tops. These are filled with old photos, video reels, VHS tapes, negatives, undeveloped rolls of film, and dozens of aluminum slide magazines, the metal still gleaming as if new. There are a few small envelopes and plastic bags, and a handful of loose two-by-two-inch slides and dozens of crumpled old photographs, some of them half melted, stuck to the bottom.

The stuff in those bins has traveled. In the 1980s, when the material starts to take up too much space in the living room, Bob dumps everything into brown file boxes and stacks them in a corner of the basement marked for deep storage. They sit there untouched for a decade, right next to the lumbering old oil burner. When Bob and Sheryl sell the white house with the picket fence in the mid-1990s, moving about a mile away to a smaller house in the middle of the woods, they clear out the basement, consolidating everything from those cardboard boxes into new plastic bins. They take the bins to the house in the woods, put them in the back basement hallway, and promptly forget them. The bins linger there for twenty years. When I visit, I stub my toe on them in the dark, as I fumble for the ceiling pull chain dangling from the single light bulb. After Bob's death, the bins are moved again to Mom's new condo, to a shelf in the garage, until she decides, at long last, to get rid of them. After all of that, they are given to me, and sit in my basement, gathering dust and sawdust, as I move from New Jersey to Indiana to Rhode Island. The blue lid has cracked by the end of these journeys, and someone has tried to fix it with clear packing tape. But the fix is imperfect, and the lid no longer grabs the sides, no longer stays down. This, in the end, is how precious photographs become forgotten, nearly become landfill.

"I gave that stuff to you," Mom tells me, "so that you could do whatever you wanted with it." I open the bins and get to work, and find that, inside, the material long ago sedimented into layers by type, slides and photographs and videocassettes, arranged like the strata of a mountain, impacted and heaved by the decades of movement from one dark corner to another.

It takes weeks to go through all the slides. The metal magazines need to be disassembled and the slides individually extracted. And then each slide must be inserted into an old-school viewer, so I can assess, discern, and appraise the image. The slides in magazines, at least, are organized chronologically. The loose slides are a different story. They are random in the way of a box of junk at a flea market. There are thousands and thousands of loose slides. Most of them, I come to understand, are about vacations taken in the 1960s, or cocktail parties at Virginia Terrace, or picnics taken at the canal near the Delaware Water Gap. Some of them are images of us. Mark comes home from the hospital. Bear has a broken leg. This is the hardest part of the process: looking at each slide, all of them the same on the outside, trying to make sense of an image that was important to Bob fifty years ago.

After a week, my fingers sifting through the loose pile, I find one that stands out. The paper mounting is darker, mottled with smudges from repeated handling. A label tells me that it was printed in Seoul years ago. To my eye, this slide has had a sort of wanderlust of its own, drifting in this itinerant bin from the other side of the world, somehow ending up in the tangled pile of detritus, the remains of Bob's intellectual life. The dirtiness of it—those smudges, those scuffs—are the story. This slide has lived.

Anna, as a child in Seoul, dancing onstage.

The image on it is, at first, confusing and unfamiliar. A small child stands onstage, dancing in a blue-and-white outfit. A small, ornate red hat is fixed to the top of their head. This seems like a play of some kind, because there are shadows cast by a strong spotlight that illuminates most of the stage, which features a village backdrop, complete with a stone-and-stucco house with a thatched roof. The child is in mid-motion, arms sweeping from left to right, and the spotlight captures an iridescent sheen on the front of the costume. It is clearly a hastily taken snapshot, because it is slightly out of focus, the angle all wrong. Another small child stands offstage, in the audience, in the shadows of the foreground. A cut runs through the middle of the slide, and a thin blade of light pierces the top part of the image.

I have never seen this image before.

I text Mom. "What is this? Who is this?"

She, too, has never seen this image. Or she has no memory of it. "Try your sister," she advises.

I turn to Anna. I send another text, along with a hasty snapshot. "Is this you?"

She calls me immediately, in tears. She has never seen it either; and yet it is her.

In fact, it is the only photograph she has of her childhood before she came to New Jersey. Lost, for fifty years, in a pile of Bob's random photographic souvenirs. Mom wonders if it was included in the materials sent over by the adoption agency, after Anna's hurried acquisition. I'll never know how it detached from that tiny archive, or how it fell into that loose pile that moved from basement to basement, from file boxes to plastic bins, that traveled to five states before it was opened. It is a marvel, I tell myself, that the slide has survived. Its very existence defies chance.

Anna joins us in 1977, when she is thirteen. She comes from Seoul, South Korea. From the same city where that slide was once processed. She shares an origin point with Bug.

"Two of every race."

Unsurprisingly, there's a degree of wrenching serendipity in her story. Through the late 1970s, Bob and Sheryl continue to work with the same adoption agency—Welcome House—that brought them Bear and Bug. "Work with," in this context, means a lot of different things. At one point, they serve as a stock couple in promotional stills on brochures. They are enlisted to offer lectures to prospective parents, sharing insights gleaned from their experiences in a multiracial homestead. Their experience with our quartet makes them knowledgeable experts in adoption circles. They are a photogenic pair, and we are a good-looking quartet. One week in late 1976, in the midst of their ongoing commitments for the agency, they are recruited by a social worker for some light acting. They are to appear in a documentary on the international adoption process that is being filmed for a Philadelphia television station.

"That was our second film," Mom says, adding, "I don't remember the details of the first." I sit still and listen, quietly transcribing.

They are to take on the role of a couple for some background footage, providing a visual to match a voice-over narration. The storyboard calls for them to be seated in a social worker's office, where they will be presented with the biographical story of a child they can adopt, after which the social worker will present them with a photograph of the child in question. They are supposed to appear to be listening, to lean forward, to nod enthusiastically, and to pretend to graciously accept the opportunity. There are cameras and lights everywhere in the room, and the director is fussy, calling for numerous retakes. Bob and Sheryl think that the whole affair seems farcical, except that the biographies and photographs presented to them are quite literally real. During the first few takes, the photograph they are given is of twin seven-year-old boys. They burst out laughing when they see it. They have two near-twin boys at home already, both of them six. They couldn't possibly handle four boys of the same age. The laughter irritates the director, of course. But Bob and Sheryl aren't trained actors, they explain. They can't fake a feeling. To showcase sincerity, they need to be presented with someone who might actually appeal to them, someone they might actually want to incorporate.

The social worker looks at them carefully. It has been a long day. The lights make the room hot. This is just background footage. Fifteen seconds of screen time. Still, she takes a deep breath, thinks about what they are saying. With a nod, she reaches down into a file drawer, pulls out another manila folder, and swaps in a very different story and photograph. This time, there is a photo of a young woman with straight brown hair, green eyes, and a slight smile on her face.

Anna is an orphaned half-Korean, half-white child. She has no living relatives. Not much is known about her father, except that he is European or American. Her mother has died recently, leaving Anna in the hands of the Sisters of the Good Shepherd in Seoul, a Catholic order dating back centuries with a close focus on the stewardship of young girls and young women. Stern and scrupulous, the Sisters have identified Anna as a singularly urgent priority: an older child with strong moral promise who is approaching a legal tipping point, at which she will be too old to easily relocate. She continues to show great potential, even as time goes by. Indeed, as a sign of her gratitude for their efforts, Anna has taken the name of the sister who watches over her and has shown herself to be gentle and kind and helpful.

This is the backstory shared with Bob and Sheryl, the story that is meant to tug at their heartstrings as the cameras hum and the lights blind them. It works. Her story is compelling enough to make them appear truly interested. While the cameras roll, they lean in, flip through the dossier, point out details to each other, and ask questions of the social worker. Suddenly, the director yells "cut!" and the scene is over. Bob and Sheryl untangle themselves from the electrical cords, leave the room with a nod of thanks to the social worker, get into their car, and head back to the white house in the small town they call home.

Here, serendipity comes into play. On the way home from the film shoot, Bob and Sheryl talk about the child in the picture. They have an itch they can't scratch. From the house, they call the social worker, and ask—this time for real, without cameras or studio lights—if the girl in the photo is still at the convent, waiting to be adopted. They have made this kind of call before. They know what they are getting into. Sheryl is already drawing up a list of things to buy, organizing the house to make room for one more body. Even so, they are nervous, excited. The child is still up for adoption, they learn, but there are legal and administrative challenges. For one thing, she is still in Korea. Bob secures a visa and a passport, on the off chance that he might need to travel, thinking that it might help if he is willing to provide transportation and an adult escort. The passport comes through in November; the visa from the Korean Consulate General's office in New York is issued a month later. He is never called to go, but he is ready to make the trip alone if necessary.

"We wondered if we would even be allowed to adopt her," Mom adds, making these challenges seem almost insurmountable. "Somehow," she adds, "it got done." Her phrasing is curious. When I call attention to her use of the passive voice, she says something that reminds me of our earlier conversation about Doylestown: "Let's let that one slide." Some stories can't be told. Fifty years later, and Mom still worries about rules that might have been bent on her behalf. Still worries, too, that it might cost us something if that bending is brought into the light.

With legal issues somehow resolved, the rest of us need to be brought into the conversation. Bob and Sheryl call for a family meeting at the kitchen table. Such meetings are solemn, dramatic occasions. The four children—Bear, myself, Bug, and Mark—sit on the sides, while Sheryl sits at one head and Bob sits at the other. We fidget, waiting for the official start. Suddenly, it begins. We hear the intake of breath and turn. "We are considering adding another child," Bob says, his eyes moving around our quartet, assessing our mood and our feelings. He tells us about Anna. Describes her to us. Tells us that she is all alone, without any family in the world, and that she needs a place to live. In some detail he lays out the story of her difficult life. His eyes are pinched and his voice is gravely serious, as if this were a murder trial and someone's life hung in the balance. In his mind, I think that is true. Anna's life, as he sees it, is threatened. We miss the notes of seriousness in his voice and his manner. We are small children, so we buzz with excitement. A new sibling sounds like a lot of fun.

To welcome her, the family stages a typical homecoming gathering. A tight circle of aunts and uncles who live nearby are invited over. The driveway is kept clear of cars so that kids can ride bicycles, or play in wagons, or just run. A picketed gate closes off the driveway, so there is no need for any parent to worry. The bulk of the action, as usual, is on the back patio, where two picnic tables and several folding chairs provide ample seating. Welcoming streamers and banners are hung on the garage, with letters so big that they can be read as she comes up the driveway. "Welcome Home, Anna!" A white layer cake from the nearby Raritan Bakery is served, with the same hospitable message scrawled in neon icing. Cold cuts and bread and condiments are laid out carefully for sandwiches. Sheryl has made batches of sun tea for the occasion. Family members with cameras take photographs of the spread, of the banners, and wait for Big Red to arrive, wait for Anna to join us.

Bug came with nothing. Bear brought that small brown duffel bag. Anna materializes in our midst with an explosion of brightly colored silk, bringing several beautiful traditional Korean dresses—ceremonial *hanboks*—including one for Sheryl. The dresses are beguiling, rich with unfamiliar sheens and unexpected sounds when they move. They vibrate with an intense strangeness. At night, she dons them, plays the music of her homeland, and dances for us. The thing I remember most vividly from her arrival is a tiny thing: a miniature golden lantern, small enough to fit in the palm of my hand. There are bright red tassels attached to it, dangling from the bottom, and the peaks of a pitched roof. I remember sitting on the floor of her new room, listening to the sound of Korean music playing from a cassette recorder, and to the sound of the silk *hanbok*—the *shh-shh* of iridescent fabric, as Anna dances—while I twirl the lantern, and let the tassels drape onto my skin.

There is heartbreak in all of this, too. The heartbreak of the loss of everything she has ever known. The streets. The people. The smells. The flowers. The taste of the cuisine. The sounds of the marketplace. The voices and faces of friends who became something like family. Heartbreak measured in the miles we drive to attend Korean-language masses in Philadelphia, or to find Korean grocery stores where she can get the food she loves—kimchi especially, but really anything that she can draw together into a meaningful facsimile of the foodways of her childhood. Seaweed wrappers. White rice. Soy sauce. Packaged ramen noodles. She learns to make kimchi at home. We learn to eat with chopsticks, seeking a common culture in the house that will include her. She speaks some English, which means that she can express herself, give voice to her lamentations, plead with us to search out whatever can be found of Korea in central New Jersey. "She missed her culture," Mom remembers wistfully. "We did what we could. It would be so much easier now."

Inside the picket fence, we understand Anna as mixed. No matter how scrupulously Bob might represent our color-coding outside, or present Anna as Asian to the rest of New Jersey, her presence and her sense of self are a countervailing force. We eat together as a family every night at six sharp. As we do so, she eloquently explains what it was like growing up as a mixed person in Seoul. And she is older than us, so she is often out of the house, doing things that fascinate us. Working at a nursing home. Going out on dates. Living beyond the picket fence.

Anna reframes our family conversations about racism. When she goes off to college, and then to Jersey City, and then to work in finance, she finds herself isolated again, subject to ridicule and isolation because she isn't "pure" or "full blooded." She reports back to us, sifting through her own feelings, trying to find her place in the world. We sit at the kitchen table, eating the feast that she has prepared, listening while she bemoans the anti-Korean racism of her Japanese bosses, or the anti-mixed prejudices of Jersey City's Korean community. The conversation is passionate, tearful—shocking, and yet also ordinary and routine.

If you're me, you sit on the side of the big table, looking around. Your parents preside, and you see yourself in their faces, their skin, as they speak. But big, mixed, adoptive families work on different angles, shadows, and tones. Your sight works in several different ways. You look around the table and you see loved ones, you see brothers and sisters, and you see difference and color. Bear grabs a fork from a bucket in the middle of the table to eat. Bug takes a drink of water from a Hamburglar glass. Mark wipes the corner of his mouth with a paper napkin. Your eye catches all the alignments and, on the inside, you struggle to reconcile them, to bridge a gap that is centuries old. *Two of every race*, a compositional construct with a terrible history that unites and divides. Surveying the group at the table, you never manage to reconcile all of these things. You can't because they are irreconcilable. You are nine years old, sitting at the kitchen table, fidgeting with your chopsticks, serving yourself some rice, watching the light reflect off your sister's tears as she confides in you about the slurs she hears in the workplace, slurs directed at her with a sneer and a raised eyebrow, slurs she hears in the grocery store where the Korean ladies meet to talk about soap operas. One part of you is heartbroken, crying with her, and that part uses her surface as a mirror. "Before I ever saw myself, I saw my sister." So says Birdie, the protagonist of Danzy Senna's novel *Caucasia*, a meditation on the lives of two sisters with different skins, their family torn apart by the visual details of racial sight. You look around and see Anna, Bear, Bug, and Mark. You see your sister and your brothers. You see yourself in all of them. You see a vast chasm, too.

9

Along with the plastic bins that Sheryl sent over years ago—the ones that contained that single slide of Anna—there was a large silver metal toolbox filled with 9 mm film. The toolbox is old. Bob spray-painted it silver at some point, and neatly stacked the reels and boxes inside.

When we are younger, the old blue-green projector and the rickety screen comes up out of the basement often. Sometimes, as is true when Victor and Malini come over, there are daytime matinee performances, with friends and family there to join us. But mostly, these happen at night, whenever Bob is in the right mood. We'll drag knitted blankets and pillows and cushions into the room and curl up in them together. We'll arrange a tray of snacks on an old ottoman. For Bob, setting up for these events—especially the slideshows and movie nights where we watch pictures of us on the portable screen—takes time. The movie projector is especially troubling. The film needs to be wound carefully through the maze of wheels and guides. Inevitably, something goes wrong before things get started. Bob will fuss over the machine, getting angry. And then, with a pop, the immersive magic of the big screen brings his memories to life. The anger dissipates instantly. He presides as emcee, narrating the story of each image and scene, and the light from the projector illuminates the room with the intensity and vibrancy of each frame.

These are Bob's memories, Bob's slides, Bob's movies. The old-style reels of film and rectangular sleeves of slides are his, all carefully labeled. And they aren't meant to be forgotten. A lifelong lover of the camera, he doesn't believe in hiding this material. It deserves exposure. It is his idea, unsurprisingly, to capture the family history and to bring us all together for regular and repeated viewings, a weekend tradition that is eventually lost as new technologies emerge and as we all grow up. The projector breaks. The film grows increasingly fragile. But until we give it up completely, Bob speaks of his slides and home movies with all the charismatic authority of an outlandish Hollywood producer. He quizzes us on uncles and aunts and cousins we have never met; asks us to celebrate the 1950s cars, with their arch fins, their chromed grills, their pastel colors; lectures us on the virtues of the front stoop attached to his parents' brownstone on Virginia Terrace.

When we finally grow too old to sit still for these performances, Bob takes care to keep the reels of old film clean and safe, locking them all away in that tight, silver metal box, far from dust and dirt. I imagine him finding the box at the flea market, scraping old paint off the exterior, sanding it down, and painting it silver so that it will stand out in the basement—making it a suitable treasure chest for his precious memories. That same hermetically sealed environment degrades the film over time, producing a chemical reaction that cannot be undone. Bob doesn't know that. And when the metal box is passed along to me, as a part of Mom's housecleaning bequest, what I see is an extraordinary regime of care, with unintended and terrible consequences. Most of the older material is lost. But not all of it.

There is a booming, if specialized, business these days in converting this kind of ancient tech into something that can be viewed on a laptop. I carry the box downtown, and the man who receives the stacks of old film reels calls me weeks later to confirm that most of them cannot be saved. "I'll do what I can," he promises, referencing the rest. The largest reel is labeled "1971–1974." The years are written in Bob's handwriting on the side of the metal can. The man feels confident that he can restore that one, the one that matters most to me. He delivers the contents on a small flash drive weeks later.

This is Bob's favorite reel. I know it intimately, in the way that one knows one's hands by sight, knows all of the whorls and veins, scars and nail beds. The material on it strays outside of the dates on the label. It opens with Bob and Sheryl's wedding in 1968. We watch them make their vows, kiss, and leave the dimly lit church. Parish gold and silver winks in the background shadows. Stained glass is everywhere, letting outside light into the space, projecting the outline of saints onto the interior walls. The bridesmaids wear gold dresses and white tops, and long green ribbons in their hair. Bob and Sheryl laugh as they run down the steps of the church. It has started to rain and everyone is still throwing rice and opening umbrellas, but they are young and don't much care about the mess. At the curb, Sheryl clutches a bouquet of yellow roses in her white-gloved hands while Bob absentmindedly brushes the rice out of his hair, a yellow rose pinned to his lapel. The camera follows them into the car. Sheryl puts her head on his shoulder. They are absolutely, luminously, beautiful. We cut to the reception, and the background aesthetic changes from dark stone and plaster to honey-colored wood paneling and fluorescent lighting. The camera catches a seascape out the windows. They are at the low-slung River House in Fair Haven, New Jersey, a small banquet hall, looking out onto the Navesink River. As they eat the first slice of cake, Bob winks at the camera. Sheryl, more serious than he, points to the cake's abundant layers, explaining to the cameraman all the work and thought that has gone into the confection.

On the rest of the reel, there is abundant footage of me, of other cousins and uncles and aunts, the first wave of the next generation being received by the last. Everett and Mary, our maternal great-grandparents, come all the way from Iowa to visit and play with me in the front yard. The new fence is on prominent display, its pickets brilliantly white. There is a long recording of a parade in town, taken from across the street by Bob's brother Jerry. The focus, though, is on the young couple and new homeowners, not the parade. Bob leans proudly against his fence, wearing a blue button-down shirt and holding his camera. I've seen his photographs of this day, but this part of the reel—taken by his brother—captures him as an object, as another face in the crowd. Bob studies the parade like an anthropologist, still a stranger in this small town, still trying to understand the place where they've settled. Sheryl wears a printed shirt and holds me in her arms. She stands just outside the fence line, making small talk with another new parent.

Like everything else in that silver box, these are fragments of time and space spliced together. I recall them as a single unit of memory because that is how we first encountered them, as a group, witnessing the entire reel, with all of its discordant jumps, in sequence as Bob narrates to us. Bob strings these jumbled memories together. This is his mixtape.

The last four minutes of this reel are of us—or some of us, at least. We've jumped forward a few years. That apocryphal trio—me, Bug, and Bear—in the driveway, all on scooters or tricycles. Our cousin Kate, also newly adopted from Korea, arrives. This is a more recent piece of film, taken a few years after that descriptive scrawl in Bob's handwriting would suggest. And perhaps right after Bear's arrival. The three older kids ride up and down the driveway, laughing and playing. Mark is a toddler, wandering in and out of the shot. Bear and I ride side by side, laughing and shouting, showing off. The cousins are in the backyard. The gate is closed at the end of the driveway. The fence keeps us safe.

The final ninety seconds are, to me, the most extraordinary. The

Peter, me, and Bear in a still from one of Bob's home movies, taken around 1977.

footage comes from around 1977, right around the time that Anna joins the family. Bear and I are about seven. Peter, who is a year older, is visiting. The three of us are clowning on the front porch. I'm in the middle, as Bear and Peter wrap their arms around me—and Peter, ever the goof, is holding a small Batman figure on my shoulder, adding the superhero to the mix as well. Even though we are being recorded for a film, we pause to pose, freezing for a portrait, and the camera takes it all in carefully, moving left to right, from Peter to Batman to me to Bear. Bob, the man behind the lens, zooms in on Peter to catch his expression, which is deadly serious, as if the gothic detective has actually joined us in formal pose.

As we come down the steps, Bear speaks animatedly to Bob, who is recording. He gestures urgently, with a smile, and pulls Peter along with him down the driveway. Pushing me aside, he asks Bob to capture this ceremonial walk with Peter, to memorialize their togetherness. Bear has been living with us for a few years, and he has already learned enough about our family—its workings, its logics—to realize that such a memory will, by virtue of this recording, become the stuff of those evening shows, the ones where we dig into the blankets, the lights flicker from the projector, and Bob takes us on a tour of our history. Bear wants Peter—and his time with Peter—to be a part of that moviegoing experience. They take off together, then, down the driveway, looking back over their shoulders and smiling. But I tag along behind them, my hand reaching out for Bear's, my arm trying to connect with his body somehow. He is focused on Peter—his other brother with whom he has so much more history—as they walk arm in arm for the camera, toward the white picket fence. Their reunion is magical, a reconnection of extraordinary depth and meaning. All I can do is try to keep pace behind them as they move down the driveway, walking together for the first time in a long while, at home and at peace in this magical place, so very far from Saigon.

In the end, it is Peter who finally recognizes me, who notices my hand, my yearning for affiliation, and who reaches out graciously, drawing me back into their liaison. As we turn around, now three abreast, and walk back toward the house, Peter, in the middle, wraps his arms around both of us.

10

They see our skin first. Bear, Bug, and me.

We arrive at Christmas mass dressed up in our very best outfits, enshrouded in bulky winter coats. The weather is bleak, even for December—dry, cloudy, and cold. There is no snow on the ground, nothing to make the scene seasonally idyllic, to make it look cinematic, or like a Currier and Ives print. The ushers standing outside rub their hands together for warmth and manage to smile wanly each time they open the church door for a parishioner. Despite the cold, they are on the lookout for something very specific. They ignore Sheryl and Bob. They look past Anna. They zero in on us right away, and then hustle over with their solicitation.

"Would you three bring the gifts up?" They stoop down as they ask the question. One of them looks over at our parents, who loom in the background. "Dressed as the three wise men?"

There are other children there that morning, of course, but there are none with the same glossy racial magic. We stand next to each other, Bear and I in matching coats, gangly preteens, our mismatched skin tones reflecting the speculative future. And, for those ushers, the biblical past.

"We could use your help . . ."

Dad and Mom agree readily. We are assembled for just this sort of enlistment.

The optics of our family allow for a regular double take because our various configurations project different meanings. There is the larger, fuller ensemble, of course, a diverse and spectacular collection of the world's peoples in a single American home. And there is each of us alone, our individual flesh, each shimmering with a specific meaning. The white child, the Black child, the Asian child, and so on, all stereotypes brought to life. The full collection—eventually eight, including our parents—is like a walking and breathing rainbow, a Benetton advertisement brought to life.

Bug, Bear, and I are a special triptych, a delicately matched set of types, self-consciously representing three different races to the almost exclusively white members of our Catholic parish. All roughly the same height and age. One of us is blond with blue eyes, one possesses dark-brown skin, a small Afro, and doll's eyes, and one has short, straight black hair. We are meant to be seen as a smaller group, an easy shorthand vision of what the future might hold. We're older now, and ready for our own close-up. Three children, three races, walking into a church together, showcasing the orchestration of difference into harmony. That is a part of our charm on Sundays, whenever we go to mass. Or when we go to the mall, walking side by side in a row behind Sheryl, or in a single-file line through the clattering food court. Or when we get on the bus, sitting next to one another as we slowly make our way to school on a rainy morning. Or when we show up at family reunions and cling tightly together.

Next to my desk, there is a small framed picture of the three of us, taken just after Bear's arrival. We're seated on the old, tattered green couch in the living room, and we're all so small that our legs barely extend beyond the edge of the cushion. I'm centered, bookended by Bug and Bear, and the three of us have big, laughing smiles on our

Three of us on a couch the summer after Bear's arrival.

faces. Bear is holding a paper airplane in one hand, his torso bunched with excitement. Bug has pulled his legs up and is sticking his tongue out. The photo is staged, for sure. And not by us. Nevertheless, we're obviously enjoying the camaraderie, mugging for the camera, loving that we are three and not just two or one.

Alone and together, we are many things, but we are always an impossibly wild yet willful experiment, conducted in the public eye and subject to the approval of a thousand strangers. The ushers at the church, blowing into their gloves to warm their fingers. The bus driver, surveying us as we take our seats. The clerk at the mall, watching us enter a store, lined up like ducklings behind Sheryl to get clothes. Wherever we encounter them, our vast audience is heavily invested—in either our success or our failure—and their gaze is invariably discerning and penetrating. As we walk through the church doors that Christmas, heads turn, look us up and down and sideways, and never turn away.

The church is new to us. In those days, we hopscotch from parish to parish, trying to find the right fit and the right pastor. This parish is young, and convenes in a quaint old Reformed Church in nearby Three Bridges. The modest building has white clapboard sides, creaky wooden floors, and darkly veneered pews. I study every corner, looking for evidence of Protestantism, but find nothing. It is close to the white house. The drive from home takes just a dozen minutes or so, even if the actual melodrama of it takes longer. Dad, who always prefers to be early, will hustle us into Big Red, that eye-catching, road-cone-orange Chevy Suburban that comes to be associated with our appearance. Inevitably, Mom will be late leaving the house, which means that as we wait, we will listen to our father grouse and complain, and then honk the horn, and then bellow out the window, calling out her name. Once we blast off, the massive, outlandishly colored car carries us swiftly along the barely developed country roads, the orange clearly visible against the dull brown palette of winter in the hinterlands of central New Jersey. The church ushers probably see us coming for miles.

I hate that colorful, clownish car, with its oversize royal blue crest, its bright white roof, and its whitewall tires. I hate the way it invites the public gaze, the attention we draw when we are in it, the overt stares and the covert surveillance that the car inspires. I do loathe that car—but I love it, too, for it is also our collective conveyance, a vessel big enough to ensure our safety.

That day—that Christmas, when the ushers greet us excitedly, our skins vibrant against the grim winter—is not the first time that we are approached to bring up the gifts, though no one has previously asked us to do it in costume, to dress up as the heralds of the Messiah, the bringers of gold, frankincense, and myrrh. But it is right after the new parish opens, and there is an air of improvisation around that day. Instrumentally, they always need a comely trio to carry up the offerings to the altar at the front at just the right moment. Maybe the founding pastor of this all-too-new parish has rallied around the notion that our troupe is to be celebrated and told the ushers to be on the lookout for our special set. Maybe the ushers themselves expect our arrival and feel that our spectacular association is for the greater good. Maybe the idea of the costumes comes to the priest suddenly, like a thunderclap. Maybe it is the holiday, since Christmas mass is a once-a-year spectacle, with much larger numbers of attendees and significantly more ritual theater. There is, after all, the smell and smoke of incense, and the clang of the mysterious brass vessels trailing smoke. There is the sprinkling of holy water, randomly cast out into the crowd by the stern priest. There is the story of the virgin birth, the miracle of a prophesied savior born of the desert. The legend of Gaspar, Balthasar, and Melchior, the three "wise men of the East," who follow the North Star to the infant Messiah. Maybe we are a part of that ritualism. There we are, conveniently: three young boys, three races, in a community devoted to the rule of three.

We sit near the back of the church, in costume, mumbling the words to the prayers we are still learning in catechism classes. The room swells with the voices of parishioners declaring their shared faith.

"For us men and for our salvation he came down from heaven, and by the Holy Spirit was incarnate of the Virgin Mary and became man."

We wait in the vestibule, with our snowy white beards and our jewel-toned robes—looking more like Disneyfied wizards than anything else. To avoid stumbling over the hems, we walk carefully up the center aisle of the church. Bear and I carry the bread and the wine in delicate crystal, while Bug grasps a wicker basket of cash, that mass's offerings, in his hands. I remember the abrasive texture of the polyester in the robes, the plasticity of the crowns, the faux-gold trim glued onto the cuffs, the jittery rattle of the crystal on silver trays. And I remember earnestly believing that this is all completely normal, this mixed-up racecraft, as scholars Barbara and Karen Fields would call it, this division of the three of us into racial avatars, into holy wise men, into the stuff of fantasy. Normal, that is, because this mythos is a part of everything we do. At the same time, I feel a hundred pairs of eyes on us that day. *A hundred pairs of eyes on us every day.* And while I understand that sensation to be ordinary, at least for us, it is not one I enjoy.

Heads turn. Pews creak. The room grows quiet. Those fake beards and cheap, colorful robes make it hard to see the racial melodrama of our grouping, our white, yellow, and black coding, our role in the community as an augury of hope. Hard to see, but not impossible. And there is an encouragement hidden in the costuming, a draw to our audience to look, and then to look again.

A palimpsest is a manuscript that has been reused, on which the erasure of old text is incomplete. The effect is startling, as one encounters the bright, clean text of the present, under which the ghostly remainders of what was once there linger. They are just barely visible, yet one is drawn to look closer. That urge—that urge to focus in, to make sense of the half-erased, blurry, and fragmentary original text—is what makes the palimpsest so interesting. On that Christmas Day, that is what we are: a palimpsest, a dyad of symbols, with bright colorful costumes superimposed on our still-legible, racialized skin. The ushers aim to entice the audience to cheer our performance of the biblical adoration, to witness the sublimation of our racial positions to our ceremonial function, to enlist our natural integration in the effort of the holiday. The so-called wise men, after all, aren't the heroes of the story; they're heralds, drawn by the starry sky to worship the newborn Messiah. Having us carry the gifts up the center aisle, in our cheap Woolworth's beards and our flowing robes, sends a powerful message to a new parish, formed at the far edge of white flight, in the

midst of the age of Reagan. It confirms, in the softest tones imaginable, that if the future is going to be confusingly diverse, it will at least
still be Christian. And that the worship of the Messiah—for us that
day, a tiny plastic infant in a straw-filled manger, just down from the
altar—will continue, no matter how the nation's demographics might
soon be altered.

Now offstage, we are hustled out of the costumes and returned to
Bob and Sheryl.

The priest's voice calls out: "Behold the Lamb of God, behold him
who takes away the sins of the world. Blessed are those called to the
supper of the lamb."

And, once more, the parishioners respond, their voices drawn
together by decades of rhythmic repetition. "Lord, I am not worthy
that you should enter under my roof, but only say the word and my
soul shall be healed."

Our enlistment is not over. And it began years earlier. So long as we
are a cute trio, they will watch for us, fingers crossed that there will be
three. First, it is Christmas. Then, they want us to do it at Easter, since
we were so good at it the first time. Sometimes they want us to perform at Saturday afternoon mass, without the costumes. Whenever we
make it into the church without a request, I breathe easier. Sometimes,
though, they find us in the middle of the mass, and, sidling over like
conspirators, they stage-whisper: "Can you three take up the gifts?"
The pattern repeats so often—and at all of the churches we attend—
that I lose track of the details, the dates, the priests, the homilies, the
unique sound the pews make when the audience turns to watch. I
am five years old. I am thirteen. We are in Three Bridges. We are in
Flemington. It is cold. It is as hot as a furnace.

So long as we are all an ensemble, we mean something.

Something about the recollection of this experience unnerves me.
Growing up in this family has made me comfortable beyond measure
in non-white spaces, and anxious in those spaces where there is only

pale skin. It has made me bold when acting alongside a racially mixed troupe in private but displeased with the spotlight, with white spectatorship, whether it falls on me or on all of us. I recognize the multiracial ensemble as a controversial sign. I also know what my skin signifies.

Some family stories are tragedies, while others are funny and irreverent. And some are inspirational. Our story is all of that. And it advances here, with the three of us—Bug, Bear, and me—walking up to the altar, costumed and bearing gifts, the smiling priest watching us shuffle, the parish enthralled by the spectacle—because that is where our story has been headed all along. It is inevitable that we will end up presented to the public like this, a gift ourselves, harbingers of the glory that is to shine down on everyone, a reminder that integration can be amicable, peaceful, and loving. Portents and people, costumed as ancient magi, we are assigned a role without a script for a public that sometimes smiles—but often grimaces—at our arrival.

A symbol, though, is not a real thing. Our magical, hypnotic surfaces make it hard to see our individual humanity, our individual quirks, our unpredictable personalities. We are not wise men. We are not actually heralds of the future. We are three children—hammered into a relationship as brothers, clinging to one another, laughing uneasily at the droll racial comedy of these costumes.

11

"I am ten." I say this out loud to remind myself that I am more than old enough to ride my bike alone through someone else's town. We have arrived in Peterborough, a New Hampshire hamlet, earlier that day, stopping off to see family and friends at the start of our summer vacation. I am determined to check out the local catchall store, where I know I will find some Star Wars figurines. *The Empire Strikes Back* has come out that summer. I am fairly obsessed, but Bear is wary of the town. So I go alone.

Ames—the local version of Woolworth's—is in a plain and uninspiring strip mall near the edge of town, backed up on an undeveloped bit of wilderness. If you do an end run around the mall, there is a long path that splits a stretch of scrubby pines out back, offering a shortcut to the home of our local host, an educator and volunteer fireman named Jim. I know that the shortcut will save me time and figure that it is safe, so I turn off onto the path, my bike tires finding easy purchase in the sandy soil.

It is not safe.

"There he is!" A chorus of angry voices, all shouting, comes from the barrens. Off to my left, I see a half-dozen or so white faces, not much older than mine. A chaotic chase ensues for what must be less than a hundred yards.

"N——! Get the n——!"

With every syllable, the voices get closer and angrier. I feel like my heart will explode.

Capture is inevitable. I try to outrace them and then just give up, anticipating the worst. Once encircled, though, the encounter takes a strange and awkward turn. We sit still in the heat of the afternoon, our pale pink knuckles clenched tightly around handlebars, the sun glinting off BMX chrome. Our chests heave to recover lost breath. I am certain that at any moment they will surge toward me in a wave and beat me down. But they seem confused about what to do next. Having caught and cornered me, my pursuers have no real plan to do anything.

Except, that is, to threaten my older brother—Bear, nearly the same age, wearing matching clothes, but dark-brown skinned, not white like me—who has had the good sense to know that the sight of a Black boy on a bike riding through the woods in rural New England will only make for trouble. He was spotted when we arrived, pulling into town in Big Red like a traveling carnival, and this group has obviously been on the lookout for us ever since.

"You're the n——'s brother," one sneers. He takes a deep breath, almost gasping for air. "Get him out of town."

This time, when I hear the word, I am transfixed by the gravity and complexity and danger and oddness of that moment. I become detached. I take stock of my own panic, that fear that rises up when you are being chased. I hear, behind those words, the boys' spiteful recognition that my skin is as white as theirs. And I recognize the danger, the crackling atmospherics of racial hate, their baleful anger that my brother is anywhere near their town, their homes, their families. Their absolute, unshakable conviction that he is alien, unwelcome, abject, Black. His Vietnamese history is, in this context, unseeable and undiscoverable.

With a desperate surge, I break free of their circle. They refuse to chase. Having delivered their message, and having no other plans for me, they let me go. I know, then, that my whiteness ensures my secure retreat.

If I close my eyes now, I can remember it like it was yesterday. I can smell it. Feel the sun on my face, the grips on my bike's handlebars, the raised pattern in the rubber. In my dreams, I always outrun them and escape.

A former professor of mine, Clem Price, upon hearing this narrative, tells me that you aren't truly an American if you haven't been chased through the streets with someone hollering the word n—— at your back. He offers this as an expression of solidarity, wanting the young white man in front of him to explore more deeply the connections between his research interests and his personal life. Perhaps this is true. Perhaps racial violence does indeed confer the stripes of real citizenship if, like Clem, you are Black.

For me—a white kid from central New Jersey—the primary lesson that day isn't quite so simple. Because even as I feel the terror of that moment deep in my bones, I have also already learned that my white skin can inoculate me against the logical end point of the pursuit. I am never in real danger. I will have no cuts or bruises that day. If the chase has to be real for Clem's truth to hold, then there are only difficult, convoluted lessons to be learned from that New Hampshire afternoon. Because, in the end, even if those boys have called me a n——, tracked me urgently across town, and trapped me in the piney woods behind the five-and-dime, they never once lay a finger on me. Bear, more alert than I to the racial electricity of that day, has anticipated this sort of encounter. He stays in our guest's home, where he is protected. Closer to Bob. If it were him and not me ensnared by their trap, the ending would surely be bloody.

I rush back to the home of our family friend and share everything. I remember the adrenaline rush as I escape, the panic in my voice,

Sheryl's concern, and the shame of telling the story in front of Bear. Of repeating that word in front of him. I recall our host's dismay. Our parents' anger. Thanks to Bob's frequent history lectures, we all know the violence encoded in the word's two syllables.

Jim, our host, is well connected. He knows the boys, knows them from the details of my description of their bodies, their skins, their bicycles. Later that evening, while we are all out at dinner at a local Italian restaurant—the kind of family-style place that has red-and-white-checkered plastic tablecloths—he spots one of the parents of the offending children in the room. They are out dining with another couple. Jim is well known and well liked in Peterborough, an unimpeachable leader. Together with Bob, he approaches the table, describes what happened, and brings the parents over to the table to apologize to me. I don't remember there being any defensiveness. I don't remember Bob or Sheryl or Jim being angry in that moment. Just earnest.

The parents walk over in my direction, their hands clutched in front of them in a demonstration of concern. I stand. "We're so sorry. We'll talk to our son. This was wrong." They lob these words in my direction, but their eyes repeatedly dart over to Bear, who sits on the far side of the table mutely. And then, after taking him in, their gaze sweeps over the whole of the table, the entirety of us.

As quick as a light switch, another odd sort of displacement happens there—a sort of displacement I have encountered before, in which Bear exits stage left while I take the spotlight on center stage. In which the challenge of racism and anti-Blackness is transmuted into an easier public conversation about integration, a conversation in which we are all equally invested stand-ins, all envisioned as champions of the project. This means, as I learn, that I am likely to be chased, threatened, and demeaned, even if I am largely inoculated against actual violence or harm. It also means that when those things happen, the apologies come to me—not to the group of us, nor to Bear. Integration is an easier object of attention, not Blackness. A white-dominant integration in which Blackness has only a token representation. White people apologize to me, that is, because I am white like them, and because I represent an integrated future in which white people still play a meaningful role.

Still, I know even then that the "N-word" is a foul term, and that the chief offense here has been to Bear—and not to me. I recognize the spotlight—turning toward me and away from Bear—as a problem, even as I am transfixed by the brightness.

"We're so sorry." Bob and Sheryl watching in the background.

"This was wrong. We teach our son to do the right thing."

My spaghetti with meatballs is getting cold. My fork has pasta and sauce twirled around its tines. The outside light reflects off the plastic tablecloth. I stand still and at attention after the apologetics are over, as the parents talk it over among themselves. All the while, I stare right at Bear, look right into his eyes. He stares back at me. His own plate is untouched, too. I see no hint of what he is thinking or feeling. There is no reaction to his displacement, and to their eagerness to apologize, without prevarication, to me, not to him. No ripple on the surface to read. No sense of any fear, any terror, at the mention of that chase in the woods. He waits for the theatrics to come to a close, and for me to be seated. Then, at last, we both eat.

12

The house is a glorified log cabin, and until high school we stay there every summer for a month. Dark brown, with a big screened-in front porch, it is set up on a hill overlooking Haunted Lake, just outside of Francestown, New Hampshire. It is one of maybe a dozen camps on the lake, all of them isolated, sequestered into little private coves. The lake is impossibly quiet at all hours of the day, and while we can't be seen, the sounds of our play echo across the water.

There, we are idyllically alone. Unwatched, in the woods. We have a small sandy beach to ourselves, along with a roped-off swimming area. There is a public beach a few hundred feet away, around a slight bend, not close enough for any interaction and not directly in our line of sight. On the other side of the lake, there is another small cove, rocky and with no beach access. Our family photo albums are rich with images from this tranquil place. I recall the black rubber inner tubes we use to lazily float along the shore's edge, how they get hot in the sun, and how we cool them off by flipping them, allowing the water-cooled surface to press against our skin. I remember the smell of the water—a slight, sweet smell—and the sound of it lapping against

At Haunted Lake in New Hampshire with Bear, Anna, and Mark in 1979.

the inside of the inner tube. At night, the thunder of frogs and toads is overwhelming.

What I remember most about this place—beyond its silence, its languid pace, and its piney scent—is the absence of any sight lines, of any watchers, of any gaze. So much of our existence is determined by our publicity, and those woods, so "lovely, dark and deep," as Robert Frost once put it, offer us a rare chance at a still, serene privacy.

We are there, of course, because of Bob.

Bob is shamelessly in love with the wilderness of New Hampshire, and he feels it is in our best interests to be outdoors, in the bright sun and the clean air. He got the idea of New Hampshire in his head when he was young, and it has served as a kind of mythic representation of untrammeled and undeveloped land, in the spirit of Thoreau. In February of 1971, he and Sheryl leave me with my grandmother (Bob's mother, Agnes) to scout out possibilities. They travel into the far north of the United States in the middle of winter.

"We arrived in a fierce snowstorm," Mom recalls, "and stopped at a realty office in Rindge, but the realtor would not or could not show us properties because of the storm. So we got a room at the nearest motel, where the manager knew another man named Jim, said if anyone could sell us a property, it would be him. So, the very next day, with the state of New Hampshire being adept at clearing roads and getting on with business despite blizzards, we met with Jim, who did indeed sell us a property and became a lifelong friend."

Jim. Tall, lean, and with tanned skin. Intellectually omnivorous. Talkative and charming. And with a thick New Hampshire accent. A volunteer fireman with a radio transmitter always on his belt.

It is Jim who finds us a small parcel of undeveloped land, a long-term prospect for a summer home. Jim also connects us with the owners of the little cabin, which we rent in the meantime. And it is Jim and his family we are visiting that day in Peterborough, when those boys chase me, trap me, and assault me. An innovative educator well known everywhere in the state, he has lovely, sad eyes with serious creases at their edges. Those eyes watch us. And I always feel that he sees us all, sees how we work—and don't work. Once, years later, I remember turning on *The Phil Donahue Show* after coming home from school, and I find him there on the screen, soothingly talking about some local school reform he is championing. He is a wonderfully exuberant man, and exactly the kind of big-hearted person Sheryl and Bob feel comfortable bringing into our private lives. When we are with Jim, strangers stop us on the street to talk to him. He is, I realize, another version of Bob.

Jim's oldest son, Nathan—in his teens, and movie-star handsome— is also the first person to ever show me a real handgun. I remember Bear and me standing in the grass at their home, holding the heavy, nickel-plated pistol, passing it back and forth as if it were red hot.

The weight and size of the piece—so much heavier than I've ever imagined—is terrible.

Bob loves the lake. Getting ready for the trip up to New England takes time and effort. He packs up Big Red until every square inch is filled with something we might need. He has fashioned a boat rack out of two-by-fours and old strips of green carpet, and loads the big, bulky sailboat he has bought onto the roof of the car. When the day comes, we get up—or are carried, asleep—to the car well before dawn. He wants to avoid New York City traffic, but he also wants to get to the house as early as possible, with hours of daylight to spare, and that means hurtling across the George Washington Bridge at 5 a.m. When we finally arrive, he will head down to the water before we unpack anything. He has a pair of old leather sandals he will wear for the trip—with strips of recycled rubber tires for the soles. He will step out of those, sink his toes in the water, and stare out over the lake.

Each summer, Bob will draw out a twelve-tine metal rake from beneath the house and devote himself to removing as many rocks from our roped-off swimming area as possible. He will draw them to shore, or simply heave them deeper into the lake. Over the years, he manages to successfully transform the mucky, stony waterfront of our access point into something more beach-like. He wants soft sand underfoot. There is an epic patience to the work, to the slow labor of more than a dozen years, excavating the small granite rocks out of our swim area. But this glacial pace allows him to exorcise his organizational demons even while he is on vacation. It is a central element of his own rest and recovery. And—as importantly—it gives us a safe refuge to play in the shallows. And after years of effort, only a few outsize rocks remain.

In the early 1980s, the owners of the little house at the lake decide to stop renting the property in the summers. We drive up one last time to say goodbye to the place. I weep as we leave it, not really understanding why it has felt so safe, so free, so without social oversight.

We try spending the next few summers in different campgrounds—taking the family Winnebago from Maine to Vermont—but those are always more public adventures, framed by the gawking stares of neighboring campers, who always seem fascinated—or focused—on our tonal variations. We always seem to be the ones integrating these spaces. We never find a place to be alone together quite like that lake.

I returned to the beachfront recently, paddling by canoe from the other side. It is a warm, sunny day without wind. As usual, there is no one around. There is a blue heron skimming the surface. As the canoe slows down and I near the shoreline, I marvel at the lasting effects of Bob's work. Beneath the surface of the water, I espy the lake bottom, still swept clean of debris, with the exception of those few massive granite boulders that were too big even for Bob to remove. I remember those big old rocks from the listless days of summer so long ago, from the hours spent floating on an inner tube with a scuba mask on, watching fish and memorizing the underwater topography. As in a dream, a small family of sunfish darts out from beneath the canoe.

"How astonishing," I think, peering down. It looks like he was here just yesterday, like no time at all has passed. I draw my eyes up, expecting—and hoping—to see us all together on the beach once more, casting our lines into the water, fishing for bass and pickerel. Wishing to see him—to hear his voice—just once more.

13

Bear and I share a paper route. We are old enough—twelve—to ride our bikes across the pleasing smallness of our town. We are a duet well known enough that people—strangers to us, but not to our parents—pull back the curtains to watch for us, anticipating our arrival in the late afternoon. Almost every customer on the route is a node in Sheryl's network. They have our route well plotted and carefully timed. We don't understand the network, but it is easy to spot. For my part, I just assume that it is totally normal for customers to greet their newspaper carriers in person every day.

The *Courier News* arrives mid-morning on weekdays and early on Saturdays and Sundays. A stack of papers is wrapped tightly in a clear plastic bag so that they stay dry until we can deliver them. When the bus lets us out after school, we race upstairs and get changed into what Sheryl calls "play clothes" (old jeans and old sneakers). Then, we head out, rain or shine, to make the circuit, burdened with an oversize canvas satchel stained with newsprint and unclassifiable grime. Weekdays are the best because the paper is lightest. Weekends, obviously, are much worse. There are comics and advertisements and special supplements. The paper weighs us down, especially at the start, and wears us out. Also, weekend deliveries are morning deliveries, which means they interrupt cartoons—and sleeping in.

Instead of splitting the route, we agree to alternate days. Subscribers watch us come and go, day after day, Monday after Tuesday, white after Black, in an endless loop. We split the work and the cash. We get an envelope of tips—a buck or so from each house, and more on the holidays—once a week.

There is, of course, some high comedy in this alternation—and some melodrama as well. For the few people we don't know, there is some guesswork, as strangers try to understand our relation. "Didn't I see another young man," I might be asked, "deliver the paper yesterday?" And there is the inevitable excitement, for us, of seeing these same strangers at their most intimate, when they least expect us. There is the perennial bachelor—balding, with a small potbelly, and the erudition of Thurston Howell III—who is always in a bathrobe on weekend mornings, talking to his neighbor in the breezeway. There is the lonely Thai woman—short and plump, at home with an infant—who has known us since we were little, and who loves to talk to us about her daily excitement (and slow us down) if she catches us on the front porch. She watches for us every day because our arrival breaks up the monotony. Her doubled isolation—a woman at home with a child while her husband is at work, a Thai woman in a white community—means that she sees us as kin somehow. She will talk to us for as long as we will listen. It helps, I think, that we share the load. Every other day, one of us stands on her front porch, clinging to the railing, looking for a sign that we can leave.

Far and away, most of the drama on the route is about dogs. There is one ranch house at the top of a hill, just past the bachelor's house, with a brace of snarling dogs who routinely chase me. An Irish setter and an Alaskan husky. Months go by where I cannot deliver the paper to that family, but Bear never seems to have any trouble. Another house has a Doberman, which seems terrifyingly fast and hates us both. My heart races as I approach this home, a small brown saltbox. The plastic recepticle for the paper is out by the mailbox at the curb, and the dog—I am 100 percent certain—is in the unfenced backyard listening for the sound of my tires. I glide to the box, my foot poised on the pedal, ready to accelerate. When he comes sprinting around the corner with a low growl, I throw the paper at the house and hustle away.

Our differences are manifested in our bicycles. Bear's bike is strong, practical, useful, and generally beat to hell. He is a risk taker, eager to test the limits of the machine. His bike has scars. Chips in the paint, chewed-up metal, bent pedals, a torn seat, frayed cables.

He has scars, too. When he first arrived, we went to a small playground behind an elementary school—the two of us and a few of our cousins. There is a pyramid of tractor tires meant for climbing, and Bear scrambles right to the top. Then, convinced that he can do anything, he jumps and promptly breaks his leg. For as long as we've been together, Bear has been climbing and testing, adventuring and falling. Leaping and breaking. Out of a tree. Off of his bike. On the playing field. Sometimes, of course, his body fractures, or tears, or breaks. A leg. An arm. A collarbone. Sometimes the object breaks. A branch, a ladder, his bicycle. Sometimes he comes out of it stronger, more resolute. He is always willing to take the chance, to see and find out.

His physical confidence is, to me, astonishing—even magical. Years later, in college, Bear gets into a bar fight with a stranger. Glass is broken, and the fight leaves him with shards embedded in his forearm and his hands. This is a consequential thing, causing him considerable pain over the months and years that follow. One day, he shows me his scarified flesh, and reveals the outlines of the tiny pieces of broken glass beneath the skin. These things will work their way to the surface, he explains, and then eventually they will just tear through the flesh and pop out. "I was playing Frisbee," he tells me, "and it just came out." It sounds horrific, but when I try to envision it, I see dazzling, bright, gleaming jewels—all cut with precision—just falling out of his skin painlessly. His hands and arms dripping with green and red and blue and white stones, which he will shake off like they were droplets of water. And I imagine Bear watching this all with bemusement, staring down at his arms and watching them shed these signifiers of wealth and royalty. Every jewel a reminder of his strength, his courage, his penchant for risk-taking.

He has a bike that fits his personality, his recklessness, his scars. His bike has seen things and done things. And so has he.

That is not me. I move slowly and with caution. My knees have no scabs. My shoes have no scuffs. My shirts are never torn. Boys, the saying goes in the early 1980s, are either astronauts or astronomers. It is clear to everyone—and to the two of us—which of us is the reckless, heroic explorer.

My bicycle is precise, delicate, and kept clean and well oiled. I built it, piece by piece, with money earned from the paper route, assembled it in the basement while I was home sick for several months with mono. Now, out delivering papers in the late afternoon sun, it sparkles with chrome details and a gold anodized aluminum frame and handlebars. When it gets scratched, I mourn. I am not a swashbuckler, not like Bear. I ride my bike carefully, safely, reasonably. "Within bounds," I say to myself. "Within limits." I fuss over the smallest scratch. On the bike. And on myself. I never once break a bone. Not a leg. Not an arm. Not a collarbone.

After I dash away from the Doberman, I pull over and check my bike.

It takes me longer to deliver the papers. Bear hurls himself around town, sailing in the air after hitting a small bump, cutting over lawns and corners. I ride in straight lines, avoiding the mud, the puddles, the slippery gravel. It takes me longer because I am so much more vigilant and so much more reserved.

Our route is a big circle through town with about forty stops. Our neighbor, Mrs. Davis, is the last person to get her paper every day, because we turn right out of the driveway, not left, to get started, and then we wind our way all around the whole town before getting back home. She is the final node in Sheryl's network.

Mrs. Davis is an older white woman with tightly curled brown hair and a deep Alabama twang. Small and gracious, she is unfailingly polite, sewing patchwork baby blankets for each arrival and generally watching over us in the way of older women of a certain generation, with her kids all grown up. We are found family. Her daughter is our school bus driver. Her son once played Minor League baseball. She wears old flannel shirts and jeans, and has the look of someone who might play a farmer's wife in the movies. She drives a tractor to mow her lawn—a high contrast to the rotator push mower we use to cut ours—and, on really hot days, I am deeply envious of how quickly she does it. Courteously, she knows that she can't see us in the back-yard, but sometimes she can hear us; when she does—if she is staking a tomato plant or transplanting some forsythia—she calls out loudly to say hello. She just wants us to know she is present, in case we decide to experiment with curse words or say something gross, because she recognizes the importance of the grotto. In a hundred ways, then, Mrs. Davis's color-blind kindness and gentility disrupts the grotesque stereotypes of southern racism. We all love her.

On weekends, we get to her house right at breakfast time. One day, the door sweeps open and she takes the paper from me directly, I can smell bacon and sausage and eggs and pancakes and biscuits.

"That smells amazing," I tell her. *Amazing* is a big word for me at twelve. So is *cool*. But *amazing* seems more appropriate for an older, southern white woman. Mrs. Davis thanks me with a hearty laugh and a grin. I peer around the corner with big eyes to survey the kitchen table. Everything is there on the table, including tall stacks of pancakes as beautiful as an advertisement on television.

I really mean the compliment. Sheryl prefers to leave us on our own for breakfast, which usually means cold cereal.

"Amazing . . ."

She laughs when I say it again.

Mrs. Davis invites us over for breakfast the next weekend. Bear and me, her two adjoining paperboys, brothers under the skin. We are giddy and enthralled by the greasy, fatty abundance before us, ravenous in the way of middle-schoolers. There is no room for conversation. We just point frantically to each other. Mrs. Davis, always mindful of appearances, stays in the back of the kitchen, on the phone with Sheryl the entire time, a node in the network in perfect working order. Bear and I are too focused on the food to notice. Brothers under the skin— and above the skin, too, in that space where we are watched and measured and supervised. And, in this instance, kept safe.

14

Our parents met by happenstance in a small law firm on Cliff Street, just a few blocks from the county courthouse in Somerville.

On break from college, Sheryl takes a summertime secretarial position at a law office in the county seat. A family friend who works in the office keeps watch over her. Bob is there, a young lawyer finding his way in the Jersey suburbs and eager to make a name for himself. They meet, there is a connection of some kind, and Bob quickly lets the family friend—a silver-haired, bespectacled senior partner in the firm—know that he plans to ring her up, to meet her again, and ask her to lunch. The family friend, ever the watchful ally, promptly telephones her parents.

"This is just a courtesy," the family friend tells Jeanne and Tom. He is a fast talker, smooth and confident, and the words come out reassuringly. "This probably won't lead to anything." Then a pause. "He is, however, a Catholic." In the early days of this union of very different family histories, Bob has two strikes against him: he is Catholic, and he isn't Old Stock.

Though anti-Catholic prejudice has diminished considerably since the early twentieth century, the news spreads fast about this commonplace, minor difference. The romance advances and becomes more serious. Family elders are stirred to act. Grandma Mary—the matriarch of Sheryl's family, and the head of the Cedar Rapid Pratts— flies out from Iowa, because she is concerned, and ready to intervene, if necessary. But, as Mom remembers it now, Mary is charmed by Bob, who she finds quick-witted and funny, and quickly and quietly drops her concerns. Sheryl writes a long letter defending her position—and her right to marry whomever she wants—but the missive isn't necessary in the end.

Grandma Mary is a prim, polite woman, not one to get on a plane lightly. "I wasn't pissed off," Mom tells me now when I describe the conversation to her that way. "I valued her opinion. It was upsetting to me that she had misjudged Bob and that she had sidelined my own decision."

It is hard, at first, for Sheryl's parents to accept Bob, with his boisterous Irishness and Germanness, his front-stoop ethnic volubility, his hard-charging family full of Jesuit priests and New Deal liberals, and his family's commitment to the city as a political ideal. He has drunks in the long family tree, including one (the subject of family gossip) who was struck dead by a streetcar after an all-nighter. They must faint when they learn that Bob went to a Jesuit prep school, a Jesuit high school, and a Jesuit college, and that he is a fervent believer in all the lowbrow Catholic mysteries, the alchemical switch of wine for blood, bread for flesh, the miracles that adhered to saints' bones and shards of wood, the unthinking adoration of statuary and stained glass. Surely they are concerned, too, that the Vatican might clandestinely seize the apparatus of the country, since one never knows where the scheming Jesuits might lurk.

Bob's parents reflect the hurly-burly, garlic-and-whiskey-flavored democratic politics of big cities, like Newark and Trenton and Jersey City. His father, Gerard, is an affable, progressive educator in Jersey City's Snyder High School, the kind of big-city public school that serves, in an ideal world, as an engine of social advancement for the children of immigrants. A short, stocky man, the elder Guterl has a charming smile, wears steel-rimmed glasses, and is quotable and lionized in the city. He teaches law school at night at Fordham University. Bob's mother, Agnes, is a small, sweet people-pleaser with a silver beehive hairdo, who loves strawberries and hugs and is afraid of cats. She never learns to drive. She is a master of casserole cooking, a world-class mid-century-dessert maker, favoring Betty Crocker recipes and anything else that has the ring of "instant" or "modern" cooking. Agnes is always feeding, touching, and holding you. Gerard passes away before we are assembled, but Agnes lives on—and later moves out of Jersey City to be nearer to her children.

Growing up, *Grandma* is almost always reserved for Agnes, who welcomes all of us—our expanding brood—into her home with a warmth that lingers even now. When we are sick, Agnes will come to the house, fixing us sandwiches, and chat about life in Jersey City. Sitting on the couch with us, she will watch reruns of *The Danny Thomas Show*, *The Lucille Ball Show*, and the soap opera *Santa Barbara*. Watching the soaps, she takes a passionate dislike to the worst of the Capwell family, especially Mason, the snide know-it-all son whose arrogance is unmatched. Agnes makes no distinction between those of us who are adopted and those who aren't, those who are white and those who are Black or brown. When our youngest brother, Eddie, runs into trouble later, Mom invokes Agnes—watching from the afterlife—and asks him to try just a little harder to please her. And it works, at least for a while. Whenever we arrive at her house, Agnes has a hot dish with a thin layer of fried onions on top and a Jell-O mold dessert ready. That tiny, perfumed Irishwoman sees our family as a reflection of her son's genius and courage, and with such unbounded faith that *he* believes it. Because Bob, for Agnes, can do no wrong. And even if Agnes might be mystified by what she sees behind the white picket fence, she has enormous respect for her son, the confident ship's captain.

Bob is white, then, but he isn't the same kind of white as Sheryl. His Catholicism, and his more conventionally urban, checkered Ellis Island–immigrant family history, mark him as dingy and racially suspect.

The difference between the families can always be measured in plastic. In the Jersey City brownstone of Gerard and Agnes, the plush Victorian furniture is often insulated by the prophylaxis of the plastic slipcover, as if these are Agnes's most treasured pieces, and they need protection. Any high-traffic area not covered by plastic is covered by something else. Armrests are covered with lace doilies or covers made of fabric that match the chair. And yet every single space in the brownstone is used, and none of this furniture is off-limits. We are always on top of one another everywhere, a demonstration of affection and welcome. If the brownstone feels small, we can always go sit on the stoop, with its vistas of the rest of the block, or play ball on the street, which dead-ends in front of Agnes's door. Jersey City feels big, complex, and variegated. Skin tones. Languages. Clothing styles. Accents. It looks and sounds like us. And the plastic on the floor, on the couches, and on the tabletops feels like a logical part of the middle-class-respectability politics of any American city. It feels welcoming. It reminds us how hard Gerard and Agnes worked to get that furniture, to buy that brownstone, to make it into a home.

Sheryl's parents, Tom and Jeanne, live in Ewing, New Jersey, a lily-white suburb of Trenton with spacious, perfectly manicured yards and single-story ranch-style homes. In Ewing, we learn, there is just as much plastic, but it is in rooms we never, ever use. A long rubber runner runs from the front door straight through to the back of the house, where there is a small mudroom off the garage that we will cram into. If we come through the front door, the runner serves as a conveyor belt, hustling us into the back—or, even worse, into a windowless basement playroom, with a small handful of games and toys. Scrupulously attentive to this *cordon sanitaire*, we pass through rooms with glorious, dark-hued furniture, through groves of pink marbles and purple mahoganies, and emerge elsewhere. Acres of space in the house in Ewing seem to be walled off from us, protected against our mere passage. We use the plastic utility sink off the kitchen to wash our hands. The other, more formal hallway bathroom has perfumed Dove soap, which we understand to be precious and lovely. On the rare occasions when I get to use that second bathroom, it is magical. I wash my face, and let the bouquet intoxicate me.

Bug is an easy adoption for the Pratts to understand. A small, discrete addition to an otherwise familiar white nuclear family. They buy into the mythos of the model minority, and see Bug as easily assimilable. As they see it, the generations on display in that photo from Easter 1971, can absorb a single Asian, especially one from Korea, the "good part" of the region. Tom and Jeanne are taken aback, though, by the sudden, whirlwind acquisition of Bear. "I'm sorry?" Tom says incredulously, when they are all on the phone during that wild weekend, and our parents are sharing the news that there is a child waiting for them in rural Pennsylvania. "I may have misunderstood you," Tom continues, stammering.

The call is an FYI. An afterthought. Nothing more. Bob and Sheryl need no advice. "We made the decisions independently," Mom remembers. I ask her whether her parents ever say anything specifically about race when they are approached in this manner. Mom answers guardedly. "I'm sure they spoke a lot between them," she says, closing off the conversation, hinting that the adoptions mark a generational rift.

"Bob and I," Mom tells me, "were adults and weren't interested in seeking permission. We didn't follow any path that either of our parents would have imagined," she tells me. Adoption was new in the 1970s. She adds, "They didn't understand," referring to her parents.

"Adoption was new." I roll that idea around in my head. It is and it isn't new, of course. White missionary families were drawing together vast families for most of the Cold War, the scale of them a reflection of God's dominion and American grace. These families, I know, were few in number, quirky features of the postwar world, and objects of popular interest, like exotic curiosities profiled in *Life*. The Holts. The DeBolts. Mom is a homecoming queen in her New Jersey high school; a graduate of St. Olaf's, a small, overwhelmingly white liberal arts college in Minnesota; raised in largely segregated neighborhoods by parents who are either disinterested in or opposed to integration, to mixture, to diversity itself. They find Bear's adoption shocking. "Bell-bottoms were also new—and popular," I respond. "International, transracial adoptions might have been new, but they also seem pretty rare even in the 1970s. They were radical, in a way. That took guts and courage."

Mom ignores—or deflects—the mild compliment. This is simple, she insists, and I'm making it more complicated. She read Jim Bouton's essay, she responds, as if that is enough. As if just reading a short piece ever makes anything happen. "That made an impression on me. The DeBolts. Those were models that I was aware of." And then, without a breath, back to her parents. "It never occurred to me to take their counsel. I had been an only child. A closely supervised, well-doted-upon, and loved-abundantly child. At some point that became suffocating. It made me want to leave and be away."

"Be away." She means "run away," I say to myself. Sheryl sought distance from a kind of constraint she couldn't quite name. I recall the brief dust-up with Grandma Mary over Bob's Catholicism. And her desire to be independent, or out in front of her family.

Our story begins in so many different places. In our living room, a slim, black volume has sat for decades on the shelf. It is a genealogical history of the Pratt family—of Sheryl's family, that is. The history begins in the tiny coastal town of Old Saybrook, Connecticut, a creaky, clapboard-sided community routinely used as a backdrop for cliché-rich Hollywood horror movies set in small-minded New England. One weekend, years after we have all grown up, Sheryl sets out to dig up that past, to confront family records. Exploring the town with Bob, she finds a monument to William Pratt, her distant ancestor, a Pratt Street, a building with "Pratt" scrawled on the side, a half-dozen historic homes and public houses and inns with the Pratt name affixed to their colonial, clapboard frontage. When Sheryl asks for a tour of the local cemetery, a local guide happily obliges, sharing the heroic history of the early settlement that is so meticulously laid out in that slim black book. But then, he also shares the disturbing truth about William, whose arrival on the continent can be dated back to the first few ships.

Early settlers were particularly cruel and vicious, the guide tells Sheryl, and William Pratt was one of the very worst. Serving as a lieutenant under Captain John Mason, Pratt was tasked with the prosecution of war against the local indigenous Pequots, who were a major brake on the expansion of settler dominion. During the so-called Pequot War of late 1636–38, Pratt helped to lead the troops during the Battle of Mistick Fort. Facing resistance from an armed encampment of Pequots, Mason and his lieutenants set fire to the wooden structure and cut down with their swords anyone who tried to escape. Pratt personally guarded the exits. At least four hundred Pequots—men, women, and children, many of them unarmed—died that day, and roughly half of those were burned alive. The dead were everywhere, and movement around the encampment was obstructed by the sheer number of bodies. From beginning to end, the slaughter took an hour. Fleeing the scene, Mason, Pratt, and the rest of the men were attacked and—if reports are accurate—killed even more Pequot men. These losses, the guide explains, are understood as a major turning point in colonial history, leading to the weakening of the Pequots, the lopsided conclusion of the war, and the establishment of English domination along the coastal territories. For all of this—for his participation in the bloodiest battle at the close of a long and bloody war—Lieutenant William Pratt received one hundred acres of land on the edge of the Connecticut River, just upriver from Saybrook.

"It was a gasping 'Oh no' moment," Mom recalls. She calls her parents, but Tom and Jeanne aren't interested in revising the family history. They enjoy the celebratory, made-up history of settlers in tri-cornered hats and Indians with feathered headdresses, planting corn and making peace.

Sheryl sits alone with the enormity of this tale, the weight of this realization. Those streets, those statues, those commemorative materializations, that headstone, they are all honoring her ancestor for the merciless Battle of Mistick Fort, for the burning alive of men, women, and children. There, in her mind, was William Pratt, guarding the exits with a sword in hand, fingers clenched around the grip, white skin on the leather strapping of the hilt, staring down those trapped inside, rallying the troops to do the same. There he was, listening to the screams and cries inside, brandishing hard steel, and returning those who sought to escape back into the inferno.

15

The meeting of the mothers takes years to happen. Oceans need to be crossed. Wars have to end. Fate and luck have to intervene.

The first fleeting steps toward that meeting are taken when Bear is in the eighth grade. A handwritten letter from his birth mother— she is always Mae to me—comes in the mail, postmarked from Vietnam. Sent originally to Welcome House, it has been translated so that Sheryl, Bob, and Bear, having lost most of his ability to understand Vietnamese by then, can read it. And it is the first contact the family has had with her since 1975, since that dramatic exodus in the final hours and minutes of the American presence in Saigon.

Sheryl shares the letter with Bear and a considerable amount of discussion follows. That first letter and the letters that follow "really messed with my head," she tells me, confessionally. Committed to an open family, she and Bob take Bear to counseling, to sessions that are organized by the agency. This is a delicate moment, and they need help to get through it. "I was able to say to Bear: 'I'm afraid to lose you.' And he was able to say to us: 'I love you and don't want to go home with a stranger.' Through counseling, we were able to say that to each other."

Before counseling, though, there is the immediate shock that comes from the sudden, lurching reactivation of a connection we have all assumed was permanently severed. Severed by distance, by time, by the aftermath of the war. Bear sits on the living room couch in tears, the letter in his hands, struggling with what it all means. Bob sits down next to him, and puts his arm around him. "You're really lucky," he says. "You have two mothers who love you."

This is an existential crisis, not a legal one. Mom is clear about that. We have papers from the agency, she recalls, which Mae signed, stating that she gave up the right to her son "forever and ever," Mom tells me. They are signed and sealed with a ball of wax over a red ribbon, the sort of paratext of officiality that is reassuring. Along with that black-and-white photograph of his Vietnamese family, those papers are a part of a small personal archive of estrangement that Bear carries with him as he grows up, all of it carefully arranged in that brown vinyl duffel bag brought over from Saigon.

"Do you have that document, bro?" I call Bear and ask him in the present.

"I'll check," he responds.

Later that night, he sends me copies of the formal legal documents, and the letters written by Mae when Bear was just about to enter high school.

"I'll quote these tenderly," I tell him.

The first letter, Mom recalls, is a translated plea for reconnection, but it also contains first-order requests for financial support. More specifically, Mae needs medicine, and basic painkillers like aspirin, which are hard to get in Vietnam. Mom and Dad look into shipping her these and other medications but are frustrated by the transnational impossibilities of the late Cold War.

Mom writes back to Mae, hoping to reassure her that Bear is fine and doing well, updating her on some of the milestones of his life. She sends pictures.

Slowly the correspondence grows. Bear sends Mae a letter, chronicling the details of his life in suburban New Jersey. The bus rides to school. The sports he plays. His favorite foods.

Mae's second letter, written in English, comes a year later. It includes seven pictures of Bear and his siblings. It also opens with a gracious "greeting to your present parents," to whom she defers repeatedly in the letter. Hoping to jog his memory, Mae recounts an experience in nursery school, when Bear was three, when she would leave him at school for the week, and he would "cry and sing for cookies and candies." She asks for a copy of his birth certificate, which she needs in order to get out of Vietnam. And she pleads with him—twice in the closing lines—to get his brother and sister, Peter and Amy, to write, too. Bear is the good son.

In her third letter, she praises him for fulfilling the duties of an obedient child to his present parents, referring back to a letter that Mom has written. Bear has finally gotten Peter to write, and Mae thanks him for that. The two women—his two mothers—are jointly proud of Bear, she writes. "Don't be sad," she admonishes; "be happy and accomplish every task assigned to you. All that I want is love," she clarifies, for him and for us. "I am now forty-eight, and my hair has gone white. Although I have to work very hard to earn my living, I am always proud of you. Never forget your duties to your parents," she closes. "Bear in mind that your parents' merit is very great."

The conversation continues after that, steady but occasional, until years later, when Bear has earned his engineering degree at Villanova, and he and Peter are living together in DC. Mae has come to live stateside with their sister, Amy, in nearby Virginia, after trying to leave Vietnam for decades. Warming relations between the two nations and her advanced age—Mae is over sixty-five now—mean that she can finally follow three of her children to the United States. Bear, in the end, helps get her American citizenship, bringing her story full circle.

Bear thinks that his mothers—and Daphne, Peter's adoptive mom—should meet. At Bear's request, Sheryl and Daphne go down to DC to meet Mae. Amy's mother has been invited, too. But, Mom tells me, she did not want to join them that day. She also didn't support earlier efforts to reconnect the three kids when they were younger, keeping Amy away from her brothers. Mom, who is not superstitious, still finds it eerie and unsettling that Amy's adoptive mother dies on the day of the meeting in Virginia.

That day, then, Amy joins the group, offering much-needed linguistic diplomacy in a room where Mae speaks no English and Sheryl speaks not a word of Vietnamese. Mae, Mom remembers, is "very sweet." The three women share pictures of the boys. Mae has brought some, too. There are no pictures of the children's fathers. When Saigon fell, Mae explains, she cut them out of all the pictures, so that she wouldn't be held accountable, either for her racial transgressions—all three of their fathers are Black—or for her union with soldiers from an occupying army.

There is such "a warm and loving feeling," Mom says. The room smells of tea and spices. Chinaware clatters on a tray. Soft cotton napkins lie on the table. The three mothers sit together, their hands touching.

"We'd brought a gift for her. She'd brought one for us. We talked for hours, with Amy providing translation. She got up and stood in the middle of the kitchen. And on the floor, there was a clean cloth. And then she squatted down and cut everything up expertly—the kids had gone to an Asian market to collect things for her. A feast was prepared. I couldn't tell you how many dishes, and many of them I didn't know. We sat down. The food was laid out on a table. Mae excused herself. And returned in a minute totally cleaned up and wearing a lovely dress to have dinner with the family."

I ask her whether the meeting of the mothers resolved any of the concerns left over from that first letter, the one that shook her, that left Bear in tears, that brought Bob to the couch with his arm around his son. The letter that pushed them into counseling. "Absolutely," she replies.

"And what of Bear?"

"As an adult," she replies, "it was time for him to make some choices. His own choices."

He chooses connection and affiliation.

Mae is the hero of Mom's account. "She had been through a lot," Mom discloses admiringly. "She was the tenth sister in a large family, she tells me; she was called that, too: Sister Number Ten. She did what she had to do to make money, serving as a serial secret wife for GIs. She sent money back to her family. She was a survivor." Her voice cracks at the end. I hear, in Mom's voice, an emotional reverence for what Mae confronted, endured, and triumphed over, as a strong woman forced to make difficult decisions. I imagine her and Daphne

The second meeting of the mothers, with Mae, Sheryl, and Bear.

and Mae, three women having a formal sit-down Vietnamese lunch, all of them charged with taking care of these extraordinary children. I think of the combination of random luck and personal grit that brought them all together in that space. And I remember the vast structures that propelled them to far corners of the earth. And the ocean of white supremacy that lay between their continents. I try to imagine what it means to Mom to stand on her side of that ocean, and on top of those same structures, and to look to the other side of the globe to see the bare outlines of Mae's life.

"That day was magical," Mom remembers. "It was so wild that we were all in that room together."

Not long afterward, Bear brings Mae up to New Jersey to meet us. The event is Tom Pratt's birthday. In its own way, it is a dramatic, interesting juxtaposition of lives, the WASP elite sharing a meal with a Vietnamese immigrant. It is probably uncomfortable for Mae, who is surrounded by people who do not speak her language. And it is certainly awkward for the Pratts, who are upstaged by this small, stooped figure with a soft voice. Everyone wants to meet Mae, to hold her hand, to hear her voice and her laugh.

I thank her for entrusting us with her son—with our brother—and squeeze her tight. She puts her hand on my arm, and it is so tiny, so light.

"Why do we call her 'Mae'?" I ask Bear, thinking that it is an Anglicized name she took up when she moved to the United States, when white American tongues had to struggle with her given name. Thinking it, but not knowing it for sure, now that I've seen her letters to her long-lost son, letters signed with her birth name.

"You're saying it wrong," he laughs. "We both are. It is *mẹ*. Our voices are supposed to hesitate in there on the *e* sound, giving it a sort of half syllable to elongate it. It means mother in Vietnamese."

He introduced us years ago and never explained. I'd been calling her Mom for years.

16

Sheryl believes in the bucket and the bell.

Both are dinnertime shortcuts, urgently needed in a family that expands sideways with unnatural speed. They keep her sane. They make it possible for her to work, to complete a graduate degree in education, to advance her career and still put dinner on the table for six children.

She understands manners and etiquette, of course. When she and Bob host their gourmet dinner parties for adult friends, the table is set with fine china and polished silver, wedding gifts from the Pratts, with everything in just the right place. Multiples of each utensil, polished to shine brightly. Napkins folded perfectly. Two—or even three—kinds of stemware. And small details I never understand until much, much later in life.

The bucket is for us, not for the fancy dinners. A big, unpainted wooden bucket with slotted subdivisions, stuffed full of mismatched spoons, knives, forks, and paper napkins. When we sit down to eat, we reach into the bucket and take what we need. If we bother to set the table beforehand—and usually we don't—we just give everyone whatever is in the bucket, along with a hastily folded napkin. Sheryl doesn't supervise such things. We avoid any assessment of propriety or etiquette. And after dinner, we wash the utensils and put them right back into the bucket.

The bucket is the materialization of Sheryl's midwestern practicality and her keen sense of what really matters. She is a believer in thrift and simplicity. She has committed to raising the family, but that, to her, means encouraging independence. "You all did your own laundry once you turned eleven," she tells me now, admitting that she chose the earliest date when we could reach the controls, that the off-loading of labor and the instillment of self-reliance went hand in glove. Her commitment also means, again, that she creates shortcuts. It might take her five minutes to set the table herself. It would take her longer, at least in the short term, to teach us how to do it, to repeatedly instruct us on what goes where. That is five minutes she doesn't have. She gets a bucket, fills it with cheap stainless cutlery, and keeps it out at all times on the kitchen table.

The bell—and later, a large iron triangle—calls us to dinner, and saves Sheryl from having to hunt us down. It is a big brass thing, with a long wooden handle, and a resounding, unmistakable clang. The "moaning and groaning of the Bells," Poe once wrote, capturing the sound of church discipline, the hegemony of the bell in the steeple calling the flock to dutiful worship. Our bell calls us to the kitchen table, whether we are in our rooms or on the other side of the block. You can hear it almost anywhere in town, it is so loud.

The bell replaces a high-tech intercom system that Bob has installed inside the house and that never seems to work. He has always been a fan of some new technology—something with a lot of razzle-dazzle— as the solution to what is basically an old, even ancient, problem: too many kids scattered over too great a distance. Bob is the first to have a CD player. The first to own a computer with a word processor. Sheryl, again, is practical. She prefers the typewriter. A bell is old and reliable technology. She doesn't want to yell or search for us. She doesn't want to have to chase down kids on foot. So she deploys a sound that is absolutely unique in our little town: that loud, clanging, unmistakable bell.

If we are still out at six—playing at the local firehouse or riding bikes in the street—she will stand on the back porch and ring the bell several times, loud and clear.

We all know that dinner is promptly—religiously—served at 6 p.m., sharp. But, still, we wait for the bell. If we are down the block or around the corner, we wait to hear it, summoning us. It is the bell that rings us home.

Racing up the street, we will zip up the driveway, jump off the bikes, rush through the heavy wooden back door, take our shoes off in the kitchen, and pretend to wash our hands before sitting down, still panting.

Once we are all seated, and after a perfunctory grace, dinner is a jubilant free-for-all. Bob will share some moral fable from work, some apocryphal story about a bad decision with horrible consequences, which we are supposed to hear as a warning. And we will lean in, jostling for the serving spoon. Most of the time, there is a single dish for dinner—a casserole of some kind, pork chops, fried chicken, fish cakes, or the family favorite, macaroni and chopped meat—and an obligatory salad, often just chopped iceberg lettuce with cubes of cheddar cheese in place of breadcrumbs. There is no tolerance for individual preferences or dislikes, no special side dishes for a child who doesn't like this or that. Only a regular rotation of the same dishes. Sheryl is an excellent cook—and Bob, too, for that matter—but they prefer, at least for us, low-intensity, easy-prep dinners without a lot of cleanup.

Whatever is served, it is a cacophonous process to actually get food on your plate. You pass your white dinner plate to your neighbor, enlisting whoever is closest to the casserole dish to load up on your behalf. There is no orderly passing of the plates in the white house with the white picket fence. Instead, there is the pleasurable chaos of that merry disharmony, all of us shouting over one another—and at one another—to get what we want and then laughing our way through dinner.

17

It is almost dinner on Sunday, and Bob is struggling to balance the checkbook again. The Green Room is filled with groans and sighs, his chair creaking with the weight of his restless and shifting body. We can hear the carrying-on in the kitchen.

Bob is a township attorney with a small local practice and a sterling reputation, but he isn't, as he often says, "made of money." Paying the bills for a large family is a dark art, requiring risk and imagination and illusion. His single biggest irritation in the epic monthly challenge is the electric bill, an easy target—and a relatively insignificant one, in the larger scheme of things. During the month, if he finds a light that has been left on, we'll receive a lecture, even if our only crime has been to be standing in the general proximity of the switch, even if we've been doing nothing. If he goes upstairs and finds an unattended radio playing, or a fan running in an empty room, he will bellow from the top of the stairs. And when he writes out the checks, he remembers every miscue.

The percussive impact of his complaints makes us all nervous. "The electric bill is too damned high!" "Who left the light on!?" When you hear the volume escalate, you vanish. If you hear footsteps, it means that he isn't asking the questions rhetorically—he is going to seek out the offending party and take his time explaining to them, in precise detail, the costs attached to every second of illumination in a 60-watt bulb.

As he sees it, we are setting money on fire.

Every Sunday morning the ritual begins. We return from church, and Bob settles into his chair. He will lean back and read each bill one line at a time. Then he will exhale loudly, and look up at the ceiling, and open a few more. The exhales evolve into mutters and then into exclamations of disbelief and incredulity and outrage. We know the cycle, so once we hear him open the rolltop desk, we simply scatter. No one wants to be nearby when the numbers don't add up, if only because he becomes grouchy. As middle-schoolers, we want to come home and lie on the couch and watch TV all day, but if Bob is paying the bills, the TV is off-limits.

At the time, Bob's eccentric and emotional bill-paying theatrics make no sense to me. Some of this anxiety, I'll admit now, flows from serious fiscal precarity. As a small-town attorney, his income is unreliable, and his expenses—with five (or six) fast-growing children who need clothes and food to eat—are surging indecently. In any given month, the electric bill might actually be the difference between a good Sunday night and a bad Sunday night. And the frequency of his encounters with random lights left on drives him insane. He will dash outside sometimes, even in the winter, to look at the electric meter, hoping to see that it isn't moving at all, that the instrument measuring household use is still and quiet. And he will drop his shoulders in agony when he finds that it is spinning at a fast clip. No one points out that he runs the television continuously in the background while paying the bills.

His solution, in the end, is to offer a collective incentive program—dessert at a local restaurant named Peachies if we keep the bill below one hundred dollars. We don't do dessert at home until much later, when he becomes a judge and the checking account is comparatively flush, so an evening in a restaurant with the full brood feels plush, even lavish. And, as kids, we haven't yet—or, at least, I haven't—begun stealing small change from his wardrobe, then dashing across the street for a candy bar before he comes home from work. Our regular dessert in the lean years is a bowl of cereal or a slice of white bread covered in butter and sugar, which we all find delicious. A fancy dessert at a restaurant is a serious enticement, one that Bob—who has a sweet tooth—also enjoys. I doubt this incentive actually changes our behavior, as the bill still fluctuates wildly each month. But we rally, if only rhetorically, and encourage one another to be thrifty. Those are glorious days when, at the end of all the groaning and murmuring and rocking back and forth and staring at the ceiling, Bob strides into the kitchen and announces that we've tightened our belts and shown admirable restraint. When that happens, it is magical.

This particular weekend, we are lucky. His financial alchemy works and all the bills are paid. Even better, the electric bill is eighty-nine dollars! It takes about ten minutes to get us all in Big Red. I am the first one in the car, leaping into the back row to avoid any arguments. Bob is next, taking the wheel and counting the seconds. We are both impatient. He runs his fingers around the edge of the steering wheel. Everyone else moves so slowly. I am in agony as Sheryl, as slow as a sloth tonight, locks the back door and climbs into the front passenger seat. It takes another ten minutes to drive there, and then about twenty steps to get to the door. There is a quick shuffle to get us all through the doorway. We run the last few paces to our table, elbowing one another to get the inside seat.

Peachies is full of dark wood, low-slung ceilings, and stained-glass lamps decorated with fruit motifs hanging over each table. I sniff the air as we take our seats, and it smells slightly of beer. But I don't care. The vinyl seat, I notice, is sticky. Telltale signs, I am certain, that on weekend nights it draws a rowdy adult crowd. I still don't care. We wait at the table, playing with the sugar packets, squirming with intense anticipation. We begin to bicker, to joke, to rib each other. At last, our waitress—with a great flourish—delivers a half-dozen over-size glass bowls, filled with ice cream and bananas and chocolate and sprinkles. We are instantly silenced as she hands them out one at a time, making a big show of it. As we dig in, savoring this real and true dessert, a rainbow of colors from the swirls and patterns of the stained glass falls on our skin. My smile widens as we all exchange knowing winks and nods, and relish the fruits of our haphazard austerity.

Keeping so many children productively engaged—and providing them with allowances—requires a mad genius for organizational schemes that will bring us all together to work, not all of which will be successful. When we are younger, raking leaves, folding laundry, and shoveling snow are common tasks, but growing older means that we need systems and structures to keep us busy and imprint us with a good collective work ethic.

Raking leaves with Great-Grandpa Everett in the front yard.

When left alone indoors, we bicker over the television remote (whoever holds it, the rule goes, makes all the decisions), or we drift apart, retreating to separate bedrooms. If they find us lying around watching television or playing video games, they send us outside, wanting us to enjoy the yard, the sunshine, the vigor of the world outdoors. And to do so, if possible, together, playing basketball in the driveway, or repairing our bicycles. We resist these efforts, preferring to be typical adolescents, lounging and doing nothing much.

A better solution—one that draws us out into the spotlight and gives us some spending money—is devised by the time we are in high school. By then, Bob has mastered the art of the yearlong and summertime "public works" programs, in which major tasks, some of which take weeks or months, are outlined, and we are contracted to complete them. Bob works alongside us, of course, enjoying the camaraderie and the exercise, and modeling a commitment to hard, physical labor.

The white house with the picket fence is, of course, a never-ending project. So, too, is the yard. We scrape and paint the entire house several times, even paint the garage for good measure. We tar or seal-coat the driveway annually. We carefully strip the kitchen floor of linoleum, scrape off all the adhesive, and finish the pine floors with multiple coats of polyurethane, using steel wool and sandpaper between coats. We strip the paint off the doorway moldings using scrapers, marinating in the toxic fumes of Zip-Strip. We install beadboard ceilings and wainscoting, predrilling holes and using a nail punch to finish the job right. The basement is constantly in need of painting and straightening and decluttering. The picket fence surrounding the property is repaired and painted every summer, lest it lose its luster or appear unfinished. Seasonally, there are leaves to be raked, lawns to be mowed, flowers to be watered, and the driveway must be cleared of snow. We install railroad ties alongside the driveway, adding several parking terraces, and move a truck-bed full of red shale stone into the new parking spots. New creations make for new regular work. Sweeping the stones from the parking terrace off of the driveway then becomes a task, too.

Assigning inside chores, he has to be creative, because there are simply too many of us. One of the worst is the cleaning of the first-floor shower, which he insists needs to involve car wax, so that the fiberglass shell will shine. The worst, that is, because you get the car wax under your fingernails. And also, of course, because try as we might, we can never discover the idea behind that particular chore, which always feels like invented labor, created on a whim so that Bob has the right number of jobs to assign every week. Still, we work hard, even when the assigned chore seems like make-work. "Stick-to-it-iveness" is a big concept for Bob.

The most prominent public works project we complete is the regular Sunday afternoon washing of "the fleet," composed of the half-dozen cars we keep in the driveway. Bob is a loyal consumer, trusting that personal relationships will get him a good deal on the lot. He loves a blue-chip bargain, and he has no interest in buying new, flashy cars for all of his children, many of whom have suspect driving records and a devil-may-care attitude about personal safety. In some cases, we figure out a way to buy our own cars—by his junior year of high school, Bear, for instance, has procured a thirsty, primer-gray Datsun 240Z. Most of the time, though, we rely on a set of hand-me-down vehicles, or cars purchased from Bob's "guy," who knows how to get cheap, old used cars that are, as I recall it, also garish and unattractive. Big Red, with its vivid flame-orange paint, is the hallmark vehicle—and was purchased new, as Bob often tells us. It is joined by a host of old station wagons with zero sex appeal, or sedans so plain and ordinary that even the federal government won't buy them. Exceptions to this pattern are rare. For two months, I have a sky-blue Peugeot with five hundred thousand miles on it. The engine cracks shortly after we get it. After that, a hunter-green Pinto station wagon, with an exhaust system that deteriorates after a year. And after that, there is an Oldsmobile station wagon with faux-wood paneling. And after that, a two-toned brown Chevette, which belches out clouds of smoke when I take it on the highway. These cars don't last long. One Pontiac is thirty years old with a massive engine and it thrives—until Bug drives it into the side of a bridge. (He is fine.) Bob, of course, struggles with the insurance costs, and elects to eliminate collision coverage on the fleet as a way to save costs. Despite their limited lifespans and lack of sex appeal, these cars all need to be washed and vacuumed, waxed and shined up every weekend.

For most of the 1980s, the family Winnebago is a part of the fleet. This white-and-green behemoth is, like nearly every other car we own, a little long in the tooth. On one trip, the gas pedal becomes disconnected, and Bob—who loves elaborate mechanical fixes—has to rig a cable through the floor of the vehicle. He moves a folding chair into the central aisleway of the vehicle, right behind the driver's bucket seat. A child is assigned to sit there and pull the cable on command whenever we need to accelerate. We all love the massive bench seat on the passenger side, the built-in seating area in the back, and the dozens of gizmos that allow the thing to unfold, once parked, into a mini–hotel room that fits all eight of us. The Winnebago is, in short, enormous. I spend hours washing and waxing that car.

In general, it takes teamwork to wash so many cars. If you are around, you are awake and washing cars in the driveway. Everyone gets a single task, which Bob attempts to distribute on the basis of skill and size. Maybe, if you are younger or smaller, like Mark, your job is cleaning the hubcaps. Maybe you are whitening the whitewalls, or maybe you are applying Armor All to the tires to make the black rubber shine. If you are larger and older, maybe you are on vacuum duty, or waxing the car, or wiping the wax off, or washing windshields with glass cleaner and newspapers.

And when we sometimes run out of home repairs and renovations and chores, or when necessity dictates that we do something different, Bob will recommission us, offering a tiny wage as an incentive for nonsensical make-work. Once, he has Bear and me move a massive pile of stones from one side of the yard to the other. Just because. Another summer, discouraged by a muddy puddle in front of our house beyond the picket fence, he decides to have us build a retaining wall several feet back from the curb. This entails removing the earth, shovel by shovel, and carting it all the way to the back of the yard. We slowly make a massive pile next to the garage. Along about fifty feet of street front, on a public road, we hammer railroad ties into the earth with steel tie-rods, cut to length with a hacksaw. We line the road with loose stone—stone that was delivered at the top of the driveway—on the back side of the yard. The hum of activity, the twist and torque of young bodies in motion, the world's ideal synchronicity, as Bob sees it, draws the right kind of attention. One high school friend—Timmy, an Irish kid we call "Mick"—finds it so compelling that he joins in, stripping off his T-shirt and getting into the mix with Bear and me. Timmy shows up every day for a week, and works so hard that Bob ends up paying him. The bikers and construction crews and lollygaggers who linger in front of the general store every day at lunchtime watch us and gauge our progress.

Mark is the only child who resists the chores, the work, the contracted labor. Younger than us three principals—and much younger than Anna—he playfully avoids doing the dishes for years. He never once takes out the trash, fearing the opossums who live in the shed, where the garbage cans are kept. He is too small and too young for the massive earthmoving schemes, and too old to shine hubcaps. Always the "little brother," he publicly resents the exclusions, but also takes sly and secret pleasure in these escapes. Years later, when Mark is in college, Sandi (who is now my wife) is brought to meet the brothers by Anna, our matchmaker, as if to choose a future husband. Mark is asked to take out the kitchen garbage, and he collapses in loud protest, reverting to his preteen histrionics. We all laugh. And stone-faced Sheryl, who is always protective of Mark, thinking that the older kids exclude him, hands him the plastic bag and points to the cans. That night, finally, Mark can't avoid his responsibilities.

The work we do together, the way we change the house and the yard, is our practice of family. Once, after too many of his weekend shirts have gone missing, Bob has us create a wall of plywood cubbyholes in the basement, running from the floor to the ceiling, labeled with each of our names, in which a basket is deposited. The project takes several weekends. The idea, we are told, is that if you find someone else's laundry in your pile, you return it to their cubby. Beyond the useful busy-work, there is an ethics of personal responsibility in this ambition to create fairness through structure, and also an ethos of group care and mindfulness. We are supposed to look out for one another, take care of one another, be self-aware. We are supposed to stand before that array of plywood boxes and see "us." It is a noble effort, but, without any supervision, it quickly becomes a farce. If your clothes are dirty, the cubbyholes make it easier to find clean clothes that belong to a like-sized sibling. Bob's shirts continue to go missing. So do mine. So do Bear's. Usually, we learn later, Mark is the thief.

We never use them correctly, but the cubbyholes remain, transformed over time—another set of ruins, reminders of Bob's extraordinary regime of work and discipline. When we finally move out of the house, we leave the cubbies for the new owners.

18

Bob has large hands, a tall, rangy body, and a full head of soft brown hair. Handsome beyond ordinary measures, he looks quite a bit like Atticus Finch, the upright lawyer with the fantastic posture who champions color-blind justice in Harper Lee's New Deal South. Or like Gregory Peck, I suppose, the actor who takes on the role in the 1962 film, which we all watch on repeat in school as we grow up. The similarities go beyond a striking physical resemblance to include their small-town residences, their shared love of the law, and their firm commitment to racial justice, as they understand it. Both are revered as saints. Both are workaholics. Both men sermonize, in an Old Testament baritone, about racial matters at home, about the consequences of prejudice, and hint at the justice that is sure to come.

Atticus, I think, is a boring, two-dimensional scold. His courage is limited to wordplay, to eloquent, gravelly sermons about humankind's better nature. Bob, I learn as I grow older, is a man of contradictions, a wide-eyed visionary, a prophet, and an endless source of fascination. He preaches the gospel of disaster at the kitchen table, but punctuates the sermon with a wink. His life elsewhere is another matter.

On a personal level, Bob is delightfully quirky. He is a firm believer that if you brush your hair vigorously you will keep it forever, so he keeps a pair of paddle brushes in the big, tall wardrobe next to his bed, and will—each night—sweep his hair straight back for a few minutes. *One hundred strokes a night*, he will admonish, offering guidance we routinely ignore. Well aware of the power of his beauty, he exercises regularly, playing tennis or golf, later using a cross-country-ski machine he has in his bedroom, or the home gym he has installed in another bedroom. He has more clothes than anyone else in the house, perhaps more than all of the children together. He shares a long closet with Mom, and then claims a large hallway closet, too. He has seemingly infinite rows of heavy leather wing-tip shoes. If we need a little cash, he offers us a quarter for each shirt ironed or each shoe polished. We never run out of shirts to press.

In life, Bob eventually finds a job that embodies his contradictions. He becomes a judge, supervising the execution of state rules and the use of the state apparatus to discipline those who violate the rules.

He is an enthusiastic reader, and makes sure the house is filled with books. He loves studying the American Civil War, and reads every biography of Lincoln and Grant he can find. He loves pulp fiction of the "beach-read" sort, from John Grisham to James Michener to Tom Clancy. He loves the self-appraisals of great, world-making men, from Dag Hammarskjöld to Sidney Poitier. And all manner of encyclopedias. And almanacs. And terrifying true-crime stories. Building bookshelves is one of the things we do growing up, another necessary work assignment. The house has several built-ins, and our parents purchased some bookcases when they moved in, but those fill up quickly. To save money, we build bookshelves for our bedrooms, for the Green Room, and even for the bathrooms, until every room overflows with books on all topics.

When we have all left home, and when our parents move into a new house in our small town, one of the first things Bob does is build a new set of floor-to-ceiling bookshelves for the downstairs hallway bathroom. We only learn in adulthood, of course, that it is odd to have a full library in the bathroom.

The bookshelves are cheap yet sturdy things, made with pine boards and a handsaw and not much else. I remember working with him on my own first bookcase—a small, three-shelf thing that I eventually stain mahogany. I make the top shelf too short, and so the books can't stand up, and the bottom shelf is too tall. It would survive a hurricane, though. The imperfections of the piece—and the absence of the finer craftsmanship typical of cabinet-making—are familiar, representative of what we all build together, everything without a formal blueprint. So, too, are the strength and the durability.

Bob has a penchant for elaborate organizational schemes. At work, where he has competent office staff to diligently follow through on his plans, his hunger for a methodical tidiness is an asset. He is renowned for computerizing things that have never before been computerized, and this becomes a part of his brand as a judge. He brings order out of chaos, putting schedules, briefs, and decisions online before most people even know what that means. At home, though, he lacks the patience to follow through on most of his ambitious schemes. As a result, the house is pockmarked with relics of earlier efforts—names written in the mid-1970s atop coat hooks, cubbyholes for shoes and laundry built in the 1980s; all linger on through our college years. Folders in his desk with labels that bear no relationship to the material found inside date back to the purchase of the house. At his cluttered basement workbench, he has several label makers, but the labels he sticks on everything to denote some item's proper location are mostly unhelpful. The sprawling pegboard tool organizer on the basement wall is famous for having a system of hooks and labels but no tools. The failure to maintain order, of course, is simply a matter of numbers. There are more of us, and we are not a disciplined bunch or orderly bunch, the "invulnerable tide" against which his systematic impulses wage a long, hard, impossible-to-win fight.

An order-obsessed man has brought together an offbeat crew and is desperately trying to harmonize it into a family, one at a time—and all together. That takes planning, but it mostly takes discipline, practice, habit, and repetition. There is a reason he loves those platoon movies, like *The Dirty Dozen*, and a reason why he watches them over and over again: he is entranced by those first-act theatrics, wherein a handful of assorted and divergent personalities are forged into a steely team moving in rhythm, usually by a singular authority with an iron will. After that, everything goes smoothly. Real life is messier. We never get out of the first act.

Sheryl insists only that we keep the bathrooms clean—and that we keep our shoes and coats out of the kitchen. She grows tired, as time goes on, of sharing a bathroom with so many boys, none of whom seems to be able to hit his mark. In our teens, we receive an instruction manual from her, with a detailed description of how to pee correctly, where the cleaning materials are, and why we all have a moral obligation to not urinate with what, to her, seems like reckless abandon. Beyond the bathroom, she wants the first floor to be free of our mess. Tired of all of the shoes she finds in the kitchen, she gets into the habit of simply throwing them down the basement stairs, leaving us to sift through the mess at the bottom and find the matched pairs. Eventually, this determined removal of clutter expands beyond shoes to include coats and anything else that should be elsewhere. When she is really angry or disgusted, the bottom half of the basement stairs will be covered in snow jackets, boots, backpacks, and school shoes. The clutter that represents us lies down there in the dark, pressed up against the oil burner and the concrete wall, but the kitchen is clean and orderly.

An easy, natural moralist, Bob presides over family meals and shares with us the cautionary tale of the day: the exploding birth rate in China; a drunk driver in nearby Somerville; an abusive husband he has seen in court. He is also a profligate spender. When he can't find something he needs at his workbench or in the garage, he gets another at the local hardware store. He is the only person I have ever known to buy a car whimsically—a dark-green Ford minivan, meant to replace Big Red—on his lunch break, and with a credit card, so he can get the points. For someone who fights with the checkbook every month, I never once see him restrain his impulse to spend money.

There is something enticing to me in this portrait of a man obsessed with labels, with grand, outlandish structures, accomplished at the courthouse but cursed with a lack of committment at home. Something dramatic, or larger than life. Something wonderful. Something tragic.

Dad misses the release of *The Royal Tenenbaums* by a few months, having passed away in May of 2001, but he will always, in some way, remind me of Royal, especially in these earlier years. Much more so than that proverbial white savior Atticus Finch. The film, directed by Wes Anderson, is the story of a prodigal father who attempts to repair his relationships with his children once a rival for their affections emerges. Royal's efforts are frantic and bizarre—at one point, he fakes stomach cancer; at another, he takes his grandsons to a dogfight—and impossibly baroque, in the manner of a Rube Goldberg device.

At first blush, the comparison to Bob might seem inapt. Royal is, by his own admission, an "asshole"—or maybe just a "son of a bitch." A serial schemer, liar, and prevaricator, outlandish and easy to ridicule, he is ostracized from the family after the discovery of an affair, and tries—over the arc of the film—to weasel his way back into their good graces only when his wife is finally, after over a dozen years of estrangement, ready to move on. His every word is untrustworthy. (Bob, in contrast, is a scrupulous truth teller.) In the end Royal fails to save his marriage but manages to win back the hearts of his children, a trio of malcontents with spectacularly unresolved issues from childhood. His death closes the film, and the family creates a tombstone for him with a blunt and astonishing and impressive untruth—"Died Tragically Rescuing His Family from the Wreckage of a Destroyed Sinking Battleship." In life Royal is unknowable; and so, too, is he in death.

And yet, I cannot help but think of Royal as analogous to Bob. There is Royal's confident optimism, his infectious faith that he can worm his way out of any jam. There is also his sartorial swagger, the glorious wool coats and suits, the sense of a singular personal style. Although he loves his children, Royal nevertheless treats them super- fluously, is if they were—together—no more (and no less) than a beautiful pocket handkerchief, a detail of his heroic persona, another reflection of that poise. This leads him, in the end, to expressions of extreme befuddlement, as if it is impossible for him to truly under- stand what he has brought together. "I never really understood us," he tells Chas, his son, in one rooftop confession.

The very same sort of wild and speculative personality drives Bob to imagine us, to build us, to assemble us. And, as is true of Royal, it is never entirely clear to me that he has fully grasped the thing we become, even if he boosts us repeatedly as if we were the singular hope of the world. Like Richie and Chas and Margot, we are symbols of our father's greatness, Fabergé eggs meant to overwhelm the eye and to reflect honor back upon their maker.

19

I am in the hallway of my middle school, a seventh grader nervously aware of the public eye.

My teacher has asked me to wheel an overloaded media cart to another room. The cart is top-heavy with a big, boxy television, and a VCR on the lower shelf. When I enter the classroom, there is a snort of derision, which I know is an acknowledgment of recognition. There is more to come. My fingers curl around the cool metal frame of the cart in anticipation as I shift the cart into place.

Someone in the back of the room calls out in a stage whisper. "Hey, it's N——— Lips!" A knowing laugh crackles the end of his words. The room responds with a low, collective giggle. The words echo off the cinderblock walls. The teacher in the room proceeds with his instruction obliviously, diagramming a sentence for the class on the blackboard, barely pausing to acknowledge receipt of the cart, not hearing the insult. The laughter continues, animating the room. People sit up, smiles on their faces. They look closely. My fingers slip from the frame. Head hung low and shoulders slumped, I duck out, shamefaced, instinctively touching my mouth, searching for something.

"N——— Lips."

That nickname—a very little thing, when measured against the sordid national context of the 1980s—is another reminder, as I see it, of the naivete of our family's progressive narrative. Not everyone, I realize, has heard Bob's kitchen-table sermons about the ark, about the global catastrophe around the corner, about the glorious future predicted for our rainbow tribe. Far too many feel empowered by the Reagan-era disdain for Blackness—empowered to see race everywhere, to call it out.

"N—— Lips."

I remember first hearing this racist epithet in middle school, a shocking, searing complication of my whiteness. It sticks, following me everywhere. For the rest of junior high, it often feels as if I am greeted with it at every doorway, in every hallway, on every playing field, and at every party or social event. I expect it. Each time, the words strike me with bare-knuckled force. Flinching, I reach up to my mouth, feeling for my lips, discerning their shape and outline, their racial character.

"There's N—— Lips!"

It isn't so much the newly diagnosed Blackness that leaves me twisted on the inside, but what I presume is my strange, mixed-up racial location. I have been seen, re-envisioned, and given a new name. And I am, by that act, transformed. That nickname compels a new ritual, a nightly adolescent inquest, in which I survey myself in the mirror, considering my skin, defining what feels inside and outside of whiteness. These racial mappings are, in the end, reassuring. The rest of me, it seems, is "fine." Straight blond hair. Blue eyes. Pale skin.

My lips—the very instruments of expression and intimacy—are apparently otherwise. There is, back then, no language to capture the experience of racial contingency, no common sense that race is a mutable, flexible thing, that identities are relational, or socially and politically determined. We all understand race as self-evident, as something that is right there on the surface, to be seen and marked and recognized without debate or effort. I am white. Bob and Sheryl say so. My classmates see something else. It must be there, somewhere, in the details of my physiognomy. If it is seen, it must be real.

At night, by the flicker of the television or in the privacy of the bathroom, I conclude that my classmates look at me, look at Bear, look at whatever is presented to them in national popular culture, and see a physical resemblance. And, being young, I agree with them, not knowing, really, what that means. In private, when I hold up two mirrors so that I can see my profile and assess for myself what Blackness might look like to others—to see how it can be measured by those who see me—I see a fullness, an abundance. I hold a pencil or a ruler from the tip of my nose to my chin and tighten my lips to make them smaller so that they won't protrude so far and won't interrupt that precious line. I practice holding my mouth closed, so that this obvious Blackness might be obscured. I stare, with painful envy, at those I perceive to be unquestionably white, with perfect profiles, thin, Anglo-Saxon lips, and constrained, civilized mouths. I learn to cover my mouth with my hand while listening or laughing. When it is my turn to talk in class, I am stubbornly silent.

In the spring of 1983, when I am twelve, I tell my parents—confess to them—that I feel, in a word or two, racialized in the wrong way, that a bright line has been drawn between my physiognomy and my family's diverse composition. I might never escape that nickname, which I now hear everywhere. It disrupts the story of us, the supposed simplicity of my position as one of the two white children. And it makes me feel—as that word is meant to do—less than human.

Perhaps Bob and Sheryl wish to redraw the color line more clearly, if only to soothe their child. In any case, I am taken to a local plastic surgeon, who promises to give me the racial clarity I so desperately want. A simple set of cuts, a summer of recovery, and all will be well by eighth grade. There will be a reveal at the start of the next school year. At the time I understand it as a sort of racial editing, aimed at clarifying for our public (and for me) the color line in my household, to firmly and permanently mark myself as something other than my brothers and my sister. To affirm, once and for all, my whiteness. To escape an epithet I already know to be hateful and dehumanizing, a racial curse I have already experienced once before, in the piney woods of Peterborough.

I expect a miracle. An end to what I conceptualize as an indeterminacy that makes me stand out. The surgery on my troublesome bottom lip is painful, involving a single cut across its width, the removal of a ribbon of flesh, and the use of a thick suture line to hold it together while it heals. Coming out of the medical office, the pain intensifies as my lip swells. I cry as we wait for the pharmacist to prepare the pain medication. I expect to see the difference immediately. To see, that is, the thin profile of the white mouth I want. Instead, revealing the truth in a bedroom mirror as soon as I get home, I find a swollen, purple mass, glistening with dried blood. It seems a haunting joke, to have sacrificed my own flesh, and to have been rewarded with a mouth that is vile and unseeable, a comical mouth that needs to be hidden.

I grab a bandanna and veil myself. I retreat to my bedroom and stay there for weeks, staring at my mouth in the mirror, wishing for what I understand to be a repair, a restoration. When that long cut across my lip loses its tenderness, I run my fingers along the sutures, restarting the inquest, guessing my "progress." When the sutures come out in the middle of the summer, I keep my makeshift veil on, waiting for the tiny red tracks they've left behind to vanish. I want to emerge perfect, without a single reminder of the surgery—or of the past. And then, one August day, finally contented with my look, I fold up the bandanna, leave my room, get on my bike, and go looking for my friends. No one comments on my absence or my return. And, at home, no one asks me why the surgery was necessary.

I can feel the sutures now, if I concentrate. I recall their texture, their tightness.

When I arrive at school in the fall as an eighth grader, I proudly offer what I think is my newer, whiter, European face to this discerning audience. But they care not a bit and shout with glee:

"N—— Lips is back!"

Even now, reading these words to myself, I am struck by an acute, visceral recall of this final reveal. That after a summer spent in isolation, healing from surgery, gauging my new look in the mirror, I can be so instantly deflated, so inconsolable. So thoroughly complicit, I now know, in the project of anti-Blackness. The unease that comes from this memory captures my general discomfort, in those years, with the whole of our radical experiment. I cannot celebrate the social magic of our ensemble that sometimes works, because Blackness has attached to me, with consequences; I cannot reject our deliberate, machine-like production either, because that same attachment is evidence of love, of kin, of family. What is the sign of the family? Or of our individual and collective physiology? What is the sign of the Black child behind the white picket fence? Of "Black" lips on a white face?

In *The Souls of Black Folk*, W. E. B. Du Bois recalls the moment when "the shadow swept across him." Playing an innocent card game with a group of children, an exchange of pretty little *cartes des visites*. "The exchange was merry," he remembers, "till one girl, a tall newcomer, refused my card—refused it peremptorily, with a glance. Then it dawned upon me with a certain suddenness that I was different from the others; or like, mayhap, in heart and life and longing, but shut out from their world by a vast veil."

The passage is famous. It is the cornerstone of disciplines and fields, an epigraph to hundreds of books, a wellspring of sentiment for generations of those marked in the same fashion. Most of those who write about Du Bois dwell, as he does, on the aftershocks of that moment, on the perverse acquisition of a "second sight" into the workings of humanity, and on the determination to "wrest" away the "prizes" accorded to Du Bois's peers and yet still denied him based on some divisive illusion. When I first read it in high school, I am struck—awestruck, even—by his admission that race is made, not born, and that it can materialize with a thunderous suddenness, that it can happen to you in moments that will be cauterized into memory as if into flesh. It is an explanation, to me, of so much.

From the moment that I take in the words, though, I also recognize that Du Bois's insights about the color line and Black life do not apply to me. And can never apply to me. On my skin, on the superficial scar that still runs across the inside of my bottom lip, one finds not the imprint of Blackness but of whiteness, not the memory of the color line but instead the dictates of anti-Blackness, which instruct on racial clarity, with often terrible consequences. One sees the evidence of my youthful attempt to realize, on my surface, that divisive illusion.

Du Bois set out to turn racism into a wellspring of understanding, among other things. Over time, he argues, an accumulation of these moments—a young girl refusing his card, the denial of funding for a PhD in Berlin, an encounter with a lynched man's body parts in a butcher shop—can turn ordinary flesh into scar tissue. And, when that happens, when the encounter with race isn't singular but oft repeated, then your racial life becomes a matter of recounting the origins of each scar—each a memorial to a wound imperfectly healed, and of translating for future generations what literary critic Hortense Spillers has called the "hieroglyphics of the flesh." At every turn, then, there is the flesh and there is scar tissue. And there are memorials to the past waiting to be seen.

20

Every story has a turning point. Or two. Or three. And this is one of ours.

In the spring of 1984, as eighth grade comes to a close, we are ready to adopt again. "Ready," in this context, means that we have caught our breath and felt reasonably in control. The first few adoptions were so reckless and so urgent. This time, we are more deliberate. There is a boy we might bring into the family, a young African American child, who would be our first domestic adoption. Bob and Sheryl organize some family meetings to discuss the process, make a trip to New York City, and reconfigure the house. We all drive out to the Bronx Zoo in Big Red, where we are introduced to our prospective brother and his attentive social service agent, and we have a wonderful day hiding in the gopher tunnels, running and laughing together on the garden pathways. It feels perfect. All that remains is the paperwork.

One afternoon, I am sitting outside, trying to impress a white girl with long brown hair while waiting for the school bus. Shannon is a well-traveled transfer student, newly arrived from California. She has long brown hair feathered back and a habit of wearing Van Halen T-shirts and tight blue jeans. She lies on her back, sunglasses covering her eyes, her face expressionless. I have a crush on her and think that our impending addition will show a unique flair and catch her eye, maybe even make me seem interesting.

"He is coming from the South Bronx," I say casually, as if it were the most exotic place on earth. I imagine that this sounds sophisticated, or internationalist. Or that the South Bronx is Los Angeles, or London, or Nairobi, or Tokyo, or Paris. It is far away. It is cosmopolitan. Big tall buildings and bright lights. We live in a small town, far from the city.

Shannon, of course, is tragically uninterested in any of this.

"That's cool," she says, her eyes hidden behind the mirrored lenses. I try to add more detail, to share some of the philosophy behind the family, to explain why he matters to the idea of "us," and what his incorporation heralds. Shannon, the love of my life at fourteen, gives me no indication she hears any of it.

His name is Eddie. He joins us in the summer of Vanessa Williams, the first Black Miss America, who appears nude in *Penthouse* and will soon lose her crown as a result. In the late summer, Bear and I search for that issue of *Penthouse* as if it were the holy grail. It is the summer, as well, of *Purple Rain*, of Run-DMC, and of Whodini, all competing on the local radio stations with hair-metal bands and New Wave. The summer, more seriously, in which we first hear about crack cocaine and first confront the desolate failures of the war on poverty, and in which we come to envision ourselves as a platoon engaged in a domestic rescue mission.

The first photo of Eddie we see is taken when he is six. It is a classic American school picture, with the light blue backdrop that is streaked like a cloudy sky. Eddie is looking off to the right. The back of the photo gives his birth name, and his age as six. He is wearing a way-too-big button-down pink shirt with a wide, white collar. His hands are folded in his lap, and he has a shy little smile. It is an adorable photograph, meant to tug at the heartstrings.

*Eddie, in a school photo shared
with us as we considered another
adoption.*

"He looks like Webster," we agree, referring to a character played
by Emmanuel Lewis on television, another adopted Black child. The
resemblance is undeniable, we think, and also emotionally compelling. Webster is a preternaturally smart speck of a child, cute as a
button—and button-sized, too.

The photo circulates at the official family meeting, where we discuss our aims and ambitions as a group. We sit at the kitchen table,
listen to our parents present the options, pass the small, cropped photo
around the table, and then share our feelings. The original idea, as I
remember it, is that we might adopt a child of color from abroad with
more pronounced special needs, a physical disability, a missing limb or
two. Bob encourages a completion of the set, a Black child to match
Bear. In opposition, I imagine a sister named Amy from India, a young
girl with leg braces, someone smaller and younger, who I will carry up
and down the steps.

As we plot the adoption in the mid-1980s, we still cite the lesson of the DeBolts, a far vaster assemblage than ours, built of bodies broken in war and poverty, all redeemed (or so their award-winning documentary assures) by what is presented as an ingenious American system of parenting. We recall the clatter of metal and plastic, of the prosthetics. The beaming, grateful faces. The satisfied, self-congratulatory tone of Bob and Dorothy, so thrilled by their creation. "Amy" is, then, a straightforward conjuring of the DeBolts' extraordinary Black daughter, Karen, born without arms and legs, a girl with a big laugh and a dazzling personality. We have always been mesmerized by the video footage of Karen, swimming in the family pool getting herself dressed without help, and trying to make snowballs with her "hooks for hands."

I am still keen on Amy, but we agree, as a group, on Eddie. Mom remembers now that some of us are concerned about having a sibling with visible and disfiguring scars. She won't name names. "Isn't that terrible?" she adds, rightfully indicting us all.

Once committed, we are unified, together championing a single sweeping explanation for the choice. We hope—like many others—that such a small child can be extracted from the rotten city, his "natural goodness," as the philosopher Rousseau would call it, restored to its original brilliance, his future reassured by our racial comity. Such hopes are marshaled against the Reagan era's divisive racial politics, which militate against housing projects and basketball courts and graffiti and seem determined to burn Black neighborhoods and Black life out of existence. "Just Say No," First Lady Nancy Reagan admonishes Black children, all of them—as she sees them—potential drug users, offering little beyond that instruction to help combat what the news media describes in almost genocidal terms. We are built for this sort of thing, we know. Opening our home is something we can do, a small act of great significance. Conservative racism is on the ascendancy, liberalism appears to be dying, and we are the only solution within arm's reach of Eddie, the only group ready to save him from the intractable problems of cityscapes and the rising tide of avowedly racist policy-makers. When we are told that he will die without us, we believe it. We ready the gate at the end of the driveway, preparing to open it up and draw him inside the picket fence.

The youngest of our group—the cute child in the pink shirt—was born in the city. Popular culture represents his home-scape as the stuff of legend and stereotype, an apocalyptic shadowland of burned-out buildings. The adoption agency presents him to us as a walking, breathing tragedy: the son of a crack-addicted, alcoholic mother, his body weak and marked by physical and psychological imperfection. The state viewed Eddie as broken, cast aside by his grandmother, and laundered through a carnivalesque sequence of foster homes. He comes with a backstory we all understand. Under normal circumstances, left alone in the Bronx, we are assured by the agency, he will become a foot soldier in the coming drug wars, a bit player in the all-too-real New Jack City of the early 1980s. We imagine the Bronx and the city more generally through the prism of *Life*, which has broadcast dystopian street scenes nationally, and through gangland movies like *The Warriors* and *Escape from New York*, which make us shiver with fear. Forsaken and left behind, we imagine, Eddie will drift in and out of the prison system from the start, his childhood quietly revoked without comment, his impoverishment predicting a grim criminal-justice profile. To illustrate this terrible fable, the agency shares that the state projects that he likely will not live to be thirty.

The appeal made to us—once more, the family of the future, headed by a white patriarch—is to save Eddie from a fate that is described as otherwise ineluctable. This call to take up the work of salvage is undeniably racist, resonating on some lower frequency with our intended purpose. Ripped from what conservative America has defined as a desolate dystopia and relocated to our idyll of white picket fences and little red schoolhouses, his story, it is assured, will take a different turn.

The public presumption is that he can be reformed, reanimated by that unparalleled engine of success: all-white, small-town America. His childhood—including his right to public education, to innocent bike rides, to tinkling laughter on the playground—is to be vouchsafed. The supposed inevitability of his criminality will be, at the very least, suspended. Tired of the decline of cities and the intractability of the race problem, the public seems to wait for—and to want—another bootstrapping narrative to emerge, one that celebrates the white-headed household. The country yearns for another Phillip Drummond, or another George Papadopolis, a new sitcom dad to preside over the melodrama of kitchen-table integration. Our adoptive family, then, is enlisted as an engine of "reform," offering a liberal multiracial pedagogy of incorporation and integration at a moment of catastrophic state failure. In an increasingly inequitable world, "we" are presumed to offer the closest thing to an ideal. This is what we are told, and it is what we tell ourselves.

We are wrong. It is important to acknowledge that. Wrong, that is, to think, imperiously, that he needs fixing or saving. That is the inherent logic, though, of the large multiracial adoptive family, where salvage and rescue discourses abound. Where concerns about over-population and catastrophe, no matter how charitably manifested, are always rooted in the deep, rich soil of racism. We know only what we have been built to do: to repair, to retrofit, to resurrect. We will fail, in the end, to equip Eddie to survive the sea of misrepresentations he confronts. We fail because we misdiagnose the changing world around us, assuming that the white picket fence is a great wall around us, that it can withstand anything. We fail because we worry about apocryphal encounters with frog-mouthed bigots in fedora hats, the racist villains of too many Hollywood movies, and because we miss the new, less obvious carceral infrastructures emerging all around. We believe, mistakenly, that we are magic. Not understanding our mistake, we miss the clash between our family's symbolic potential as a single, dazzlingly futuristic unit and the powerful, growing swells of anti-Blackness, which repeatedly threaten us as well.

We see none of this at the time. In the present, I ask Mom if she has warm, treasured memories with Eddie. If there is some untroubled souvenir from the early days, just after he joins us, when everything is going well. Every arrival creates a memory like this. Bug and the long ride home from JFK. Bear and the plastic slide. Anna and the swirl of silk dresses. She is silent for a minute, choosing her words carefully. "I might," she says. It is hard, she continues, because "it was difficult from the start."

We organize a welcome party, she recalls, just a few days after Eddie joins us. He is six. The entire extended family, roughly thirty in number, arrives in our small town. We keep the driveway clear for the younger kids on bicycles and order a big sheet cake for the backyard. Bob grills hamburgers and hotdogs. The boys all play Wiffle ball in the side yard. The older ladies sit at a picnic table and reminisce. Everywhere Eddie looks, someone calls out to him, inviting him to be a part of something new and different, something materially far beyond what he has experienced. Just as the party gets started, though, he grabs our aunt Joan's purse and makes a dash for the end of the driveway, and then turns right to go down the hill and toward the old firehouse. He runs as fast as he can. He is hoping to get back to the city.

Bear runs down the hill after Eddie, catching him easily. As he walks his new younger brother back up the hill, he explains that there is no longer a need to steal.

We all laugh, Mom remembers. It seems, to her, like a humorous, fish-out-of-water kind of story. Like something that Arnold Jackson might have played for laughs in the early days of *Diff'rent Strokes*, when the Drummonds' Park Avenue penthouse seemed so glitzy and so elevated that it must be off-planet.

21

"Would you have married me if you hadn't grown up in your family?"

My wife, Sandi, asks the question seriously, holding me hostage to the terrifying abstraction of the average white man. She has read a rough draft of this manuscript. Her working hypothesis is that the experience of the "we" is value added, that it disrupts the abstraction. Without it—without the experiences that allow me to use that first-person plural—I am irredeemable.

"Of course," I purr, reaching out to touch her hand, stroking her skin with a mischievous finger. "How could I not?" I am trying to turn it into a joke. We have been married for a quarter century. My voice and my smile tell her that I hear the humor in her question.

"I don't think so," she rejoins, pulling her hand away and furrowing her brow, signaling concern. My wife, a friend likes to say, is coy like a knife. "I wouldn't have married you," she continues. "You would be different. I would have steered clear of you."

"How so?" I wonder aloud.

Neither of us is sure how to answer. And neither of us really knows how to be sure, or what to measure, what to assess in testing any prospective answer. All of this is said, of course, in the wake of the forty-fifth presidential administration—"the late unpleasantness," as we call it now, a euphemistic reference to the terrible half decade that commences on November 7, 2016, when the election results are reported. Our daughter, upon hearing them, wonders aloud whether Sandi—brown skinned, the descendant of slaves and planters, coolies and explorers—will be deported. Or Uncle Bear. Or whether the same will be true of Aunt Indy, Sandi's sister. Five centuries of enslavement and empire loom as a backdrop to our discussion and that question: "Would you have married me if you hadn't grown up in your family?" If we give that history too much mind, those centuries swell up, and we might be crushed

Four of us, days after Bear's arrival, 1975, celebrating his incorporation with cake.

by the weight of everything—the wholesale extermination of the brutes, to paraphrase Conrad—that came before us, the viciousness of everything that produced us and that bound us together historically.

"... if you hadn't grown up in your family?"

My family. Our family. Another intimate construct.

Our parents are saints, or so we are often told. They have built a big, bold, audacious rainbow family, with which they mean to change the world. It doesn't work. Or, at least, it doesn't quite work the way they—or any of us—expect. We are built to be different, to be unique, to conjure a new future. We are built to stand together. The world ends up changing us, warping our mission, at least a little. And, one after the other, we are bruised, or broken, or just plain wrecked. As a whole, we are ruined and cast aside. The world moves on to other things, too—to other radical idealizations of the future. Scattered, buried, and gathering dust, we are relics of a radical innovation with consequences.

A relic is a dangerous thing, though. A relic is invested with ancient power and meaning. A relic is from long ago, its survival often a matter of chance. A relic is precious, whether it is carried aloft on a feast day or hidden inside a temple or a museum. A relic can kill. A relic can inspire.

Sandi has no time for relics. Many in her family fled a CIA-engineered race war for the United States, Canada, and England, but they didn't escape the collateral impact, the psychological marks that attend forced articulations of diaspora. Other family members stayed behind and tried to build a newer, better independent country. Her parents left for New York City when she was young, and, as a consequence, she will tell you that she is defiantly and unapologetically from Queens. This means something important to her, this chosen touchstone in one of the world's most demographically diverse communities. She has no patience for the predominantly white American fetish for an unusual background, for the self-serving idea she routinely encounters in the broader nation that surprisingly global and off-white racial inflections make one's story unique, or worth sharing. "In Queens," she tells us routinely, "everyone had a story about international migrations, racial complications, and mixed-up identities. So, if everyone around you—everyone in school or on the block—has a story like that, what else do you have? What else can you bring to the table?" When she talks to Jelani, a friend who grew up in the same neighborhood and who went to a rival high school, they laugh about the simplistic pretentions of a fanciful origin story, the kinds of stories occasionally profiled on those retail DNA specials on PBS, where everyone looks to find that one tiny detail—that grandparent from the mystical faraway—that they believe makes them special.

"Please," she says, derisively, when she hears a friend invoke a distant West Indian connection, "what else can you bring to the table?" Actions and experiences matter to her, not the cheaply acquired identities that distract and refract, the costume jewelry of modern American life.

In her terms, Bob brings a lot more to the table. He has abundant imagination and conviction, and a bold idea for a big multicolored family. He has a keen sense of what this family might stand for, what it might dramatize for a post-civil-rights-era nation torn apart by war, violence, and racism. Like many before and after him, though, Bob shares this interest in finding some obscure, random ancestor, some genetic flourish that will enrich what he sees as an otherwise all-white background. In fact, on the application for his first adopted child, he lists himself as part "American Indian," a reference to a long-lost French Canadian grandparent on his mother's side, a woman with Native blood and heritage. "Race and Nationality Background," queries the 1971 application to be adoptive parents. "Caucasian—German, Irish, Fr. Canadian, Am. Indian," he responds, squeezing the typed words onto a single blank line. This genealogical factoid—a wish for something other than white, a remote claim made against steep odds—is a part of his backstory.

And, on some level, this claim repels me in the present. Nauseates me. Does this line—this throwaway, reckless reference to an Indigenous heritage—make it easier for him to adopt my brothers and sister? How is it read by the adoption agents? Do they imagine that they are placing children of color in a household with off-white connotations? Does it, in some structural way, make the adoptions easier?

Sandi finds him amusing, even now, twenty years after his passing. He told us that he wanted "two of every race," just like Noah, building the ark, right before the world was cleansed by a wrathful God. When he met my wife, he joked that he had forgotten to collect two Native Americans to complete the matched sets he had assembled. And he added, with a smile, that I had brought home the wrong kind of Indian, thinking that my intended's roots could be limited to the subcontinent. She laughed, thinking him outrageous, and gently mocking him for misunderstanding her genealogy. All such adoptive families, she knows, are playfully, recklessly engaged with race and identity. Some endure. Others collapse under their own weight. A few wreak havoc on the world. A relic is a dangerous thing.

"Hey," Sandi asks, pivoting to a new subject and shaking me out of this reverie, "remember when we took the DNA test?"

I do. The test comes in a small, innocuous box. It is a gift from her sister—a half-serious excavation of our entangled histories. She has gift-wrapped us a box with test tubes and a padded envelope.

We spit in the tubes and send them back. My results return first. "You're like the Benjamin Moore color wheel for white," she jokes. And it is true. The easy assertions of biological truth in the report—"45% Irish"—are laughable, but there is also an undeniable reflection on the page of family histories, old and new. Ireland and Germany, England and the Czech Republic. No surprises. Not a hint of "Native American." Just a teasing, unexpected reference to "1% Sicilian," which feels

A young Bob in profile.

like the kind of surprise that corporate HQ might write into any such report, a necessary precondition for the "ah ha!" moment they want to create for every customer. In the age of genealogy as big business, that 1 percent is an invitation to pay for the subscription service and to keep digging.

"Yes," I say, with a shrug. "That looks right." I would say the same thing about anything.

I cannot share Bob's fascination with the obscure, long-past historical fact. I cannot list myself as part "American Indian" because he machined me into a white object, without what he would see as exciting variation. For far too long, I know, many white folks have concocted such distant ancestors. So many, in fact, that the 1925 Virginia law that codified the "one-drop rule" and forbade marriage between

two different races had an exception for those who claimed a distant Native ancestor. The "Pocahontas exception," it was called. Such
fantasies of meaningless difference insulate against guilt. And that
insulation is an enticing marketing device in the dawning age of the
majority minority. I cannot, then, imagine clinging to a fake Indian
ancestor conjured up by my father, or to the mystery of that "1% Sicilian" that has been customized for me by a corporation that artfully
provisions racial "facts." I cannot derive from any of this a sense of
the exotic possibilities of the self. A distant Native American relative;
a long-lost Sicilian connection. All of that seems farcical to me, or
dangerous. A pointlessly exotic detail that only confirms the value of
whiteness in the end, like the tiny drop of black pigment added to the
"optic white" paint in Ellison's *Invisible Man*. In this family, I am the
stylized white child, one of two, a matched set without complexity
or ambiguity.

Sandi's test comes back a few weeks later. She muses that the delay
must reflect her more complicated DNA. Perhaps, she jokes, they
needed a bigger computer? Sure enough, when it arrives, we find that
her report is basically a kaleidoscopic population map of Queens, of
the Caribbean, of Asia, of Africa. She has all the world's diversity in
one body. And she laughs it off, too. As anyone from Queens will.

"What else can you bring to the table?"

The laughter is one of those things we never address, but it is a constant part of the backdrop whenever we talk about race. I'm reminded
of Alice Walker's notion that laughter is "tears turned inside out," an
insight that flowed from her elegiac account of the search for Zora
Neale Hurston's unmarked grave in Florida, and of her own unstifled
laugh in the midst of discovery. Likewise, I remember the laughter
that often greeted my own presentation of Josephine Baker's story—
monkeys dressed like children, children treated like zoo animals, a
home transformed into an amusement park. The smirks and guffaws
from the audience. Laughter in the face of race—laughter that escapes

our lips in the shadow of those five centuries, laughter that gives voice to our hauntings—is never really what it seems to be.

She returns to her original question: "Would you have married me if you hadn't grown up in your family?"

There is no laughter in it. She is coy like a knife. And the laughter, I know, is never really laughter anyway. It is always misdirection.

"You married me," I tell her out loud, hoping to sound convincing, "because I was once a part of something dangerous. And because that changed me. Changed us. For the better."

Bob tried to build an ark. I know that he constructed something else to be held within. Something dangerous.

Missile silos are hidden in cornfields. Earthworks built so long ago that no one can remember when the army bulldozers arrived— earthworks that hide mothballed subterranean fortresses. Experimental technologies gathering dust in forgotten laboratories underground. Deadly weapons enshrined in the earth's crust, waiting for a rediscovery, waiting for the day that some farmer plows too deep. A big, mixed-race family, a product of empire and war, meant to lead the way to a better American future, meant to survive whatever apocalypse is forthcoming. These are all weapons for a different age, meant to win a different war. Oversize, dramatic expressions of the state power to change the world. Touch them and you die. Plow too deeply and you resurrect them, set them off, blow them up. The blueprints are lost. The builders are gone. All of these are dangerous things.

22

When we enter high school, Bob wants us to take the faith more seriously. Immaculata is a big parochial school in the county seat of Somerville, which means a longer bus ride. The building is a vast, mid-century structure, all clean and modern, clad in red brick, despite the baroque reliquaries and medieval religiosity of the interior. The scale of it is daunting. I am struck by the ubiquitous presence of nuns— the stern, aged Sisters of the Immaculate Conception, dressed in severe dark-blue habits and frocks. The Sisters are ancient and intimidating, and some carry yardsticks in the halls, anticipating a chance to mete out punishment, but their knowledge of religious arcana is astonishing. The assignment of drab student uniforms is stifling. Shirts and ties, jackets, and khakis for the boys. Knee-length plaid for the girls. It takes a while to understand how one can inflect something so sterile with any kind of individual flair.

The year that I arrive at the school, Anna leaves for Rutgers. Bear and Bug are a year behind me. In the fall of 1984, then, I am alone in a new school—and disaggregated from the rest of us, at least for a year. I have always been a grade ahead of Bear and Bug. In Bear's case, it was a matter of language acquisition, as the school district slowed his entry to ensure that he was fluent. Mom often wonders aloud if it would have made more sense to hold me back, so that the three of us could proceed together in the same grade, especially as my grades plummet and I continue to struggle—and as Bear and Bug both thrive. High school, then, is defined by estrangement, by loneliness, and by the soft disciplinary regimes and hard religious structures of the place.

My most acutely felt memories of that first desultory year, though, are about a very private lesson learned about the perils and pitfalls of being a savior. Specifically, they relate to a surprising, ambitious midyear effort to foster a connection to a potential new member of the family—a seventh child, whom I abstractly idealize as a new sister. This follows, in a strange sequence, my earlier visualization of Amy, the sister-who-never-was, the sister with the shiny, glittering leg braces, the sister who would have needed me to carry her up the stairs, who was dreamed up during the family meetings that ultimately bring us Eddie.

As the weather turns cold, we are challenged to make a donation for a coat drive. That is, to purchase a winter coat, presumably for a child in need, which will then become an anonymous Christmas gift. My deposit of the coat into the big cardboard box wrapped in the obligatory holiday-themed paper outside of the school chapel is supposed to bestow warmth and comfort to the poor or less fortunate—and also the blessings of soothing reassurance to me. The school chaplain—a smiling, agreeable Filipino man, with a talent for reaching troublemakers—is the facilitator here, keeping the school community in the dark about who will be receiving our largesse. The point, as he explains repeatedly at a school assembly, in the hallways, and in morning announcements over the loudspeaker, is to give because it is the right thing to do, and not to expect the gratitude of the less fortunate. We won't be receiving any handwritten notes meant to soothe our guilt or burnish our self-esteem. The problem of poverty is intractable. Winter is approaching and the coats are an urgent necessity. Our contributions should, therefore, be generic, plain, and, above all else, useful to absolutely anyone.

In my fourteen-year-old imagination, I go way off script. In my mind, this gift will go to another member of the family. She— invariably, this will be a she—will be "found family," perhaps not formally adopted. She will be grateful for the warmth we provide. She will join us for the holiday. Maybe she will even live with us, bringing her parents into our larger embrace. In the back of the school bus, staring at the barren highway median as it zips past, I imagine an even bigger family Christmas by the fireplace. I see our new addition laughing and celebrating. I believe that a big gesture—an astonishing, lavishly expensive coat, a coat so extraordinary that it will elicit the same handwritten note we have been forbidden—can make it all happen.

I'm reminded, thinking back on this, of the positive, upbeat associations with the idea of adoption that swirl in my mind at that age. To adopt is, of course, to take in, to accept and to realize, to choose, to sponsor, to bring together. And our family—at the time, it seems big, bold, adventurous, unstoppable—is living proof. I recognize, in this wild fable, the occasional pleasure that I take in our assemblage, in being a part of something with an outsize destiny. And I remember the confidence that it will have no limits, that there is more to come, that we will expand outward, over and over again. Eddie has just arrived, I think. There is no reason not to continue to adopt, especially with Anna off to college. The loneliness of that first year in high school surely enhanced my commitment to the legend of us, to the very idea of adoption as a positive force for necessary social change.

I also see the racial texture of this position, this sense that bringing someone into the family is a blessing, that our function is to expand our benevolent jurisdiction, that we have near-unlimited capacity for more. If there are limits, I certainly don't know them. Not then. Not at fourteen. And maybe, in truth, I never find them. In believing this, of course, I echo the late Cold War solution to almost every human problem caused by war and empire—the arrival of exiles and refugees, immigrants and migrants—all of which are best addressed by assimilation into the white heterotopia of the American small town, the American suburb, the American family. I veer away from the increasingly xenophobic terms of national political culture. I find religion—the civil religion of liberalism—at a moment when the country's faith in the tenets of that ideology is dwindling. I am Bob's son, in teen consciousness, with all of his extravagances and fervent beliefs.

On some level, though, I know our family is not just bulging at the seams but also straining. Eddie's arrival puts us back at our limit in the white house with the picket fence. To make more room in the house, three of us—Bob, Bear, and I—turn the attic into a long, low-ceilinged shared bedroom, accessed through a small stairwell in the hallway closet. At night, Bear and I crawl on hands and knees along the four-foot peak of the room into bed—or crawl into the adjoining attic space, now occupied by Eddie. And on really hot nights, Bob puts a box fan at the bottom of the closet stairs, trying to redirect our home's single air-conditioning unit to the improvised third floor. Bear sets up an array of oscillating fans in the attic, hoping that we might be cooled down by the movement of so much hot air in the room.

Bob's efforts to pay bills and balance checkbooks on Sunday afternoons are once again increasingly stressful, his frustration now boiling over regularly. He's made some imprudent investments in real estate with a few friends and has been saddled with an office building that drains away some of our limited resources. He is forced to sell off the land he purchased in New Hampshire, land he has hoped can someday have a small house for us all to share. The added expense of a parochial high school and college is not helping. We know to steer clear of the Green Room on Sundays, then, when his mood and his frequent outbursts of incredulity and exasperation ruin the atmospherics of whatever is on television. Eventually, we know, he will give up, open a beer or have a rum and Coke, and sink into his La-Z-Boy recliner.

Then and only then—once we hear the clickety-clack of the recliner's mechanism and the soothing sounds of the television, playing some mid-century war movie—will it be safe to curl up under a blanket and watch with him.

I never for a minute, then, consider asking Bob for any money for the coat drive.

I might talk to Sheryl, who has a more sympathetic ear. But, somewhere deep inside, I know that she will just go to the Burlington Coat Factory and choose a nondescript, cheap puffy jacket. She is, again, practical to a fault. She will understand what the school chaplain is trying to do, and she will support him, keep it functional, make it work for everyone. That isn't right, I think. This person we are helping deserves the very best. Imagining that this new member of the group might join us somehow, and not wanting to provide her with a coat that might stigmatize her or reveal a class position, I decide that we need a high-end ski jacket, totally top of the line, which will cost hundreds of dollars, even then. Once more, a big gift—a gesture, an overture, a generous extension of myself—is required.

When Bear arrived, I gave him my bicycle as a welcoming gift. A gesture that was meant to express my eagerness to have another brother, and one exactly my age. There was also, clearly, a deep reservoir of anxiety and stress, a desire to overperform welcome and generosity, to snuff out any doubts dramatically. And any guilt—white guilt—which Bob instilled. This ski jacket will, in the same way, be a much nicer coat than mine. I have—we all have—exactly the kind of blue puffy coat that makes the most sense for a growing kid with an active outdoor life. It is warm. It can be easily repaired.

The jacket I have in mind, though, is full of rich color blocks, with a snappy collar. It will be so futuristic that it will come with a long label, explaining all the science built into the exterior and interior. It will have a place for ski tags, which I've seen dangling off the front of outerwear in movies—and in the hallways, on some of the wealthier white students at my new high school. It will have a dazzling array of built-in pockets. Pockets, I know, are signifiers of abundance: if you need pockets, you have a lot of stuff to carry around.

Mom, of course, is right. Better, as she might say, to buy a dozen useful coats than one flashy coat.

The jacket I own has pockets only for my hands, and a pair of broken plastic zippers that refuse to close. It is, of course, a big, blue puffy jacket handed down from one of our older cousins down the road. The material is so worn that it routinely tears, leaving tufts of white insulation exposed. Mom sews a black triangle on top of the holes, and by December there are five or six such triangles randomly spaced to cover cuts and scrapes. "You all grow so fast," she says, "there isn't any reason to buy the very best. We can make this work for one more winter." She is right. Everywhere, those days, she emphasizes the rhetoric of parsimony, mobilizing against the culture of excess. Some of this rhetoric is a matter of prudent household budgeting with six kids. And some of it goes deeper, back to the 1970s, back to our origins as a family, back to the earth-conscious, anti-corporate ideologies that lie behind the push for recycling and home-sewn clothes. Back to knee patches and elbow patches, ironed on by Sheryl at night, to the shoe whiteners she uses to "refresh" our sneakers, to quilts and blankets she has made for all of us. I barely grasp the conflict between our past and my present, being so obsessively attentive to what seem like class lines being drawn by everyone at once. My new high school is sifting and sorting us into new camps based solely on what we are wearing, despite the uniforms. I want to be wearing the right things.

I want the same for Amy. My idealized, abstract potential sister can't have a knock-off either. Secretly, then, I go door-to-door in our small town with an empty coffee can in hand, championing the school's coat drive, and collecting cash and checks along my paper route and trudging through the snow after school. Word gets back to Sheryl—her network of contacts on the old paper route is still active—long before my fundraising effort is complete, though she keeps it a secret until it all plays out. I raise several hundred dollars, which I hide away in my bedroom, and then present it to her as a reason to drive out to Hermann's, a chain sporting-goods store, and to buy the very best. Sheryl, always a brake on Bob's riotous schemes, has me admit the truth and return the money, one house at a time—which is embarrassing—but also agrees, after only a little discussion, to buy the jacket. And so, making the trip to Hermann's together, we get a bright white alpine number, with a glamorous tag and a logo right on the breast from a top brand, with purple and aquamarine color blocking and abundant pockets and zippers. We never tell Bob. With a little personal fanfare, I place it in that large cardboard box outside of the school mission.

That is the end of the story, of course. Because it has already been made abundantly clear that we will never hear back from any of the families who receive this material. There will be no handwritten notes received in the mail, expressing deep thanks, suggesting that our generosity has "made a difference." Maybe the jacket fits someone for a year before they outgrow it. Maybe it, too, is passed down, patched up, worn thin over the years. Maybe it is seen as undesirably garish and loud for some other high school kid, just trying to fit in and not be seen.

As my school bus drives into Somerville each cold day of that first year, I keep my eyes peeled for the jacket, so distinctive in its coloration. The grass has turned brown, and the median is filled with gray snow, dirtied by exhaust and the gravel kicked up by the snowplows. For the rest of that winter, I expect to spot a smiling, laughing young girl, walking to the public school up the street, her hopes and dreams now realized by that glorious coat. And I half expect, if I see her, that she will recognize me as the benevolent giver, wink in sly solidarity, and wave to me with grace and thanks. I've helped her climb the ladder, that wink would say. "Hi, brother."

23

The backyard smells of oranges the whole summer of 1985.

Anna, slim and effortlessly beautiful, is an enthusiast of the summer tan, and she likes to lie out every day with citrus-scented Bain de Soleil glistening on her skin. Enjoying her company, we sometimes join her, though I burn too quickly to stay out for long. I stay as long as I can, reading science fiction and sipping ice-cold Cokes. Bug lies out, too, a Walkman whirring in his lap, spinning the gears of a Beatles cassette. The air smells of oranges. We smell of oranges. Everything smells of oranges.

The small section of the yard tucked right behind the house is just about the only private space outdoors. The neighbor behind us has a red barn that borders the property, and our detached garage butts up against it. On the north side of the yard, a tangled forsythia hedge grows tall and deep. The result is an almost perfect square that draws a lot of midday sun and is extremely intimate. A perfect spot for a teenage girl to sunbathe, away from the prying eyes of neighbors. A perfect spot for racial satire, too.

"I think I can get darker than you." A consummate humorist, Anna says it with a straight face.

Bear laughs. He has spent his summer house-painting outside, enjoying the outdoors with our cousin Chuck, and darkening up a little each day without even thinking about it.

"I'll bet you."

Easy money, Bear thinks.

Anna takes the challenge seriously and approaches her sunbathing as if it were a real job, punching in every day and staying out for as long as she can, generously applying Bain de Soleil, which seems (with an SPF of 4) to be nothing more than orange-scented baby oil mixed with Vaseline. She squeezes as much as possible out of the thin metal tubes, rolling them up until the outside is greasy or the foil edges crack. And every thirty minutes she turns over on her green-and-white plastic lounge chair, which has thin straps and leaves lines on her flesh. Every time she turns over, she is cross-marked, as if she has lain on a hot griddle.

There are no other players in this peculiar competition. We all find it hilarious. Or are incredulous. Anna and Bear put their arms next to each other, their skin in tension, for a nightly comparison. Mark, a lifelong sports fan, narrates the daily results at the dinner table as if he were Howard Cosell.

"Anna, Bear is Black," I say one night. "There is no way you can get darker than him. No chance." I am egging her on, goading her. We are a very competitive family, and I know that this sort of big talk will keep her engaged. We all know I am right. By then, we have all been together in the summer for years and have a clear sense of what our skins need, how they respond to the sun, and how dark we might get. Mark burns within seconds. Bear burns a lot less. But Anna has issued the challenge, and so we measure their dash to achieve darker tones each day, with as much scientific precision as we can.

This is a summer of great, worrisome transitions. Anna is working at a nursing home, providing weekend and overnight care, and saving up for the return to New Brunswick and for a second year of college. Bear and Bug are about to enter high school. Eddie, still new and uncertain, vacillates between joining us and remaining aloof, finding our easy banter about race and our relative privilege alienating. He spends the summer in the county-run day camp, in preparation for what we hope will be a smoother reentry into the public school system. And yet, though we stand at a juncture, the suntanning competition—a trivial if unforgettable manifestation of our love for and pleasure with one another—is what will linger in my memories.

Bug, Mark, and I aren't fools. We know how this will end. I spend the day on the shady side of the patio, reading or napping or getting ready for work, and just generally enjoying the smell of the oranges. Anna rolls over, applies, and lies still, her headphones in her ears. She tilts at the windmill, and every day she pulls the strapped vinyl chair out, pulls out her radio, diligently covers every square inch of her body, and goes to work.

Insofar as anyone can measure these sorts of things, it is never close. As anyone can predict, Bear gets darker just by walking around and painting homes—no need for an orange-scented tanning concoction for him. He needs no sunblock at all, he proclaims, boastfully. He is trash-talking, of course. Another family tradition.

Anna, by the end of the summer, gets very tan. The sun draws out of her the warm tones that are already in her skin, already exposed to the eye. The result is an exacerbation of difference—and a clear victory for Bear. He lords it over her, as if he has won Olympic gold, marching around the kitchen, adopting a royal wave to thank some imagined audience that cheers for him.

24

Church is boring. Painfully so. Some might enjoy the conservative medievalism of the Catholic Mass, but for the six of us, it means listless homilies, corny folk-singing, and a painfully early start to every Sunday. And yet, every Sunday, there we are, squeezing into Big Red as teenagers, rolling into the parking lot, oozing out of the car like molasses, and then lining up as a family on our way in the door. Anna, of course, is always dressed perfectly, but the boys are slouched and untucked, with hastily groomed hair and sleep-lined faces. Bob—showered, pressed, and admirably coiffured—likes to sit up front, in the second or third rows. So we need to pull into the lot about twenty minutes before the start of things, lest we be broken up and have to sit separately. We are a large enough gang that we usually take up an entire row.

Eyes are always on us. I worry about our spectacle, a legacy of those earlier years when we were trotted out as symbols of the world's veneration for the newborn Messiah, bringing up the gifts. Our lack of decorum ensures that we no longer play that role, as childlike pleasure has given way to outright disdain, manifest on our teenage faces. Still, I know our undeniable appeal to the audience, our role as a public property and popular fetish. I know that we are still watched carefully. We know the stakes, and what matters. It is important to model comity, to embody the harmonious future, to show no discord. To be, as much as possible, pleasing and graceful.

And yet church is unbelievably dull. The sermons are repetitive, delivered with ennui, or even disdain. The ritualistic cycle of standing, sitting, kneeling, speaking, singing, sitting silently, and then presenting oneself to the priest for a dry host means that you can't really daydream the hour away. Every time you get settled on some fantasy, the ritual jerks you awake. There is no clock anywhere, no reminder of the authority of the hours and minutes in our regular lives. This is medieval time. To keep track, there is only our collective movement together through the ritual, the measurement of that orderly sequence of standing and sitting and kneeling, singing and praying and listening. Only when the ritual is over will we be released. Afterward, Bob makes conversation with our neighbors about the didacticism of the homily or the rhetorical moves made by the priest. Or he strikes up a conversation about some new zoning law, or the future of the church's various building projects. We hustle outside and wait in the car.

Stuck in the midst of the ritual, we find ways to entertain ourselves. It takes years for us to find the best kind of play. The challenge, of course, is to find a way to have some fun without catching anyone's attention. A stern, disapproving flick of the eye from Mom, or a muttered "Stop it!" out of the corner of her mouth, is fine—to be expected, really—but the scrutiny of the crowd behind us is not. It has to be a game without words, without any communication. A game that can be played standing up, sitting down, kneeling. A game that can transcend medieval time.

"Whomever you forgive anything, so do I. For indeed what I have forgiven, if I have forgiven anything, has been for you in the presence of Christ . . ."

Mark leans over. "How much longer?"

Bear catches my eye and raises a brow.

"Do not associate with unbelievers. For what basis can there be for a partnership between righteousness and lawlessness? What do light and darkness have in common?"

Bug leans forward, his knuckles tightening.

The first game begins without any discussion or plan, on an otherwise sunny day, as the rest of the parish absorbs another forgettable monologue. Pressed in a row, youngest to oldest, one of us tries to move the person next to them, to move them just a little bit farther away. It starts with elbows, then butts and thighs, but our varying sizes and weights always propel you away with a noticeable wobble. It evolves from there into something smaller, less easy to spot. We settle on a quiet battle on the handrail, a battle for inches and centimeters and fractions. It begins with a firm grip. You lean forward, put your hand on the back of the pew in front, and grip it tight. Slowly, you spread your hands out, never losing your grip, until you bump up against another set of hands. You plant your feet, set your jaw, and then try to move their hand a bit farther down the pew, to win just slightly more space for yourself.

Eddie finds the subtlety of this game hilarious, and has to learn not to laugh out loud when we begin. Such a thing, we instruct him, is never meant to solicit a discerning look. No one in church will ever—*should* ever—know that it is happening. It is meant to be unseeable, unknowable, approximate to the games we play in our secluded backyard. A private thing conducted right in front of the audience, under the glare of the spotlight, where everyone is already looking us over, surveying with great self-satisfaction our multiplicity. An open secret. Indeed, if you exert too much force and expand your territory too quickly, or if any movement is visible, and it is seen or recognized, you lose. The game ends. It can never escalate beyond that tiny span marked on the back rail of an oak pew.

This is the whole game. All of it. The intimacy of it—skin on skin, even in the glare of the spotlight, with the sun streaming through stained glass—is what matters. A secret, protected family game, conducted in full view of the parish, a game that avoids public supervision or judgment. While the priest drones on—". . . and so the lesson of Paul's second letter to the Corinthians . . ."— and the banal regime of church rituals continues, and Sheryl's eye flicks over to us, twitching with disgust, we play out in front, on the edge of the color line, pressing into one another, gauging our strength, our will, our commitment to public spectacles and private intimacies. We never discuss it afterward, never share a play-by-play. And Sheryl, who is always so keenly aware of our shifting centers of gravity, our tensed shoulders, our painful winces, and our labored breathing, never once lays into us.

It doesn't cross my mind to think of what this must look like, this row of children pressed close to one another, their knuckles tense with feeling, their hands in unquiet communion. The game is so intense, so physically dramatic, so intimate, I am always certain it will be noticed, that an usher will come over afterward, scolding us for making a joke of the church. But that never happens.

25

We watch a lot of bad movies together in the 1980s. When they are action movies—and they very often are—we cheer for the Black guy to live, to make it to the sequel, so that we might cheer for him once more. In those days, action movies are vitalist resources for a nation still recovering from the supposed trauma of a "loss" in Vietnam. Rich with beefcake, marbled with homoeroticism, these macho set pieces with clear-cut good guys and bad guys often feature Black characters as visual accompaniments, colorful sidekicks for the white superhero on center screen. For every Arnold Schwarzenegger or Nick Nolte or Mel Gibson there is a Carl Weathers or an Eddie Murphy or a Danny Glover. Bob loves these movies—and their simplistic commitment to compositional diversity in the service of reflexive, muscular nationalism. They seem, to him, like updated WWII movies, which he adores for their equally zealous portraits of American righteousness.

We watch with the lights on and with popcorn so that we might emphasize our togetherness and not be lost in the cinematic darkness. We learn the value of the platoon, learn that not everyone survives its engagement. With grim prescience, we augur our demise—and the demise of our Black siblings.

That is to say, most of the Black figures in these movies don't make it. So, all in a group, swaddled in homemade blankets and tangled together on the floor, we also consume visions of Black death, hoping every weekend for something different.

"I think he is gonna make it this time." Bear whispers this to himself, his fingers clutching the edges of his quilt.

On a very typical evening, we root for Master Sergeant Franklin, one of two Black characters in the forgettable *Missing in Action 2: The Beginning*. Franklin has been, as one might guess from the title, missing in action for years. Tall, earnest, and with a sincere smile, all Franklin wants to do is return home to his wife and four kids, but as a member of Colonel Braddock's captured platoon, he is instead held as a prisoner of war in a bamboo cell by the nefarious Vietnamese army. *Captivity* is too tame a word to describe the platoon's hardships. Franklin has been weakened by malaria, tortured, and subjected to all manner of perverse cruelties at the hands of his jailors—especially the evil, smug-looking Colonel Yin, the prison camp's presiding officer. His wounds have become infected. Yin, of course, is a callback to the Japanese villains of the older movies from the 1950s and 1960s, while Franklin is a perfect representative of Braddock's entire multiracial platoon, a collection of once strapping and virile and handsome and serious men, now reduced to pale, glassy-eyed, disheveled creatures, so desperate to escape that they will chance the certain death of Yin's "man-traps" of the jungle. This is no romanticized *Stalag 17*.

The looming drama of the film's second act is that Braddock—of course, the blond, blue-eyed hero of the film, played with heavy, wooden seriousness by Chuck Norris—has refused to bend or break. Meanwhile, Franklin (sympathetically performed by the actor John Wesley) is getting weaker and more diminished by the day. By this point, we have come to know the rules of this genre. Something is going to give. Either they will escape, or Braddock will fold, or

Franklin will die. And we are 100 percent sure that Braddock—with his searing sapphire eyes and his sober grimace—will *not* fold.

"He is gonna live."

There are two. Franklin is the Black guy we want to live. We care less for the darker-skinned Nestor, the obvious backstabber, who is healthy by contrast to the rest of the men, seeming well fed and well clothed. Nestor, played by Steven Williams, is a Black collaborator who has sold out his country—and done so simply to benefit himself. He walks freely through the camp and is never accosted by the guards. We don't ever learn why. He seems disinvested from any sort of radical Black politics. And we aren't supposed to care about that either. Sometimes, Nestor whispers solicitations to Braddock, encouraging him to give up the fight, to confess to his crimes, to ensure the survival of the platoon, this living microcosm of the post-civil-rights-era United States.

Nestor is Franklin's opposite—the Bad Black guy—and he is Braddock's opposite, too. Good Black and Bad Black, White Hat and Black Hat. Our man Franklin is the Good Black, the heroic sidekick, a member of the mixed platoon, with a soft street accent. He is undeniably American, with a last name shared by a Founding Father—indeed, the best Founding Father, Bob says, pointing to the shelf of Benjamin Franklin biographies above the TV. Right to the end, our man Franklin is loyal to Braddock. When Nestor and Braddock are compelled to fight by the smirking and villainous Yin, dressed in a starched, tailored uniform, the exalted Franklin—glistening with sweat, clad in rags, lurching sideways, and seriously ill—cheers for Braddock.

Bear's prayer inspires us all.

"He isn't gonna die." "Not tonight, he won't." "High fives if he makes it through this scene."

The genre's conventions advance the plot. Sensing the quickening pace, we lean forward a little.

Franklin's condition worsens. He is incoherent, rambling. Braddock grimaces and agrees to confess to his crimes in exchange for the medicine his officer needs. The smiling Yin is predictably treacherous, however, and still quite eager to "break" Braddock's will. So he gives Franklin an "overdose of opium," administering to the Good Black the kind of death that so many in the audience will already have associated with the inner city. "I do feel better," Franklin says with a smile, released from his pain, then falling limp in the arms of his platoon mates.

In the Green Room, we collapse in groans. Bear pulls the blanket over his head.

"Noooooooooooo!"

"Maybe next time, Bear."

Braddock's anger is ours. We seethe with anger. We huddle closer. I reach out and put my arm on Bear's shoulder. His hands are balled into fists.

There is, however, one more Black man in the film: the traitorous Nestor. With Franklin dead, we rally around Nestor, who has begun to resent—and distrust—Yin. Franklin's death is a turning point for Nestor. We watch as he listens in on a private conversation, and we begin to hope that he has a change of heart. That, when the final battle comes, he'll be shoulder to shoulder with the rest of this diverse platoon, including the Chinese doctor Chou, the spirited "white ethnic" Lieutenant Mazilli, and the vengeful Braddock.

Bear holds his breath. We say the words for him. "I think he is just waiting for the right moment. To turn against Yin. Maybe he will live."

Nestor, we soon learn, *has* been waiting. He doesn't make it, though. In a well-telegraphed plot twist, he redeems himself in a desperately heroic act, pulling a gun at a critical moment, saving Mazilli, and emptying the clip into a group of Yin's soldiers. As payback, he is riddled with bullets in slow motion, denied any final words. "Nestor came back to us," Mazilli says breathlessly on screen, speaking for all of us there in the room.

Now all the Black characters are dead.

The groans are louder.

"Not again!!"

"Maybe next time . . ."

The words sound hollow.

No family exists in total isolation. We are not the Swiss Family Robinson, though we sure read that story often, so much so that its details—colorful illustrations in our version, and the endorsements of thrift, foresight, mutual aid, and cooperation—stick with me even now. That is not exactly us, though. We cannot live above the world in a treehouse. A white picket fence, even one so regularly painted and so well taken care of, lets air and light through. The world comes to us inexorably.

Bear and I are fifteen in 1985, when we watch the story of Braddock and Nestor and Franklin unfold. Eddie is much younger. And the nation is right in the midst of the Reagan era, with its celebration of the white male action hero. The screens are full of Colonel Braddocks and Franklins, full of Black death and Black trauma. And full of Colonel Yins, Asian villains who have all the human complexity of a Halloween costume.

We gather every weekend—Fridays or Saturdays, and sometimes both—for a family movie night. Invariably, these gatherings take place in the Green Room, the large room our parents added to the house in the early 1970s in anticipation of their growing family. It is nicknamed the Green Room because of its lush, Kermit-green shag carpeting, its green wallpaper, and its decorations, which are in keeping with bicentennial tradition. 1776 is the room's major theme. The wallpaper is garish, I think, featuring scenes from the nation's colonial past, scenes of settlement, territorial conquest, and daily life. Above the fireplace mantel, a reproduction of Gilbert Stuart's unfinished portrait of George Washington, haunting in his repose, is affixed to the wall. He surveys the room with eyes that seem to follow you no matter where you stand. We all feel judged by Washington's slight smirk. The Green Room also contains much of the family's library, including many of the books our parents purchased on Vietnam and Korea before the adoptions, as well as various multivolume encyclopedias and almanacs, and numerous biographies and memoirs of the famous, from Washington to Sidney Poitier, to Martin Luther King, to, once again, Benjamin Franklin. In the evenings the Green Room is a centripetal space, drawing us together and into communion with one another, in a context where we are watched over by the Founding Fathers—the venerable George over the fireplace, the settlers inscribed on the wall, the Great Men among the biographies. Bob presides from a massive recliner positioned to have an ideal view of the television.

Early on, we are at the mercy of the three main networks (ABC, NBC, and CBS), the local stations (channels 11, 9, and 5 on the dial), and PBS. Cable television comes late to our little town. The VCR comes in the early 1980s. So, when we are younger, if something is on television on a weekend night, we are there to watch it, no matter how random it might seem. We watch *Roots* and *The Wiz* on Sunday nights, along with dozens of Broadway musicals, *Gone with the Wind*, *Planet of the Apes*, and whatever else they dare to air. Some things are forbidden. Often, there is a WWII movie on. Sheryl generally turns up her nose at those. Just as she does when we watch *Missing in Action 2*.

The VCR changes everything. So does the political economy of movie watching. In the mid-1980s, these movie nights are transformed by the advent of video rentals, which offer us astonishingly broad à la carte possibilities. The slides and reels of 9 mm film have long been stashed in the basement. Now the randomness of network programming drops out. Still, to be honest, at that point, it becomes less a movie night than a curated film series, with the moving object of the week chosen by Bob, who drops by the rental shop during his Friday lunch hour and chooses something that strikes his fancy. He might ask for suggestions, but he also loves bad movies and appreciates levity, and he usually improvises, depending on how the work week has ended. Often, if things have been difficult, he chooses a lowbrow action film, something starring Norris, Schwarzenegger, Stallone, Willis, or some less talented actor. These are almost entirely forgettable films, cheap knock-offs retrofitted for the late Cold War. But they also emphasize key themes for us: the value of teamwork, the symbolism of the racialized ensemble, the need to do the right thing. When, in 1987's *Predator*, Dillon and Dutch and Billy and Mac march off into the Central American jungle to search for survivors, we watch them move in delicate choreography, backing one another up, guarding the whole of their unit and the whole of the world.

Bob is particularly fond of sequels because he believes in franchises. This is helpful, because, given his judicial duties, he usually gets to the rental store too late to get the best, most in-demand movies. In those days, before Blockbuster has opened, the local appliance store has a small rental corner in the back by the VCRs for sale. New releases go fast. Sequels are always available, it seems. *Missing in Action 2. American Ninja 3. Delta Force 2.*

If there is one steady, brutal, and constant truth of these movies, though, it is that the Black guy dies before the end. Sometimes, the death is horrific. Most of the time, it is melodramatic—the film has taught us to love this Black character's spunk and humor and determination, and by killing him it encourages us to mourn. Just as often, the death of the Black best friend is a catalyst, inspiring the white hero to finish the story. No matter when it happens, though, we come to predict it, to expect it, to fear it. We start to look for the same actors, playing the same roles over and over again. Steve James, the affable, chiseled Black actor and Kung Fu master, is an idol. We mourn his sad death in *The Exterminator*. We mourn Carl Weathers, too, whether it is *Rocky IV*, where he is beaten to death by the white juggernaut Ivan Drago, or *Predator*, where he is dismembered by an alien hunter. We mourn Franklin and so many others like him. And yet we understand that the genre demands that the Black man has to die so the white man can be their hero.

A partial list, from memory, of Black characters we lose together:

FRANKLIN—A POW, murdered by Colonel Yin with an opium overdose (*Missing in Action 2*, 1985)

NESTOR—A privileged POW, who sacrifices himself and is shot down after a period of collaboration (*Missing in Action 2*, 1985)

CREED—A boxer, killed in the ring by Ivan Drago (*Rocky IV*, 1985)

WILLIAMS—A Kung Fu master, beaten to death by a Shaolin monk with an iron prosthetic hand (*Enter the Dragon*, 1973)

DRABA—An enslaved African in ancient Rome, who is killed after sparing the life of a white slave (*Spartacus*, 1960)

JEFFERSON—A redeemed US soldier, part of a platoon of criminals assembled for a rescue, gunned down (*The Dirty Dozen*, 1967)

DILLON—A CIA operative, dismembered and killed for sport by an alien hunter in Central America (*Predator*, 1987)

ELLIOT—An elite US commando, shot in the head for sport by an alien hunter in Central America (*Predator*, 1987)

TEASDALE—A schoolteacher, killed by invading Russian soldiers (*Red Dawn*, 1984)

JEFFERSON—A Vietnam vet, mercy-killed by his best friend, Eastland, after being brutalized by a gang (*The Exterminator*, 1980)

PARKER—An engineer, killed aboard a spaceship by an alien creature while attempting to escape (*Alien*, 1979)

APONE—A space marine, killed in an alien nest during a rescue mission (*Aliens*, 1986)

EARLY—A police detective, blown up by a bomb planted by a
renegade group of vigilante cops (*Magnum Force*, 1973)

COOKE—A villain, impaled by a table leg wielded by a retired
special forces officer (*Commando*, 1985)

DYSON—A scientist studying metal fragments from the future,
killed by police (*Terminator 2*, 1991)

LAUGHLIN—A member of the resistance, killed in a televised
game show run by law enforcement (*Running Man*, 1987)

KASTIGIR—An elegant, immortal swordsman, beheaded by the
Kurgen during the Gathering (*Highlander*, 1986)

Bear mourns these losses the most.

From the opening credits he openly roots for the Black guy to live,
of course, and applauds his every move. Announcing it right at the
start, just as we sit down, as we organize our pillows and cushions for
comfortable viewing. So, too, does Eddie. So do we all, really. And
when the inevitable end comes, Bear sighs. Or laughs out loud and says,
"Dammit. Next time!" Over time, of course, the laughter goes away.
Or it is transformed into a vehicle for exhausted, depleted sadness.

More than once, Bear leaves the room when the Black guy dies. Just
leaves without a word, ostensibly to get a drink of water from the kitchen.

I'm reminded now that in middle school, in the midst of one of
these weekly movie nights, we get a phone call from a friend of Bear's
biological father, letting us know that the man has died—a man we
have never known. A man we have never seen, even in a photograph.

The Black-white dyad, both in life and in films, overwhelms us.
Everything on-screen is about "us." Bear's Vietnamese past is displaced,
in the moment, by the meanings attached to his dark skin. About Bear
and me, that is. That is a copy of us on the television screen—and it pre-
dicts, I fear, Bear's inevitable death and my own undeniable triumph.
Beyond the occasional Bruce Lee flick, there is little in any of these movies for Bug and Anna. The "loss" in Vietnam, the fear of Japanese and

Chinese economic dominance, and memories of the Pacific theater in WWII mean that Asian characters are easy villains or cannon fodder. They are rarely a part of the platoon back then. They are limited to one-dimensional, scheming caricatures like Yin. Anna, at college, misses most of these films. Bug roots for the Black guy with the rest of us. Even now, though, I have no sense of how a movie like *Missing in Action 2* might pull Bear in two directions, might give him a gut-punch, with its villainization of the Vietnamese, its slaughter of the Black, and its celebration of the white savior. Bear, still sifting through his competing, intertwined racial positions, might reasonably assume that, at the very least, the Black guy has a fighting chance, while the Asian characters obviously do not. There is no inducement to root for the Vietnamese guy to live, even if that place is a part of our brother's personal history, too.

On some very basic, primal level, we know what this means for all of us—to see these platoons and ensembles come together and fall apart each weekend is to encounter a meaningful parable. The experience serves as a metaphor, a tocsin for the future. The same is true for Bob, whether he realizes it or not. His repeated selection of banal films in this genre, where predictable plots abound, clearly brings him pleasure, perhaps because he wishes to see a different American team enlisted in the service of the nation-state. Perhaps, in some way, these movies give him language and inspiration. Perhaps, too, he appreciates the narrative of the white savior and is blind to its effect on us. After all, the moral instruction of these "action" platoon films is drawn from the death of the Black character, or the damage inflicted on his body, and by the healing that comes later, thanks to the heroism of the white savior. There is, for me, something heartbreaking in these memories, these recollections of the openness with which we discuss the death of the Black figure, and in our worried solidarity with Bear and Eddie in the wake of Franklin's passing—and that of so many others.

These aren't the only things we watch, but they cut the deepest. Missing from my memories, though, is any sense of how we respond to the Black-and-white "buddy cop" films of the era. In contrast to the white savior films where the Black guy dies before the end, movies like *48 Hours*, *Lethal Weapon*, and *Beverly Hills Cop* allow him to live, to thrive, and even to have sequels where he continues to breathe and triumph. Murphy and Glover play funny, three-dimensional characters, with rich arcs, humor, and heroism. They have white partners who are, in many ways, their equals. Bear and I might see them as models for our relation, and yet if that is so, I don't remember it at all.

Instead, I remember Bear bemoaning the death of his hero—whether it is Franklin or Nestor or some other character—on-screen in those terribly imitative films. And I remember the rest of us cheering on Steve James, hoping he will live to fight another day. And crying when Ivan Drago murders Apollo Creed. It is easy to count the few Black figures that appear in earlier movies, and then to celebrate the triumphant inclusion of the cerebral Sidney Poitier in the 1960s and the smoldering Richard Roundtree in the 1970s. It is just as easy to forget how regularly the spectacle of Black death has been a feature of American popular culture since then.

Years later, I learn of the famous 1940s doll study conducted by Kenneth and Mamie Clark, which documented the psychological trauma of Jim Crow segregation on young Black children. The Clarks presented nearly identical dolls—with skin color being the singular difference—to Black children attending segregated and integrated schools, asked a range of questions to measure the sentiments attached to skin color, and determined that the Black children who attended segregated schools were more likely to devalue the doll with Black skin. The study was footnoted in the *Brown v. Board of Education of Topeka* decision of 1954 as proof of the damage done by Jim Crow, and it served as evidence that integration was a moral issue deserving of mainstream American attention. In college, I stare at the photographic narrative of the polymath Gordon Parks, whose realist images document the study in haunting detail, showing the discarded Black doll, the treasured white doll, and the face of the child who wants one but not the other. What, I wonder, does it mean when family movie night finds the six of us, lounging on sofas and curled up on the floor, watching the ensemble on-screen? What is the weight of watching the character you identify with die every Friday night? Or watching your brother be killed off so your own avatar can triumph? Or seeing yourself as the villain? Integration often comes with consequences: in the action movies, the Black guy dies first, or last. And all the villains are Asian.

Bob's movie tastes irritate us, so we seek other worlds. Over the same years that we have these movie nights, Bear and I build a shared library of speculative fiction in our shared bedroom. We fill up a towering bookshelf, running all the way up to the sky, with radical dreamscapes of futures and pasts that never were but might someday be. Samuel Delany. Nancy Asire. David Eddings. Robert Jordan. Robert Heinlein. Piers Anthony. Octavia Butler. L. Ron Hubbard. Madeleine L'Engle. After a trip to the mall, or to the library, we return to our personal library, alerting the other to some new acquisition, some new discovery. And then we dole them out. While one sleeps, the other reads, late into the evening and early in the morning. When we travel, we take a part of the library with us. We are drawn to speculative imaginings, richly textured worlds bigger, wilder, richer with possibility than life behind the picket fence. To landscapes and universes and parallel realities where the Black guy doesn't die. Where the color line is harder to find. Where we can identify with the same character.

What I remember most about our shared bedroom, filled to the brim with mind- and genre-bending plotlines about wizardry and spaceships, new worlds and lost technologies, is how voraciously Bear consumes it all. And how it sustains him in the midst of all the jarring shifts and twists of his life, his identity, his sense of self and self-worth and belonging, how he clings to these speculations in the swirl of so much Black death. As I lie in bed waiting for sleep to find me, I hear him turn the pages, searching for a better hereafter.

26

Inside Bob's large, pine wardrobe, on the top shelf, is a small dark tin, where he deposits the spare change of the day. By the end of any given week, there is quite a bit in there. I become deft at lifting the tin, gently shaking it, and gauging its volume. Sheryl has gone back to work as a schoolteacher and guidance counselor, and we are left alone in the afternoons. I am dipping into the tin pretty regularly to get a candy bar, a soda, or—later—a pack of cigarettes at the small mini-mart across the street.

One day, Bob corrals us into the bedroom—me, Bear, Eddie, Bug, and Mark. We line up in a row, shifting uneasily. Sitting on the edge of his bed, his toes curling into the tan shag carpeting, he lectures us on the evils of theft. His eyes move up and down the row. As he speaks, the back of one hand slaps the palm of the other for emphasis. Someone has been stealing from his change tin, he accuses, reaching into the wardrobe and then holding the box out in front of him, shaking it to reveal that it is nearly empty.

"Have I ever denied you anything?" he asks. "Ever?" He is not angry, only disappointed.

He insists that the guilty party step forward and say something. And then a long, long silence descends.

I am pretty sure that we have *all* been stealing from that tin. None of us has cash. Or jobs. And yet candy-bar wrappers and soda cans are everywhere. There is a constant stream of us walking across the street to the mini-mart like a trail of sugar ants, making a small purchase, and returning home for a lazy snack in the backyard. In the face of his accusation, though, I believe that there is but one ungrateful thief: me.

My heart rate surges. I look down at my feet. The silence continues. I try to feign innocence.

"I'm waiting," he declares, filling the void.

Finally, a small voice speaks up. And it is not mine.

"I did it."

Eddie. A foot shorter and several years younger than the rest. So tiny we nickname him "Flea"—though the moniker, thankfully, doesn't stick.

The rest of us are hustled out of the room. Eddie stays behind for a gentle tongue-lashing. Bear and I share a look. He raises an eyebrow. I say nothing to anyone. I never do. But I also continue to purloin small change from the tin until years later, when I move out. I take less, of course. I also never learn how Bob figures out what we have been doing. Nor do I ever learn how Eddie is disciplined. Bob and Sheryl don't really ground us or confine us to our rooms. They rely on the Catholic soft powers of guilt, shame, and remorse.

In a thousand ways, the ground is tilted against Eddie from the very start. The circumstances of his birth and childhood are terrible. His abandonment by a grandmother—as it was explained to us, when she was presented with two children to care for, she discarded Eddie, and retained his older brother—is scarring. Eddie maintains clear-eyed memories of this renunciation. He grows up doubly rejected, cast aside by a mother and a father he has never known, and then again by a grandmother who can support only one child, and who decides that it won't be him.

But this also goes deeper, into our bedrock history, into the history of the name we assign to him. Years before he joins us, whenever things go missing, we blame a mischievous sprite we call Eddie. The screwdriver goes missing? "Eddie must have taken it," Bob will say drolly, rolling his eyes. A plate is broken? Eddie again. This fantasy of a filching, misbehaving sprite helps us to avoid conflict, for sure. It makes for fewer ultimatums, fewer assemblies of the children to ferret out the truth. It also creates an unseeable phantom, a wild projection of all of our misdeeds, mistakes, and petty thefts.

There is always Eddie to blame.

We give this fantasy a physical presence, too. Over the kitchen table, there is a low, wide stained-glass lamp, the sort of technicolored fixture you might see in a pool hall or a pizza joint, with bright panels and colors. The lamp hangs from the ceiling on a chain. And on the chain, there is a small koala bear, which someone attached there long, long ago. After years of calling out the spirit, we even name the koala "Eddie," gesturing to it when it seems like our hauntings have continued, or when it seems like something has inexplicably vanished.

When our brother arrives in the summer of 1984, we give our last adoptive arrival the same identifier—a family appellation, to be sure, but also the name of the thieving spirit who haunts us.

What happens when the phantom comes to life? What happens when you bring a new child into the family and slot him into the rhetorical groove previously occupied by this phantasmagorical creature? What happens when that child is Black, and is—by virtue of that racial position—already in another, deeper groove, already predestined by the social scientists of the day to be a criminal? When every state agency and advocate for the foster system highlights for the prospective family the supposed biological associations of habitual drug use, crack cocaine, and the "handicap"? What happens when the child sees the same highlights and knows the same associations?

In all of the state's propaganda, Eddie's mother is repeatedly demonized as an addict, whose abuse of her son begins while he is in the womb. The fear—or folklore, because it seems more myth than science, even at the time—is that every so-called crack baby will grow up to be a monster. Nightly news reports villainize Black mothers, foster a culture of political panic about the damage done to the fetus after the use of crack cocaine. Convincing, scientific-looking diagrams of the crack-damaged brain are shown on television, in cop shows, in movies. Politicians deploy the image of the crack-addicted Black mother as the lowest of the low, the worst of the worst, and describe "crack babies" as the scourge of the social contract. As irredeemable superpredators. Beyond this gruesome backdrop, the world also sees his generalized Blackness as a permanent disability. So, in these moments, do the very agencies that have enabled his adoption, that have sought out our family, that have pitched him to us as "disabled." So, too, do we, as we sit in front of the television, listening to the horrific stories coming out of the city. His Blackness, in our unsound calculations, is the roughed-out equivalent of a damaged or missing limb.

Maybe, in a way, he makes the same calculation, too. Maybe all the metaphorical weight on his shoulders finally breaks him, or bends him, or warps him. He studies race, just like the rest of us in our domestic experiment. I wonder if, in that moment when we all stand shoulder to shoulder, when the tin is held out in front of us, when Bob's eyes move up and down the line, *he* might believe that he alone has dipped into it, while the rest of us stand still, quite certain that we've *all* done the same, determined to maintain silence. I wonder, I wonder, I wonder. I agonize, now, about the lessons of that lineup.

The five of us, lined up in a row in front of Bob. The shag carpeting on the floor. The tall windows looking out on the backyard grove, the garage, and the driveway. The wardrobe doors thrown open. The heavy *ka-ching* of the change inside the tin when Bob shakes it. The sound of the back of his hand slapping his palm as he confronts us. The sound of our collective exhale, once Eddie steps forward—signaling something other than relief, something more like a last breath. Every one of us a terrible thief. Just one of us burdened with inglorious stereotypes. The only one of us to admit to the commonplace crime of stealing loose change from your parents' bedroom.

Maybe Eddie takes the blame *for* us, knowing that is easiest, knowing that he is deep in that groove, and unable to slip free.

There is, perhaps, something entirely banal about this story. A tall wardrobe in the parents' bedroom containing secrets and pleasures. Children, some of them teenagers, exploring its inner warrens, some of them filled with treasure. And there is something predictable, too, in the inevitable moment when, at long last, we are all summoned to the bedroom, queued up, and asked to account for ourselves. That moment when our youngest brother takes the heat and we, selfishly, fail to stand up for him.

Race changes it into something ghastly.

Only Eddie has the courage to own up to it.

Only Eddie takes the blame.

"You want to watch TV?" Eddie asks me one afternoon, not too long after we're marched into the room, lined up, and interrogated. As always, he holds no grudge.

There isn't much on in the afternoons except for game shows, talk shows, and soap operas. Or a baseball game. And none of those interests us. If we are lucky, though, there will be some syndicated procedural on a lesser channel, something that will hook us for an hour and then let us go.

Eddie passes me the remote and we go looking for one, moving deliberately up the channels. We are lying on the old pull-out sofa, a massive, steel-framed, black-and-white-patterned thing that opens up into a queen-size bed. It took five of us most of a day to move it, inch by inch, up to the second floor, where it serves as an extra bed for guests. In a feat of strength and "stick-to-itiveness," as Bob calls it, Bear, Bug, Mark, Eddie, and I strained and twisted and torqued it up the narrow stairwell, trying not to tear the wallpaper, and getting it stuck several times. We took a break halfway through, leaving it jammed against the handrail, suspended in midair. It sits in a second-floor common area, now a teenage gathering space for us when we want to watch television away from the Green Room.

The Equalizer is a show Eddie likes a lot. Ostensibly, it is about an aging British secret agent living in Manhattan who offers his services to "the little guy," giving them a chance, as the show's title suggests, to even the score. An unknowable secret weapon, the retired-spy-turned-hero named Robert McCall resembles, to me, an out-of-shape grandfather, with his silver hair, his jowly face, and his gentleman's potbelly. At seventeen, I am perhaps too old to enjoy the camp of the show, but Eddie loves it because it is set in his dear New York City and also because of the David-and-Goliath themes that replay each week. Some poor sucker always stands on the verge of ruin, and some terrible human is always so close to getting away with it, and then—often by sheer fluke—this overweight, shabby old man intervenes decisively, using his wit, his years of spycraft, and an impressive judo chop.

I simply cannot suspend my disbelief. "This guy? Really?" We all know—after years of movie nights—real heroes are as hard as brick and muscled like cartoons. They have actual jawlines.

For one spring, though, The Equalizer becomes an afternoon tradition. Lying on the couch together, changed out of school clothes, enjoying a grilled cheese sandwich for a snack, we kill an hour and watch this amusingly simple show, a welcome distraction in a house without central air-conditioning.

As the season drags on, though, I grow more and more unhappy with it. The opening credits trouble me—and remind me of those movie nights in the Green Room, when we root for the Black guy to survive. The Equalizer's credits offer a different pedagogy. In scene after scene, a white woman does something ordinary—enters an elevator, walks by a car, strides down a hallway—only to be accosted or threatened by a large man who often appears Black or brown. The emotional premise of the show is unavoidable: New York is a city in the grips of racial crisis, bereft of law and order, and in desperate need of macho, lawless solutions coded white. I see the show as an obvious attempt to serialize—and turbocharge—the dangerous racial material of *Death Wish* or *Dirty Harry*. The show strikes me as poisonous.

"Let's turn this off," I say one day. "I don't want to watch this." I try to explain what I am feeling. I don't think this is good for Eddie. For his self-image.

"No, no," Eddie replies. "I just want to see what happens this time. Tomorrow, maybe we'll watch something different." We have the same conversation the next day. Over and over again. The intensified repetition—every day, the same white woman leaving the subway and the same looming Black figure, following her—allowing me to see the destructive totality of it all. I shudder on the couch.

Later, as the end credits roll, I ask what draws him to *The Equalizer*.

"The city," he replies, smiling, looking out the window, remembering someplace else. "I miss New York."

27

I am celebrating the end of my junior year in high school. It is the summer of 1987, which means that I have an old Rip Curl T-shirt on, a pair of scuffed jeans, and a pair of Chuck Taylors. This is my go-to look for any Friday night.

I am out looking for a place to drink with two close friends, Chris and Rob, who are similarly attired. So much of that summer is spent doing just that—trying to find some place where there might be a get-together, peeking through hedges and down driveways. This night, we stumble upon a house party in Warren, a suburb of big homes with even bigger yards and no streetlights. The three of us shuffle toward the front door. A darkened figure calls out, letting us know that this is an invite-only kind of party. We decide to drink a few beers in the driveway while we figure out what to do. We enjoy ourselves, even stuck out there, at the lonely edge of the blacktop. But we stay a little too long. Someone inside the house pulls back the curtain to see if we are still outside—and we laugh at them.

The front door opens, and for a second, we hear the party inside. The Violent Femmes are playing. There is laughter and singing. They are eager to get rid of us, though. The host has sent out a guy we know, if only by reputation. A guy named Big Joey from Roselle, a high school wrestler with a reputation for brutality. Big Joey ambles toward us, a dense mass of Italian American muscle, thick everywhere. Thick neck, thick hands, thick gold chains. He is wearing a dark tracksuit, sunglasses perched on the top of his head. Big Joey really wants us to leave. He doesn't mince words.

"Go," he says. "Beat it." He gestures to the street, plants his feet, and stands between us and the music, the food, the warmth of the indoors. He wags a finger, encouraging us to head back to the car.

We're smart-asses. And there are three of us. We start drunkenly taunting Big Joey, laughing at him. "We're not leaving, dude." And then—*Bam! Bam! Bam!*—he drops the three of us with punches to the head. I remember the thick, meaty sound his knuckles make on the side of my head. When I wake up a minute later, Big Joey is back inside. My jaw aches. We leave, embarrassed, rubbing our faces.

A few weeks later, the same friends and I are sitting on my back porch, once more drinking some beer. Three white guys, alone with our beer and our whiteness, commiserating about Big Joey. Bear shows up in the midst of our storytelling, while we are rehashing what happened in that driveway in Warren. He is outraged. Angry. Determined to exact revenge on our behalf.

Bear and I are close through high school, even if our lives have been drawn in increasingly different directions. We share that love of reading—we share a bedroom, and a dreamscape, right up to college. But he is a high school football star and a solid student. I am neither. And my friends are not his friends.

"Not my fucking brother!" he roars, when I describe what it feels like to take a blow that knocks you out. Like me, Bear is a power drinker, and his drunken boasts are magnificently theatrical. He swells up, his hands spreading wide, his voice crackling with intensity.

"Big Joey has to go down!"

Bear is a goddamned legend in those days. When he enters high school, he immediately signs up for football—a sport he has never played. He is a natural. And by the time Big Joey enters our lives, Bear is an all-state linebacker, bench-pressing 250 pounds. His helmet is covered in skull-and-crossbones stickers for "pancakes": big, hard hits that leave a man on the ground. He is a black belt in karate—and has studied martial arts with the local police chief, which means that he is "in" with the cops.

If Big Joey is thick, Bear is ripped.

Once, when I am called down to the main office for some discipline, our vice principal—who is also the head football coach—asks me if anything is going on at home that might have caused me to act out. I tell him that my brother—meaning Eddie—broke his arm over the weekend. That isn't the reason for anything I've done, of course. I am just giving him something, some fragment of domestic chaos, in the hopes that it might get me out of trouble. But the vice principal thinks that it is Bear who has broken his arm, not Eddie. He immediately sinks back in his chair, closes his eyes, and rubs his brow dejectedly, as if his best player has been lost, and as if the whole season has gone down the drain.

I catch his drift. "No," I say, "my other brother." Relief flows into his eyes.

Bear is, in a word, beloved. Coaches enthuse over his attitude. Teachers love his sense of humor. It would be easy, reflecting on this period, to think he was dissembling, gaining white favor with his athleticism and his hard work in the classroom, but despite his big, easy smile, his hard-edged flat top, and his deep baritone voice, he also has an edge. He has a penchant for wearing clothing that is torn—his muscles showing through the tears—and a long gray trench coat, an ensemble that makes him look like he comes from the future, as if he were Kyle Reese in *The Terminator*. Bear also has a true muscle car— that primer-gray Datsun 240Z, a two-seater with an engine that feels so powerful that, if you press the accelerator to the floor, you might rip a hole in space and time and punch through to the other side of the world. This is not dissembling; this is just Bear being Bear. I am in awe of his football accomplishments, and envious of his grades, which are significantly better than mine. And I enjoy moments of togetherness, our afternoon basketball games in the driveway, our shared library, our love of big, hearty after-school snacks—steak-and-egg sandwiches, Hot Pockets, cold cereal.

He doesn't always stick up for me, though. A year earlier, some older kids are picking on me on the school bus ride home, and they hold me down, take my shoes off, and throw them out the window. Bear sits passively nearby. He is already a football star. They briefly hesitate, watching him for a reaction while holding me down, trying to gauge whether he might step in. They respect him—or are afraid of him. He does nothing, though, and looks out the window with disinterest. When the bus lets us off, I chew him out and then walk in my socks to go and recover my shoes.

So I am thrilled that night, back when I am seventeen, when he stands up and declares that he is headed to find Big Joey—the all-state wrestler and occasional bouncer—and kick his ass. Thrilled because I remember that he has looked away in the past.

With abundant promises of glorious revenge, Bear grabs a friend— Dave, an easygoing, soft-bodied regular and contented sidekick, who lives just down the street—and tears down the driveway in the 240Z. We hear the squeal of rubber as he floors it once he is past the picket fence, almost losing control before turning under the railroad trestle, up along the road that winds out of town, toward Route 202. Toward the Italian American mecca of Roselle.

We slam our beers together and toast him—my magnificent, vengeful, protective, slightly older brother. And we fantasize about what he might do to Big Joey. Will he just walk into the room and punch him in the face, returning the violence that Joey meted out? Will he invoke his brother first, issuing a righteous declaration of war and vengeance?

Will he surprise Big Joey outside, dropping from a rooftop like Jean-Claude Van Damme?

The words come out of someone else's mouth. Rob, one of my friends:

"Bear is gonna open a can of Black whoop ass on Big Joey!"

My head turns down the driveway. I have dispatched my brother to get into a fight. In Roselle, the land of white people.

Voices continue in the background. My friends are thrilled, excited, cheering on the now-inevitable distribution of justice.

Then Chris, my other friend, speaks: "We turned the n—— loose!"

There it is. They have said it.

I freeze. I run my fingers along the edge of the porch, feeling the cracks between the boards, the slickness of decades of paint, remembering the effort I made to scrape and sand and repaint it the previous summer. There is a notch in one of the boards where a piece of the wood chipped away. I focus, again, on the tactile. I have understood the whole thing as a family matter—an older brother's defense of a younger sibling—but Rob and Chris, instead, are titillated by their weaponization of Bear's Blackness. I am instantly, irrevocably sober. Every scent, every sound, seared into my memories.

"We turned the n—— loose!"

They are not distracted by my sudden stillness. They don't notice the movement of my fingers over the paint on the porch, my quest for some haptic release from the moment.

I say nothing.

The wait for Bear's return is agonizing. The crickets sing in the distance. Our conversation has dwindled, and we have nothing to do but wait. Chris and Rob keep drinking—flinging the pop-tops from their Old Milwaukees into the pachysandra—but I have stopped. Bear races up the driveway an hour later, the sound of the Datsun's engine audible from a mile away in the thick of the night. We are still seated on the back porch. I am withdrawn, still contemplating the trap I've unwittingly sprung on Bear, and on myself. Having grown sleepy, my friends startle at the sudden appearance of the muscle car, stand up, and walk over, eager to hear what happened. They are animated now, jostling to get to the car first.

I am terrified. I needn't be. Even drunk, Bear is no fool. He has done the racial math, too. He isn't going to charge into some all-white party in the suburban rows of Roselle and stomp on Big Joey's head. Certainly not at the urging of a bunch of high school losers drinking cheap beer on his back porch, even if one of them is his brother. He has wasted an enjoyable hour with his Sancho Panza, the ever-agreeable Dave, driving a big loop around town on twisting back roads in that 240Z, cheating death at high speeds. He doesn't even get on the highway, fearing that a cop might pull him over. He has never intended to go anywhere.

"Did you kick his ass?" they ask.

He gives them a disdainful look. "Nah, man, we just drove around and drove really fast."

"I have *never*," Dave adds with complimentary gusto, "gone so fast in my whole life." He was pressed back into the seat by the acceleration, tossed left and right as Bear executed a hairpin turn, and he floated above the seat, momentarily weightless, when Bear hit a big hill in just the right way. He is speaking to Bear the whole time, ignoring Chris and Rob completely. Ignoring me.

The two of them brush past us and go inside to grab their own beers.

I watch them and say nothing. I am secretly pleased that Bear is safe. I am heartbroken that my friends called him a *n*———, the cheap beer and intoxicating atmospherics of our back porch loosening their tongues, releasing their deeper racism, shattering our friendship. I am furious that this—their venomous utterance—has happened in our backyard, in our guarded, private preserve, where only we, or our closest family and friends, gather. I am also angry that Bear has not stuck up for me, reading in his refusal to avenge my beating—and finding in his moonlight drag-racing on the back roads around our small town—a complete rejection of our kinship. I have allowed that terrible word to escape their lips without any response beyond my own blankness, my own silence, which they either did not notice or read as a complicit endorsement. I will cut off those friendships, but I will never forgive myself. Rob and Chris leave quietly, disappointed in Bear. I sit down on the back porch, find another beer in the cooler, and look out into the darkness of the backyard, seeing nothing.

28

I hear the word *n——* more frequently during my senior year.

High school has continued to segregate us into different grades, different sports, different extracurricular activities. And our friend groups evolve in different ways. Immaculata, our high school, is a football powerhouse, sitting right on the state's fault line between Irish and Italian Catholics. In choosing football, Bear has joined up with the most racially and ethnically integrated corner of our school. In contrast, many of my friends are white and Irish American, a potlatch of drunks and recreational drug users, most of whom have had no direct experience with people of color. Their disinvestment in the liberal project reveals the seams of our intimacies. We drive separate cars to school.

With my friends, I invite no conversation about color. It comes to me anyway.

My friends and I book a small apartment in Seaside Heights for the week after graduation, traditionally known as "Senior Week." The apartment we rent is underground, and one night, we gather together there for a drinking game. Everyone at the table is white. So is everyone in the room. There is a cheap wooden table in the center of the space, its surface mottled with dried beer. My fingertips stick to it. A small light dangles over the table.

There is a lot of laughter. Dark, perverse laughter, and sly sideways smirks. The kind of laughter and the kind of smirk that, for white people, often accompanies the thrill of saying "n——" out loud and without apology. We have been playing quarters, bouncing the coin off the table into a glass, forcing someone else to drink.

"Your older brother is a Black . . . ," one of them says.

I freeze. I note the use of the article. The use of *a* before *Black*. *A Black* sounds a lot like *a brute*. *Exterminate all the brutes*, I think, retreating into bibliographic mode, invoking Conrad, *The Heart of Darkness*, the novella's obsession with genocidal intent. I know that more is coming. There is always more. Always, in such spaces, when my friends are drunk.

". . . but your younger brother is a n——," he says, finishing the thought.

"Shit," someone adds. "That's right." Heads nod at this supposed profundity.

"Let me tell you about the difference between the Blacks and the n——s," the same voice continues, now more seriously, not wanting to miss this chance—this rare opportunity to say the word over and over again, to offer up a sociological treatise for the seventeen-year-olds gathered in a small rented apartment at the Jersey Shore.

A hush falls over the room—a joking formality, a collective intake of breath as all the other white faces lean forward while I draw back into the shadows.

He opines once more: "You see . . ."

It gets worse, louder, and more raucous. It travels the length of the apartment, leaving the table for some time before suddenly, violently returning with some gesture, or with a single word.

I look down, detaching from the conversation and focusing on my fingertips. Rhythmically sticking and unsticking them in the beer-sap on the tabletop, leaving fingerprints behind. I once more let the tactile distract from the turn the conversation has taken. No one notices that I'm not really listening. No one ever does. It is not the first time I have heard this treatise on *"the difference between."* It is not the first time—not even close—in which a casual conversation between supposed friends and trusted intimates takes a very predictable detour into American racism.

I have come to understand that this—*the difference between . . .*—is what white people talk about when they are alone.

"Your brother." Bear. At home, asleep in his bed, in our shared attic bedroom.

"A Black."

"N——."

"Exterminate the brutes."

My fingers, sticking and unsticking on the tabletop. My face in the shadows.

The not-so-secret truth of white people, I have learned, is that most of us, deep inside, *hate* people of color. And it generally takes a couple of drinks—or maybe just one—and the presumption of racial affiliation to get our tongues loose. Sometimes it doesn't even take a drink at all, just a brief window of time in which we are isolated in a space that is usually occupied by a racially mixed population. White people *want* to talk. We *want* to say "n——." The word redounds in all-white spaces. It is a magical word, full of enormous power and tragedy. The power that it brings to white people is absolutely intoxicating.

Looking back on high school, I ask Mark about this, seeking confirmation. Mark, the other white brother, the schoolteacher, the family man, another good son. Mark, with the ready laugh and the serious job, a studious man with wire-framed glasses, a superintendent and father of three. We look alike, have the same sense of humor, and share many qualities and quirks, but there is also so much that is different about our lives. We are almost fifty years old when we first discuss our shared whiteness.

I ask him if his high school friends ever used the word *n*—— in his presence.

"One hundred percent," he says quickly, without any hesitation. "In high school and in college."

He sighs, pausing on the phone. I hear his youngest daughter in the background. Yes, he confirms again, he heard the word often— and always in all-white spaces, in the context of some joke. But then, inevitably, it would be followed by awkward, unnerving apologetics, as his intimate friend group knew of us, admired Bear, and didn't want to offend. Offend Mark.

The laugh would catch in their throats. "Sorry, man," they would say, turning to him, with sincerity on their faces, "I don't mean your family."

And then, just like me, as the word bounced around the room, Mark would freeze, unsure about whether to blow up or to shrink down. Unclear what it meant, exactly, to be caught up in those kinds of apologies.

Back in June of 1988, Senior Week ends in deflation. I leave my friends behind, offering little conversation after that night, and make the drive back to the white house with the picket fence alone. It takes about ninety minutes to get from Seaside Heights to our little town, if everything goes right. If you don't get tangled up in the exodus of weekenders, if there isn't an accident on the parkway, if you don't need to stop for gas on Route 287. I get home late because there is traffic, but I appreciate having had the chance to think. Pulling into the driveway in the dark, I park behind Bear's 240Z, the flat primer gray absorbing the glare of the headlights. I look up at the peak of the roof and see that the light is on in our attic bedroom. I make my way up deliberately, shedding my shoes in the kitchen, hanging my keys on the hooks by the back door, using the second-floor bathroom, and then climbing the stairs to the attic, which we've painted black and white, so they can be seen in the dark. Bear is up there reading. He's been to the mall and picked up another stack of books to read, expanding the imaginative world we share.

"I got you something," he says, not even looking up from the page he is reading.

At the top of the stairs, a wrinkled brown bag holds a pair of new titles from an author I love—David Eddings, whose work, we agree, is so obviously derivative of Tolkien. Bear knows I appreciate the familiarity, the repeating themes of family and nation and ethnic type, the cheap, tinny echo of *The Lord of the Rings*. I crawl into bed, flip open the first book, turn on my reading light, and lose myself in the faraway fantasy of a different place, a different time, a different universe, until deep into the night. The sound of Bear turning his pages keeps me company.

29

White skin is dark magic. Powerful, but corrupted and dangerous.

I test the limits of its power, of course. In the summer of 1989, as a half-joking experiment, I attach an empty beer can to the hood ornament of my car, a big, lumbering station wagon recently added to the fleet. I drive right by the local police station to no response. I am pretty confident that no one will ever pull me over, but I keep a criminal justice–procedure textbook on the back seat, just in case, as a sympathetic prop to ensure gentler treatment. I never once need to use it.

Once we are all out driving, encounters with the police are inevitable.

Bob's response is typically color-blind, reflecting his unflagging idealism. Bear and Eddie do not get "the talk," a critical part of the pedagogy of the oppressed, wherein the parents of young Black and brown children remind them that, in the eyes of the police, they are all marked by criminality, and equip them with survival skills. *Obey. Consent.* We all certainly understand that this is true, since racial disparities in policing, in sentencing, and in the basics of life itself are regular subjects of conversation at the breakfast and dinner table.

Bob feels, though, that there should be no formal, separate syllabus for those of us in the family who are, indeed, Black. It is important, he tells us, that we all get the same lecture, over and over again, whenever the mood strikes him, that we all understand how race works. So we all get "the talk." He pulls us into his bedroom, or calls us into the kitchen, and holds out a newspaper story about a traffic stop that went wrong. "You all need to hear this," he begins. We stop whatever we are doing to listen.

The very specific lesson we all receive is a strange indictment of policing. Strange, that is, because it comes from someone who so routinely works with law enforcement. And strange because it is most often delivered at our kitchen table, the very same platform at which he will sign arrest warrants once he becomes a judge, where we have discussed potential adoptions, where we gather to have dinner at 6 p.m. sharp each and every day without fail.

That kitchen table is his lectern. It is broad and thick, made of a dark wood heavy enough that it never slips or moves. Sitting at the head, shuffling the newspaper, or drumming his fingers on the lacquered top, Bob drills us on the consequences of illegality. With great seriousness, he describes the police as incredibly thin skinned and habitually prone to terrible, ego-driven overreactions. He encourages all of us, without exception, to overperform respectful courtesy in any context in which we engage with law enforcement directly. The constant repetition of this lesson—it is a regular, sometimes daily feature of our assembly, competing with the discourse on overpopulation for top billing—clarifies the stakes. Any encounter with the cops, we think, might go horribly wrong. Nothing, Bob insists, can protect us, refusing to make exceptions for whiteness.

"Contempt of cop" is his catchphrase. It preserves the notion of law as something pure, shifting the blame for its prejudicial impact to the flawed, corruptible humans assigned as policemen. "Contempt of cop," he continues, looking at each of us in turn, "means that if you piss them off, they are going to take it out on you."

Even then, we know that isn't quite true. His passionate sermons at the table emphasize the disproportionate focus of the state on Black and brown men and women. From the safety of our kitchen table, he routinely calls out the police for their hostility toward those who are most marginalized, those who have the least, those who are prejudged as dangerous. "Racism!" he will say emphatically, gesturing to the newspaper. He outlines a set of scenarios. "You get pulled over for speeding . . ." "A cop enters a party and sees you . . ." "Someone hits you at an intersection . . ." Ticking off possibilities on the tips of his fingers, he will walk us through a sequence of imaginable mistakes and lay out the consequences, often prison time or death. His cautionary parables—usually delivered with fear and concern in his voice, to our entire ensemble, as if it matters to each of us equally—are almost always color conscious. The victim of the police shooting is always Black. The white guy is always arrested, or given the benefit of the doubt.

By the end of high school, however, we are all well aware of the discrepancy. We know that if the hammer falls, it will hit Bear and Eddie the hardest. Every time Bear peels out of the driveway, the 240Z rumbling toward the highway, we understand that his life is at risk.

On some level, this is a different kind of pedagogy than the one we know and experience. We are living in a small town, cloistered and protected at home, and don't have access to collective, community knowledge about the power of policing. The cops we know are kind and polite. We regularly encounter them on our front porch, at the courthouse, and even at our dinner table. Bob's dire warnings contradict our everyday experience—which is refracted by his public role and sterling reputation, his status as a "saint"—but confirm what we see in the newspaper and on the nightly news.

Bob does more than just talk, materially guarding us against the terrifying possibility that some of his children are more likely than others to be victims of police violence. As a state judge, Bob has special license plates on his car. These include an outsize gold crest in the middle, and his initials in big, bold letters. He loves them, loves their aggrandizing gilt tone, and the questions they prompt from strangers. To shield us all as best he can, though, Dad outfits the entire fleet with the same plates, so that wherever we are, and whatever we are doing, the penumbra of his authority is extended. Bear and Eddie are protected. And every weekend, when we clean the fleet, we are instructed to use brass polish on the symbol to make sure that it shines. The fleet is a part of our protective encasement. He equips us with staid, bland cars engineered to attract no attention, and then affixes to their license plates a gleaming, potent reminder of his status.

Our parents also subscribe to an 800 number for the house phone, so that any one of us can always call home from anywhere and at any time on their dime.

That number comes in handy. I, marinated in whiteness, use it randomly and whimsically, calling Bob and Sheryl from subway stations and libraries just because I can. Once, when my car overheats down at the shore, I call home and Bob quickly dismisses the call. "I can't help right now," he instructs. He is paying the bills. "Figure it out." I use my "emergency credit card" (we all have one) to have the car towed and repaired, and stew for hours while the mechanic works.

Some of my siblings use that 800 number for much more urgent purposes—and when they do, Bob springs into action. The same year I affix that beer can to the hood of my car, Bear calls home from a bar in Philadelphia. He is a student at Villanova, an engineering major, and the pride of the family. There has been a big brawl of some kind, and the police are arresting people one at a time, moving deeper and deeper into the establishment, approaching his position. I answer the phone. I hear a wild racket in the background and then Bear's calm voice in my ear—"Hey man," he says, with a cool casualness, "can I talk to Dad?"—and quickly hand it off to Bob.

I turn the TV down so that I can listen in. "Yeah," Bear says, matter-of-factly, "they are getting closer to me, Dad. What do I do?

Do I need a lawyer?" He gives no hint of being unusually stressed. Prepped by Bob's lectures, he is collecting information, preparing for whatever comes next.

"Just be compliant," Bob reminds him. "Put your hands on the bar where they can see them. Don't reach for your pockets. Don't resist in any way. Do *not*," he says, with heavy emphasis, "fall into contempt of cop."

Getting off the phone, Bob hustles to make a few calls. He is nervous, worried. He knows the statistics. He knows what might happen. Sheryl sits on the couch, holding the cordless phone, hoping that Bear will call back.

There is no denying that the license plates do a certain kind of work for us all. As does the blandness of the fleet. As do the 800 number and the emergency credit card. As does our homeschooling at the dinner table in the psychodynamics of American policing. In a way, even if they are rooted in a clear-eyed understanding of racial policing, these are universal prophylactics, meant to protect all of us. But, we know, they also amplify racial privilege. That station wagon of mine—with the beer-can hood ornament—is equipped with stealth technology, the uninspiring, dry dullness of its exterior multiplied by the polished state symbol on its primary marker of identification, which is further enhanced by the whiteness of the driver, by the bright white skin of my face, my hands, my visible signifiers.

A year after Bear's arrest in Philadelphia, Mark and I are moving a mattress up to Jersey City in an old minivan. We are pulled over in a mass speed trap. We idle nervously in the breakdown lane, across from Northern State Prison, the cutting edge of the barbed wire glinting in the sun across eight lanes of traffic. "I hope we don't end up there," Mark jokes. We've been traveling well over the speed limit. When the ticketing officer comes up to the window, he has a quizzical look on his face. He sees two college-age white faces in the car. He sees the forgettable, flat vehicle, as boring and emasculated as any car can be. And he sees that big gold seal on the plates, the initials, the vain expression of privilege and power.

"Whose car is this?" he asks. He is holding his ticketing notebook but hasn't written anything.

We give him the answer. He rolls his eyes, realizing what he believes to be his mistake. He takes a breath. He doesn't want to give us a ticket and irritate a judge.

"Follow me," he says, before getting into his car. And then, in what is clearly meant to be a message for us, or a challenge, he floors it, accelerating well beyond our ability to catch up. We try to follow, laugh at ourselves when we fail, and then just ease back into traffic, once more on our way. There is no ticket. We have been released.

I'm reminded of what Bear tells me when I ask him about vacations: "Wherever dad was, I was safe." That isn't just metaphorical, or affective. It is literal. Safe, in the context of anti-Blackness, means alive, alive beyond what this place wants for you. Alive and full of promise and possibility. As Bear will come to see it, Bob extends himself, as far as he dares, to make sure that his authority, derived in large part from his whiteness, travels with us, shielding us, if differently, from the police. In his case, it means that Bear survives the arrest at the bar that night without a scratch, and without eliciting any contempt from the cop who cuffs him and drags him off to the lockup that night. In my case, though, it means that I feel untouchable, doubly immunized against state violence, and beyond the reach of any authority.

30

I leave home for a big school in a poor state in the middle of the country, the only kind of place that seems interested in admitting me. I have been a lackluster student in high school—with grades that are consistently in the C and D range—so Sheryl takes the lead, helping me develop a list of right-sized schools. Sitting together at the kitchen table, we fill out the applications, substituting her perfect handwriting for my own. She figures that anything—even neater penmanship or perfect typing—will make a difference. West Virginia University has been in the news as the top-ranked "party school" in the nation. Sheryl, practical and realistic, marvels at its vast curriculum and comprehensive scale, important qualities for a prospective student with no idea about his future. "Political science?" she asks, raising an eyebrow, hoping to have me declare an interest in a major. "History?" I shrug and say nothing, so she checks the box for the first. I am imagining the parties, the bawdy wildness of hundreds of young men and women in togas, am envisioning something like an updated version of *Animal House*, wherein cheap beer and bad decisions make for a wild and reckless coming-of-age melodrama. When the acceptance letter arrives, then, we are both thrilled.

In August, we all drive out west to Morgantown, passing out of the flattened, concretized orbit of Philadelphia, through the Pennsylvania farmlands, and into the hills and mountains of West Virginia, where the astonishing scale of the natural environment makes the roads wind and climb, twist and descend. It has been surprisingly easy to leave my high school friends behind, but the long trip out with my brothers and sister is a source of deeper sadness. "You never know people until you leave them," Bob says as we pack up the car in the driveway. He pauses and turns to face me. "They will surprise you." I think about that brief comment as we head west, to a place far from home, far from us. I'm not sure if the surprise is supposed to come from me or not. The hours pass slowly in the car, each minute taking me farther and farther from New Jersey. Bear sleeps while Bug reads a thick Stephen King novel—the terrifying *It*, which he leaves with me to read in the dorm.

The freshman dorm at WVU is the size of seven or eight hotels but made of plain cinderblock, allowing sounds to echo down every hallway. The bathrooms smell like industrial cleaner, lemon-scented and overpowering. Sheryl notes that everything seems clean, while we carry my duffel bag, a stereo, a few books from our shared library, and some winter coats up the stairs. At the start of the trip, Bob stopped at a big-box store, filling up the back of the car with cases of ramen noodles, cases that we now diligently relocate to my closet. Our parents stay for a night in a local hotel and take me out for breakfast the next morning. Sheryl gives me a big hug, but the rest of us downplay the whole thing. "See ya," I say with a casual wave as they drive away. Upstairs, the noodles are stacked high. Chicken, beef, and shrimp. To distract myself, I read *It* that night, and the book is so terrifying (and strange) that I stay up all night to finish it. I am homesick immediately, and call the house every night, talking to anyone who answers.

Bear, now a senior in high school, drives out to see me in October. Mark tags along, an amiable sophomore managing the maps and rationing the food for the trip. I count the hours, and then the minutes, from when they leave home, and I wait for them to telephone my room, peeking out the windows and trying to spot the car. When they finally call, I race downstairs, embracing them both. Mark is flustered but Bear hugs me back tight. "What's up, brother?" he calls out when he sees me.

The backslapping ends quickly. They've been on the road for a while. "Let's go inside," I say, sweeping open the fire door. They remember the building from August, the antiseptic smells, the concrete walls, but a lot has changed in a month. I stop at every door on the hallway, making introductions, high-fiving new friends, reminding them to stop by later. Our plan—my plan and Bear's—is to spend the entire weekend in my dorm room, a small square with a single recliner, a set of steel bunk beds, and two small desks built into the wall. My roommate has lined the walls with posters of porn stars—more than a few of Traci Lords. There isn't anything to go see in town, I assure my brothers. "We'll just hang here and drink and you can meet everyone." "Sounds great!" Bear says, dropping his bag and sprawling into the recliner, an ancient green, quilted thing we found abandoned on a street corner.

"I'll be the staff photographer," Mark offers, as Bear and I open the bottles. Responsible to a fault, he knows that he is too young to partake in our revelry. He puts some new film in the Polaroid and hangs the camera around his neck, ready to document the evening. By the dinner hour, classmates from the floor are pouring into the room. There, over by the makeshift bar, are Pork and Dorf, the local kids with thick accents, one handsome and thin and the other decidedly neither. Ruff, the dark-haired, smooth-talking kid from California who always has a pocketknife, lies on the top bunk. My roommate, Judd, with a mullet haircut and a plaid flannel shirt, sits on the bottom bunk, making Bear comfortable in the recliner. Judd lights a cigar for him. Kenny, a one-handed placekicker for the football team, pokes his head into the room and drops off a bottle of moonshine in a Mason jar, drawing a rousing cheer from the small crowd. Rob, always with some gross bathroom joke, asks Bear questions about football. Every few minutes, a flash goes off. Mark stands in the corner, snapping away.

Earlier that day, we used Judd's fake ID to buy some bourbon to celebrate—two half gallons of the cheapest, most plentiful stuff we could find. Old Grand-Dad, a brand renowned for its volume, not its quality. Now, with the aroma of cigars and the smell of bad booze, Bear holds court, pontificating about martial arts and Asian philosophy. Even in a room full of drunken college students, all of them brimming with the thin wisdom of nineteen-year-olds, he is a masterful, world-class bull thrower, the true heir to Dad's charisma and charm. And, stepping back, I can see that my floormates love him—his comfortable middle-class tones and textures, his devotion to karate, tai chi, and kung fu. The evening goes on and on until our bodies can't handle sitting still any longer. Like wildlings, we run to get breadsticks from the grocery store down the hill. Back at the dorm, we eat them quickly, and then we all promptly throw them up. We're drunk enough, though, to laugh about it. Mark cleans it up while Judd, Bear, and I say goodnight to the tired white faces in the room, bringing the evening to a late close.

His last memory—Mark's—is of Bear sitting in the recliner while the rest of us are asleep, talking to himself in the near dark, a shot of bourbon in his hands.

Mark is a good photographer, intuitive about mood and scene. The handful of Polaroids he takes that night show Bear surrounded by white faces, flush with the drunken exhilaration of boastful homosociality. At the start of the sequence, everyone is fresh-faced and smiling. The Old Grand-Dad is balanced on Judd's lap. Bear is the only non-white person, sitting at the center of the room, sporting a perfectly shaped flattop, wearing a sleeveless T-shirt slit open at the sides, his formidable biceps on display. Judging by the series, the night unfolds quickly. Cigarettes dangle from lower lips, and bleary eyes are squeezed half shut from the smoke. The room is filled with people, young men and women brought to meet my brother—and to enjoy some free liquor. In one shot, Bear has turned away from the camera, a cigarette in his mouth, his hand raised in explanatory mid-gesture. A white woman's foot is on his lap, and a floormate from down the hall listens to him intently, hanging on every word. In another, a different set of new friends bare their muscular arms alongside his, posing to measure biceps, flesh on flesh. In every frame, Bear, in a room of white people he has never met before, is the gleaming, living centerpiece.

Bear's overnight visit to the dorm breaks an unwritten rule. Morgantown, West Virginia, is one of the whitest and most segregated places I have ever been. As far as I can remember, there are no students of color on my floor—or in the entire dorm, I am guessing. And if there are, they've been erased from my memory and from the album of pictures from that first semester. There is no discussion in any of my classes about race, not even in my modern US history course. Or, at least, there is none while I am in the room. I have no Black professors. No non-white instructors. I rush a fraternity, looking for free beer, hoping for a facsimile of the family, and find no people of color in the whole bunch, though the ice-cold Rolling Rock sure is plentiful.

Morgantown is also where I most frequently hear that word: n——. It is a part of the atmosphere, spoken casually and out loud, with a southern drawl, as a simple descriptor, as if it is a totally natural thing to be saying while in line at the cafeteria, waiting for a hard square of spaghetti loaf and talking to the next person in line about something you saw on television. "And the next thing that n—— did was to jump up and grab that ball right out of the air." Spoken angrily, as a promissory note for future violence. "Gonna get those n——s." Spoken jokingly, in laughing disbelief, as if Black folks were endlessly comedic. "Damn, that is one crazy-ass n——." It is uttered with new relish by white students from the East Coast, young men and women who have never dared to use it before and who are suddenly enthralled with it, excited to use it in the myriad all-white spaces that the university provides. They chew on the word in their mouths until it grows softer and easier to manipulate, until they know it so well that they can blow bubbles out of it.

At the same time, I see Black students, all held at a great distance, seemingly isolated from the rest of the student body. Sitting at my window, looking out into the quad, I watch the members of a Black fraternity, their arms branded with Greek letters, move together in a phalanx, a necessary precaution in the largely segregated campus. The fraternity is putting its pledges through the ringer, making them stand in the rain. I watch the rain glisten on Black skin, on scar tissue, and listen. Looking to the side, I see other white faces peering out of nearby windows. Through the walls I can feel white mouths speak the word aloud, each utterance a minor tremor. Or think it, descriptively and pejoratively. And dangerously.

Bear's visit has been a lifeline, a reminder, an echo of the past. A reintegration. For me.

It isn't enough, though. I skip nearly all of my classes that first semester, drink myself into near oblivion. My memories of those four months in Morgantown are spotty, irregular, imprecise, like the Polaroids. Walking on the train tracks late at night, drunk and with friends. Attending a local football game. Traveling to see Rob's hometown and attending a fall formal in Reston. Going to class in pajamas. Running down a hill during a massive fight. A wild night of keg-stands and five-beer funnels at the frat. A girl in my bed, talking about her love of medieval pageantry. Bear's visit is the most vivid memory. I am homesick. At the winter break, I return to the white house an abject failure, having failed four classes and somehow earned a D in the fifth. When the grades arrive in the mail, Bob and Sheryl are crushed—but perhaps not entirely shocked. I am put on academic probation and encouraged to return for one more shot, but I can't go back to Morgantown, which seems southern in all the wrong ways. I can't stomach that long, winding drive, taking me so far from our small town. I can't return to what I understand as segregation.

Just down the road from the white house, the local community college beckons. New Jersey's old county-college system is a product of the same anti-elitist liberal zeitgeist that created us, born of the 1960s and expanding along with the county. Growing up, the place is famous, to me, for its Olympic-sized swimming pool, and for its underwater changing rooms, which allow you to watch from below as divers plunge headfirst into the crystal-clear water. A middle-school girlfriend once confesses to me that she made out with her ex in the shadow of the athletics facility, and I spend months obsessed with what goes on around back, where young people retreat into the foundations to explore, to cheat, to break hearts. Those early, youthful impressions are eventually replaced by jokes. In our fairly affluent college-prep high school, the county college is derided as the "island of misfit toys," a safe space for broken underachievers and working-class stiffs taking night classes. A college for failures. No college counselor ever proposes it to me—not to the son of a judge and a schoolteacher. Nor does anyone propose it to Bear, or Bug, or Mark, or Anna. With the exception of summer swim camps, the campus is a foreign country to us.

Despite its popular representation as a repository for the downwardly mobile, Raritan Valley Community College is my salvation. This underfunded engine of social uplift, a massive, sprawling edifice of poured concrete, is one of the best structural adjustments the state ever made. It is also integrated, a striking contrast to Morgantown, where the small number of Black students eat alone, the classrooms feel uniformly white, and the reading material is old-fashioned. There is a Filipino psychology professor, who moves us through the basics of the human brain and shares with us his encounters with race while driving to work. And a cackling Samoan philosophy professor in a wheelchair, who fervently believes that "love is an attitude," and who advocates for the faculty on campus—once, by slowly marching to the administration offices during class, when professors are in the midst of salary negotiations. And a bearded old white man, passionate about the arcana of world history, who spends weeks on the global history of the peanut. And a quiet Black math professor who coaxes me through college algebra, one step at a time. A former off-Broadway actress, with a warbling, high-pitched voice, who teaches Shakespeare, focusing exclusively on the romantic comedies. And there are some of the clearest conversations I have ever had about race or race relations, with new friends that look, feel, and sound more like my family. Black and brown and Asian American students, working-class students, adults returning to school, ex-cops and corporate types and schoolteachers, all trying to recredential themselves, to restart their lives. RVCC is an institution that is meant to serve people from all walks of life, and it is a better fit for me than any place I have ever been—or ever will be. It lacks all pretension, stoically focuses on reaching its students, on methodically getting them through classes, one semester at a time, and routing them into BA degree–completion programs around the state.

I love it. Still, a sense of shame hangs over me that spring, after the confession of failure and the decision to move back home. I lie awake at night in my bed, trying to game out some plan that will speed up a return to "regular" college, that will keep me on the same track as Bear. Maybe I will join the navy, I think. Maybe I will try to transfer to some other college over the summer, so that my restart can be synced with Bear and Bug. In the end, I stay put, and spend two years in community college, learning how to be a good student.

That summer, then, we are all at a crossroads. I am settling into a pattern of return, and Bug and Bear are preparing to depart. In June, Mark records their graduation party.

It is a hot, steamy day, and almost everyone is outside, where it is a little cooler, fanning themselves with paper plates. Mark follows Eddie around the yard, chasing him with the camera. Eddie smiles and laughs innocently, enjoying the game. He is so small and so young, and so impossibly cute, wearing a T-shirt that reads "West Virginia University," a reminder that just one year earlier we hosted a party for me. "Stop recording me, Mark!" he calls out, and yet he keeps looking over his shoulder with gleeful anticipation, and his face tells Mark that he is loving the play, the innocence of the game. "Duh," Eddie says, making fun of his "dumb" older brother, taunting him. The brief pursuit begins in the Green Room and continues into the kitchen, where potato salad and baked beans and hot dogs and cake are laid out. Mark chases him outdoors, onto the back patio, where the aunts and uncles have pulled all of the chairs in close around the picnic table. Anna and Bug are there, enjoying a slice of cake. Bug still wears his graduation gown, a flimsy polyester thing provided by the school. Bob has opened up the striped umbrella. The table is covered in red Solo cups, and we catch a brief second of Sheryl leaning forward, describing her classroom to the group. An ashtray sits in the middle of the table, right next to the umbrella pole. Our aunt gives Mark a mocking, disdainful look when he briefly pauses to record her face, and then he moves along.

"Dad!" Eddie calls out from the driveway. "Mark is chasing me." He dashes around an old maple tree, and then runs to a cousin and hides behind him. Eddie is comfortable with us, playing with his brother, in love with his cousins, appealing to Bob for protection. Mark says nothing, but the appeal to Bob has scared him off.

Two of us are missing from the patio. Bear and me. Mark finds us easily. Back in the Green Room, I sit back in Bob's recliner, taking the patriarch's throne while he is on the patio. Bear, uninterested in the revelry outside, sleeps shirtless on the nearby couch, his arms outstretched, his muscular torso on full display. When Mark turns the camera to me, a wan smile is on my face. Bugs Bunny is playing on the television, but I am reading something, deep into another book. I look up quickly to acknowledge the family's cameraman, and offer a small, polite wave. "Last year's graduate," Mark says drolly as he surveys me, reminding the viewer of all that has happened in a year, that twelve months ago the party was in my honor, that I was the one heading off to bigger things. Now, Bear and Bug will soon be gone, and I am headed nowhere. But that is OK. Leaning back in that recliner, moving through another book, surrounded by the sounds of family, I am comfortable in my skin, happy with the work I am doing in community college, and glad to be home. The scene has such an easy, comfortable familiarity to it: the two of us, Bear and me, together in the Green Room, with the portrait of George Washington looming over the fireplace, and the weird colonial aesthetic of the wallpaper. One of us reading, the other taking an afternoon nap on a hot day. The cartoons of our childhood on-screen. Everyone else is outside, but there is nowhere I'd rather be.

31

The white house with the white picket fence also has an old basement. Its floors are painted brown. Its walls are filled with pine shelves. Its ceilings are latticed with copper pipes and electrical wire. During the day, a handful of slim, dusty windows provide some weak light to the far corners, and at night the vast, cavernous space is dimly lit by two bulbs that hang from the ceiling. No matter the time of day and no matter the wattage, then, there is never enough light, and there are always too many shadows.

Once, there is an incident in the basement. I'm not there. It happens after Bear leaves for college, after Bug returns home and transfers to nearby Rutgers, after I move down to the shore. I can't describe it. I can feel it, though. In the way that one can feel the ocean currents, when standing knee-deep in the water. It draws me out and pulls me down.

To me, the event—the *incident*, in family parlance—takes on a gothic weight, in much the same way that contemporary horror films build the feeling of dread slowly. The threat is felt but not seen. A fading, ghostly outline, a quick turn to face an empty wall that almost, for an instant, seems like a portal to somewhere else; a voice that is just beyond the reach of your ear; a fingernail scratch at the other end of the hallway beyond your line of sight. What you can't see, what lies just beyond your perception, is what makes you lean forward, what makes you grip the chair tightly, what makes you prepare yourself for what you know is inevitable: the actual reveal that is sure to come, the moment at which the thing is finally, at long last, right in front of you. A good director stretches out the suspense, leaving you wretched with emotional attenuation, and won't show you the thing until they absolutely must. Until your heart is pounding. Eventually, though, they all let you see it, at least once. And then you gasp. And collapse. A basement, any devotee of these films can tell you, is a helpful metaphor for what is purposefully underground, what is buried, what emerges unbidden in moments where stress and panic and even terror can tear apart a family, a life, a body.

Like any other old basement, ours is cluttered and jam-packed with entangled, half-remembered histories. Toys we've forgotten—old matchbox cars and board games—and then recall vividly upon sight. Clothing we've outgrown—or hand-me-downs we are set to inherit someday. Old coats, an array of browns and grays, that have been replaced or are ready to be repaired. A liquor cabinet that is lacquered black, its padlock a reminder of too many thefts. The family's film projector, broken and unused but too precious to cast out. Christmas ornaments and the tree stand, which resurface each year. The rumbling washer and dryer. The laundry bin, shaped like a big red pig, because it was bought for us when we were children. The massive hot-water heater, a source of pride for Bob. "It is glass-lined," he always says. His workbench sits in another corner. A wood-burning stove that creaks and crackles when it isn't inert. A massive oil tank, as solemn as a mountain. The furnace, which is prone to awakening without warning. A hulking deep-freezer. And boxes upon boxes of old files and folders, stacked high and deep, and labeled—to my eye, at least—incomprehensibly. All together in the basement, this astonishing volume of material creates a twisting maze of machinery and nearly forgotten pasts, some of which we never really knew, and some of which we remember upon sight.

In fiction and in film, a basement like ours is always a site of terror. Basements are always presumed to have hidden rooms with red-painted walls, or to have been dug in the midst of Indian burial grounds. Hauntings are real, our Catholicism instructs, and so, too, are ghosts and phantasms; the supernatural is always just around the corner, and dangerous, and ritual magic can adhere to the physical, so that any old bottle cap, rosary, or book can open the door to spirits and ghouls. The inevitable, dramatic clangor of an old house in the four seasons—the pops, creaks, snaps, groans, and mysterious gusts—add to the foreboding, the anticipatory sense of danger. If I am the only one in the inky underground, if I have been tasked to retrieve something, I will run up the stairs, hoping to avoid whatever might be lurking below the stairs.

Despite its chaotic and terrifying clutter, though, I know the basement fairly well. Periodically, when I need a little spending money, I am dispatched to warily clean it up, always in the middle of the day. This rarely means throwing things away; it most often means straightening, restacking, or boxing up what is already in the space. This means that the stacks get higher and deeper, that the walkways get more convoluted, that the atmospherics get darker and heavier. In my teenage years, when I need money the most, I become a wary steward of the wildness of that place.

The place where the incident happens.

Any attempt to create order is futile, however. Shoes and jackets pile up at the bottom of the stairs. Laundry accrues in the corners. Boxes, stacked neatly years ago, fall as time drags them down. New objects arrive. The near past is always ready to be archived, always accumulating in a pile.

We all hustle up the stairs, fearing the dark, worriedly watching the looming clutter, but the thing we fear never reveals itself. The tension builds. Our fingers tighten. Until the day that something happens in the basement.

There is a conflict of some sort. Between Bug, who is in college, living at home, and Eddie, who is still technically in high school. It happens in the basement, where the piles of things encroach on us, where intensities are accelerated by forced proximity, where the lights are dim and the shadows are dark. It starts as a minor dispute, I am sure, over some little thing, some outrage born of ego, born of some desperate sense of turf or scarcity. It grows quickly into a major conflagration. It gets violent. Again, I am not there. But I feel the aftershock of it, spending the evening on the phone and then hustling home from Long Beach Island.

Bob is on-site, cauterizing the wound, operating purely on instinct. "I wasn't there," Mom deflects in the present. "Bob handled it. He was very good at handling things."

There is a current in the house, a narrative flow that is taking us somewhere. In the brief span of time since Mark chased him in the driveway with a video camera, Eddie has grown up, becoming a teenager verging on adulthood. A year before the incident in the basement, I am watching a basketball game in Bob and Sheryl's room. I see our neighbor rushing up the driveway to the back door, cradling Eddie in his arms. Eddie has stolen liquor from the basement, taken it down the street to the old firehouse, and consumed it all in one big rush. The neighbor has heard him retching and carried him home. I bring him to the bathtub and call my aunt, thinking that she might know what to do. I hover over them, watching him vomit repeatedly. He is unconscious. He has always been a small child. Even as a teenager, he looks years younger. The locks on the liquor cabinet are installed as soon as Bob gets home. Those locks are the start of something, but we don't know that in the moment when we hear them snap closed.

Eddie has been seeing a psychologist for a few years, as we struggle to understand why he continues to "act out" in school, and as he slips out of the public schools and into the disciplinary regimes of private schools whose only purpose is to move students along briskly wherever possible and by whatever means are necessary. He is beginning to steal larger things from the neighbors—bringing home a new bicycle, a pet goat, and someone else's Alaskan malamute—and this causes alarm, or racial panic. He takes some of the junk from the basement and sells it for cash. Mom and Dad have arranged for him to see a Black therapist in nearby Princeton, thinking that some vital connection might be made, that race might enable a better repair. In the aftermath of the incident, after a hasty phone call, the same therapist facilitates Eddie's admission to a nearby inpatient medical institution for observation and treatment. Another sort of place that looms large in the gothic imagination. In my imagination, it is all brick and stucco, and covered with gargoyles. In real life, it is a two-story modernist building, an angular brick-and-limestone rectangle.

From there, the plot unfolds with a precision that can be felt in the fingertips, in the bones, in the flesh.

"Bob handled it."

At the psychiatric institution, Eddie is quickly subjected to tests and evaluations. He is medicated, an object of intense scrutiny. He fights it, of course, but the plot has grabbed hold of him. And never, ever lets him go.

Some will see this conflict—and even the consequent institutionalization—as inevitable. Eddie, a restless and insurgent teenager, has been chafing at what might, in any other context, be understood as ordinary parental discipline, ramped up to match his own intensity. Bug has grown tense, frustrated, since a return to the house. Strife in families is normal, even if that strife becomes physical. Siblings bicker. Sometimes they slap and shove. Given that we are, in some ways, a normal family, such things are predictable. Or ineradicable. Race, however, complicates what would otherwise be ordinary or expected. It adds drama, even horror, to the incident in that dreadful basement, so dark and mysterious and malevolent. Black and brown flesh, slapping, punching, pushing, in the dim light, amid the towering stacks and piles left behind, the crumbling file boxes and random miscellany. This is not brotherly play, but barbarity.

I have always felt like it could have gone either way that night. It could have been Bug who was referred out to the institution. He was angry, too. So angry in those years. Or there could have been no referral, or a renewed commitment to family therapy. Could have gone either way, except for those instincts, those snap decisions, that sense of inevitability. Bob felt the same. "Did I make the right choice?" he asked, in the wake of it all, never really knowing.

"I want to talk about the incident in the basement," I say to Mom. She sighs wearily, the thought of those decades she's tried to repress coming so speedily to the fore. She knows exactly what I am asking about. Thirty years later. All I need to say is "the incident in the basement." That is how you know it haunts us.

An "incident." As if it were merely awkward or mildly unpleasant. "An incident." A reminder that it was a singular occurrence, a simple historical event, one of many in our timeline.

"Bob handled it."

He did. Bob plays the role assigned to him with considerable, late-in-life anguish. When we speak of it—and we do, regularly—he always wonders what would have happened if we stuck it out longer, if we continued to steer clear of carceral regimes that validate medical restraint at the start. What, he wonders, might Eddie have become? Bob never forgives himself for that moment, for the urgency and haste with which he picks up the phone, calls that therapist, and enlists the world—as uneven, as broken, as treacherous as it is—in the disciplining of his son. He knows all the statistics, understands all the racial logics, has spent a lifetime building a family that is meant to undo all of it, and yet still acts in that moment as he does.

"Bob handled it."

And regrets it, forever. With the pained awareness that "the grave is a barrier to all amends, all redress," in the words of Henry Roth.

Once, there is an incident in the basement.

I can't tell you what happened because I wasn't there. I can't ask Eddie or Bug about it because they have made peace with it. Mom would prefer not to guess what happened. Trauma is often a hole in the plot, and from this point forward, there are silences and elisions in our story.

Bob knows. Knows what happened. Knows what his role was in it. And he is wrecked by the enormity of it, an enormity that makes a joke of the word we use to name it. An "incident." I am wrecked, too, even though I can't describe it, can't see it, even though it is just out of view, like fingernails on the wall, scratching a message in the plaster. Sometimes, reality is the nightmare—the snap decisions, the instinctive response, the phone call, the tilted ground beneath us, the current that draws us out, and pulls us down, that ensures that the Black child, in the end, goes to jail. One minute you are there. The next you are sucked out to sea and drowned.

A small, adorable child, Eddie struggles in school before the incident, stubbornly fighting his own "improvement." He pushes back halfheartedly but consistently against our intimacies. Keeping us at bay, he supplements hard work with unnecessary theft, mixes anger with kindness, leavens secrecy with openness. His transgressions are bourgeois quotidian, nothing too far beyond what I did at his age; there are minor break-ins and police interventions of a suburban ordinariness and a wild set of drinking binges, notable occurrences in a small white town where your father is the judge and your mother is a schoolteacher. And notable, too, in a small town where your family has been an object of quiet obsession. There is again nothing in this that goes too far beyond typical teenage rebellion, no action that—if coded white—might not be easily forgiven. But anti-Blackness—encoded in the backstory provided by the agency, discerned in the popular context of the day—labels these things otherwise. The state criminalizes his actions. And within the house, even before the incident in the basement, his halfhearted resistance to incorporation has led to a new system of borders and locks and walls, a new kind of carceral homeland with one simple goal: to restrain, rather than to reform. The lock on the liquor cabinet, I remember, clicks shut.

The clinic puts him on medication immediately.

The list of drugs must be familiar to Bob, a judge who focuses on family matters in court. They all have complicated, chemical names, communicating medical seriousness with each syllable. As days become weeks, the prescriptions grow more complex, the interactions harder to gauge, the doses doubling and then doubling again, even as Eddie is moved from institution to institution, from a small hospital to assorted wilderness schools for "at-risk kids." Bob tries to keep track—tries to organize the notes from the clinics, the hospitals, the reform schools—keeping the correspondence neat in his desk.

At each next stop, there is failure. At one "ranch" school, Eddie steals a car and burns it. At another, he escapes and eventually assaults an officer. He is in touch with us throughout. During a frantic phone call while he is on the run, I counsel him to go to the Nation of Islam in Chicago, thinking that Malcolm X's commitment to order and discipline might appeal to him or might save him.

All of this long, terrible story unfolds while our youngest brother is still a teenager, still the adopted child of an affluent pair of parents with considerable resources to spend on his behalf and a great deal of experience and the best of intentions. In white America, he is required to go to school, though the only schools that seem to "work" for him—to displace the danger, to contain it safely—are more like prison hospitals, run by private for-profit corporations.

Bob takes careful notes. Reading through his file on our brother, I discover a vast, desperate determination to protect this one symbolic body's status as a redeemable child, to find the right solution through science and medicine and therapy, to preserve his rights, broadly construed—and to redeem one's own beliefs. After a confrontation with a police officer in Colorado, Eddie needs to be transported to a new school in Texas, but as a minor, he isn't subject to the law in the same way as a prisoner. Bob, desperate to find a safe harbor for his son, taps into his network of contacts and pays out of his pocket for sheriff's deputies to transport him. Sheryl, in a parallel effort, writes long, impassioned, thoughtful letters to Eddie, over and over again, a form of perseveration, explaining the first-order rationale for the social contract, pressing him, from the only perspective she knows, the white perspective, to respect the most basic bonds of citizenship, taking up—in essence—the civic education of this man-child adrift between worlds, offering a liberal pedagogy so immanent in her loving prose.

If success is measured by a productive return to civil society, these efforts fail. Some problems are just too big to be solved by bootstrapping, by hard family work, by ideologies of rescue. Structural racism cannot be paved by good intentions and by heartfelt correspondence. And the family, even one as futuristic as ours, cannot be a remedy for the problems of racial formation, of a world in which incorporation and integration are understood as primarily operations of salvage and repair. I doubt, as well, that civil society's notion of a "productive return" would ever have been permitted to our youngest brother.

Eventually, the penal state intervenes, and decisively, so reform schools give way to jails and then prisons and then penitentiaries. Escapes lead to other, more major offenses. The school-to-prison pipeline becomes, for him, a one-way superhighway. What comes next—once he is formally branded a "criminal," once he begins to move in and out of the prison-industrial complex—is perhaps too long and too complex and too heartbreaking to narrate for the here and now.

What is clear to me in the present is this: the basement was a hellish place, and the incident there was, in many ways, our ending. Bob has his first heart attack soon afterwards. They sell the white house two years later. And Eddie, our youngest brother, never lives at home again.

32

A yellow rotary phone hangs on the kitchen wall by the front door. This phone is old. Bob once used it to call the Pennsylvania farmhouse, on the night our parents decided to adopt Bear. The wallpaper around the phone—blue and white stripes, and a stamped pineapple—is slightly darker, smudged from decades of dinner-table hands grasping for the receiver. A pair of thin radiator pipes, running from floor to ceiling, is just to the left of the phone. A nearby hot-water radiator sizzles and pops in the wintertime. A twenty-foot-long cord dangles, pooling to the floor alongside the mopboard we once stripped of paint.

That phone is important. From that one spot, you can sit in the rocking chair in the corner, or huddle on the steps to the second floor, or withdraw to the living room couch. You can look out the kitchen window and see the street, or the driveway. You can walk out onto the porch and get comfortable on the oversize wicker chairs Bob has spray-painted black. You can reach and travel to the back of the house, turning the stove off, or getting a snack from the cupboard. On cold days, you can wrap one hand around a radiator pipe, warming your fingertips, while the other holds the receiver to your ear. Even after cordless phones enter our lives, that old phone is a centerpiece of the first floor, offering a simple, reliable connection to the outside world from the most-used room in the house.

Once a week—on Sunday nights, mostly—the phone will ring.

An automated message—a soft woman's voice—prompts us to accept the charges. "Hey, guys." Eddie's voice, low and huskier than normal, as if he is trying to sound tough for anyone around him who might be listening in. A hundred ten pounds. Eighteen years old. Looking like thirteen. Trying to sound like he were forty.

The timing of the call is unpredictable, Eddie explains with apologies. There isn't much he can do about that. The line at the prison phone bank might be too long. Someone might be on the phone with their lawyer, discussing something urgent, or with a loved one, navigating some difficult issue. Some Sunday nights, the call never comes, because Eddie is in solitary, a consequence of some physical scrap with another inmate earlier in the day. Most weeks, it is just Sheryl and Bob and me and sometimes Mark. On holidays, or on those regular weekends when Bear and Anna return, there is a larger group. We will pace nervously, watching the phone, checking it repeatedly to make sure it isn't off the hook in some other room. The wooden chairs in the kitchen creak as we shift. The phone calls are serious business, and the house is uncharacteristically silent while we wait for the ring, with the TV off lest we miss the call. We jump into action once we hear the phone, fumbling for the handset, waiting for the recorded greeting to end, for the moment at which we can accept a collect call from the penitentiary. "You have a collect call from"—"Eddie," he will say, inserting his name in the recording—"Would you like to accept the charges?" "Yes!" we will exclaim. And then we pass the phone around, asking vapid questions about day-to-day life in prison, hoping to keep his spirits up—and ours, too.

The ritual receipt of these phone calls is a feature of the great severance, the loss of one of us to the carceral state following the incident.

Eddie is the first in our family since distant and drunken Gilded Age ancestors stumbled through Jersey City streets to be imprisoned. Rather naively, then, we understand prison an as entirely rehabilitative place, a conception that allows us, at first, to sit still and wait patiently while the state warehouses Eddie into adulthood. Even Bob, who provided those early lessons on "contempt of cop," trusts that barbed wire and batons ensure safety, and that prison time offers a chance for reflection that can inspire real change for recidivists. Still, we pick at the idea of the institution, probing its rationale and its public face for flaws, looking for verification that such warehousing will produce, at the close, a reformed citizen. We want Eddie to go straight, to get religion, to return to us.

Whenever Eddie begins to talk about getting out, we ask about jobs programs. If he has broken a bone or cut an arm, we wonder about his safety. "What," we wonder, "is medical care like?" We ask what he is doing with his time and what time means to him. "Not much," he will say whenever we ask, describing hours without end spent in his cell. We ask about the prison library, about book-borrowing programs, about access to newspapers. Without much thought—and certainly without a family meeting—we begin to supplement the lean materials he describes. For Bob, who trusts that the state is an honest broker, and who is himself the dispenser of legal certainty, the beginnings of his own private radicalization lie in this embittering moment, in which his son is drawn into the prison-industrial complex, and when that institution's press releases are revealed to be malevolently false.

"Did you send anyone to jail today?" we used to ask when we were younger, jokingly, at the dinner table. Bob hates the question. But he also must see some truth in it, and often throws himself into genres of court practice—family court, specifically—where he feels like he can make more of a difference, where he can sometimes turn the question back on us. "Today," he can say, "I repaired, or fixed, or restored something." And then, leaning in: "What did *you* do?" We stop asking the question after the incident in the basement, when our relationship to Eddie seems to depend on that phone cord, on its capacity to stretch all the way to Trenton or Rahway.

"Bob handled it."

Bob works the lawyers and makes sure Eddie has representation. Mom focuses her attention on understanding the prison commissary so that we can supply Eddie with food, clothing, soap, cigarettes, cash or credit—whatever material he needs. My job, as a part of this effort, is simple: whenever he asks for something to read, I send books, sometimes through the mail, sometimes through a delivery service, or sometimes offering them to the prison library. The means of delivery depend on the rules, which often seem to change. Keeping track of the rules—and they seem to only tighten up—is a part of the job, but every institution has its own rules. One institution allows us to ship straight from Amazon or from a bookstore. Another requires us to package the books ourselves and send them from our home address. In a few instances, we can send him whatever he wants, no matter the title or the topic. In most others, however, the list needs to be approved beforehand, and the approval process is Byzantine, complicated, and doomed to fail.

The job falls to me because Bob is uncertain about what to send. Our home has enough reading material to fill a small library, but our habit is to discover things that we care about individually. We get gift certificates, not hardcovers and paperbacks, and we relish the privacy of our choices. Bug likes Stephen King and horror. Bear and I prefer science fiction and fantasy. Bob loves Civil War history and thrillers—the literary equivalent of action movies—and biographies of great men. Sheryl reads fiction broadly, from Barbara Kingsolver to Toni Morrison. Eddie isn't much of a reader, and we need a scattershot approach until we find something he enjoys.

Bob keeps our correspondence—emails that he prints out and

files away in the rolltop desk. There are a number of annotated bibliographies, where I suggest this or that, preparing to send Eddie stuff that seems right, or that I have just encountered. History, fiction, memoir, philosophy, along with general commentary on the state of race relations.

I send copies of *The Autobiography of Malcolm X*, of course, along with Claude Brown's *Manchild in the Promised Land*, Kody Scott's *Monster*, and Mark Mathabane's *Kaffir Boy*. These are, as I see them, chronicles of uplift, in which the rough-edged protagonist, with nowhere else to turn, finds the courage to lower his shoulder and dig, one shovel of dirt at a time, his own way out of some personal tragedy. Hoping some general history might interest him, I also send copies of Nathan Huggins's *Black Odyssey* and Walter Rodney's *How Europe Underdeveloped Africa* and Cheikh Anta Diop's decidedly Afrocentric *The African Origin of Civilization*, a title recommended by a fellow inmate. I send him Cornel West's *Race Matters* and Andrew Hacker's *Two Nations*, which I think might be diagnostically interesting. And, for literature, I send two books I know well, Chinua Achebe's *Things Fall Apart* and Wallace Thurman's *The Blacker the Berry*, aching meditations on the cultural reach of colonialism and racism. Consciously or not, this hidden syllabus, composed of these and so many other readings, is ideologically diverse, reflecting our ecumenical approach to the problem—his jailing, his youth, his failure to complete high school—and a recognition that his miseducation has been profound.

Few of these titles resonate with Eddie. One Christmas holiday, though, I sit by the tree in the living room, the long cord from the kitchen receiver wrapped around my fingers. My toes absentmindedly sift through the delicately wrapped gifts, the foil paper crinkling when I touch it. Holiday music plays softly in the background. Eddie has phoned, and he wants to discuss the Diop book, a rich counterhistory of everything that one might learn in a suburban New Jersey school system. "Were the ancient Egyptians really

Black?" he asks. I have read the first few volumes of Martin Bernal's controversial *Black Athena*, which argues that much of classical antiquity was an offshoot of African culture, and start to walk him through the argument. He repeats the question, seeking a straightforward confirmation rather than a dissertation. "Yes," I reply. Not because I necessarily agree with Bernal, but because Eddie is, for the first time, curious about something. "He wrote that white people were barbarians," he continues; "does this sound right to you?" He wants to talk about African art, about pyramids and statuary. I tell him about the height of Islamic civilization, about medieval Europe as a provincial backwater. I wonder if the glorious past of the continent might be transformative. I hope that this reenvisioning of the continent might counter the overwhelmingly grim imagery of the present—the Somalian civil war, the Ethiopian famine, the Rwandan genocide, the long list of the Black dead in movies, the daily news cycle that centers Black criminality. The opening credits of *The Equalizer*, too. We talk for a long while that night about who writes history, and how that history gets written. I come back to Bernal, and to Arthur Schlesinger's *Disuniting of America*, and to the raging debates about national history standards, Ebonics, and a multicultural curriculum. I sketch out the cosmopolitan life of Arturo Alfonso Schomburg, the avid collector of Black history during the 1920s. I describe for him the scene a hundred years earlier, when W. E. B. Du Bois, then a faculty member at Atlanta University, listened to Columbia anthropologist Franz Boas at a commencement address. Boas spoke of the sophistication of sub-Saharan Africa, its metalworks, its civilized cityscapes. "I was too astonished to speak," Du Bois recalled in his autobiography. "All this I had never heard."

There is a pause on the phone. "Yeah," Eddie replies slowly. "I get that."

"Send me some more," he says at the end of the call. I say that I will—and that I will include a copy of Du Bois's memoir, for good measure. And then, with a note of eagerness, Eddie asks: "Who's next?" I pass the phone to Mark.

That January, though, Eddie is moved to a prison with a fixed library, a long-term assignment to an institution that forbids the delivery of any new books. With that, sadly, our exploratory Black Studies curriculum comes to a temporary end.

33

One Thanksgiving, a couple of years later, Bear gets married. Almost, as he tells it, on a whim. Disdainful of high ceremony, he plans a simple elopement and asks Bob to perform a quick ceremony to make it official. "We'll do it here, at home," Bob replies, game to organize the affair, "and I'll just include a few people. Just a handful of family." Sheryl sends out invitations over email and hustles to the grocery store to get a cake and party napkins. Bob works the phones, coordinates travel itineraries, and brings his judicial robe home. He brushes off his civil-procedure manual, wanting to make sure that he has the details of the ceremony committed to heart. A "few people" mushrooms into dozens.

They have only a few days to plan the affair, and as a consequence of the mad, last-minute scramble, there are some key people missing. Bug and Mae can't make it. Eddie is in prison. I am out west teaching. Anna is there, thankfully, an excited older sister eager to celebrate her brother's good fortune. So is Peter, Bear's half brother from Vietnam, sporting a long beard and dressed in an elaborate red silk shirt with a priestly white stole and a white turban, honoring a new pan-African politics. Amy, their half sister, comes with her hair tied back in a neat ponytail, wearing a brown shirt with tan slacks, looking like a suburban housewife. As the person who first introduced Bear to Libby, Amy presides over the room, her matchmaking prowess on display. Mark, in a white button-down and a tie, is the youngest sibling present, and serves, as usual, as the dutiful recorder, using the family video camera to capture everything.

The wedding takes place on a cold, gray day in a new house, just down the road from the white house with the picket fence. Now that we are grown up and gone, Bob and Sheryl have bought themselves something smaller, and much more remote—a modern Cape Cod with gray clapboard siding, set in the middle of the woods, where no one can see anything. The previous owners had clear-cut a perfect circle in the midst of hundreds of pines and maples, building their home in such a way that the sun is always shining through the windows, showcasing the surrounding woods as forbidding and dark. Bob spends his afternoons walking the perimeter of the property, creating a wilderness path for exercise, and planting fast-growing white pines on the outskirts. He revels in the privacy; more than that, he cultivates it. When a new development is put in next door, he fights to have the permit held up until the builders agree to enhance the line of trees over the two-hundred-yard border between the properties. While making the pathway, he finds an old stone well buried in the undergrowth. It takes him a year to dig it out, and he keeps the pottery shards and glass bottles he discovers in plastic bins in the basement, bringing them out like an archaeologist whenever we return. With curved walls made of carefully cut red shale, the eighteenth-century well is right at the end of the driveway, a visible landmark for anyone who might otherwise miss the hidden driveway. Guests coming for the wedding pause as they pull up, knowing how much time and effort have gone into its reveal. Bob loves its mysterious origins.

Pale and haggard, Bob performs the hastily arranged ceremony in his long black judicial robes. The wedding finds him weakened, struggling to beat cancer—again. His illness—first diagnosed a decade earlier—returned the previous summer when a routine blood test revealed a trend line in the wrong direction. In the past, this would have prompted an immediate and urgent response—from Bob and from all of us—with the rapid establishment of a new medical regime to which he would scrupulously adhere. This time, though, Bob puts off the start of any new chemotherapy, which he knows will wear him out. He has been fighting cancer for ten years. He knows the treatments will wipe him out and he has begun to wonder if this is the end. The pain in his ribs heralds a last act. He doesn't want to meekly retreat into bed at the end of every workday, his body drained of strength, until his luck runs out.

Instead, in the summer before Bear's wedding, he defers treatment and decides to travel to Italy, to the wine-producing Chianti region. Sandi and I tag along. We rent an apartment in the small Etruscan town of Chiusi, where old stone carvings line the streets, and every day seems to be bright and sunny and crisp. It is a glorious, but also tragic, three weeks. By design, the trip has the feel of a grand finale. Bob gapes at the vast seas of sunflowers and the cheapness of mature wine and the inch-thick steaks served with just a little salt. He wanders through towns, speaking no Italian, and orders giant blocks of cheese and gloriously overstuffed pastries. He has left his driver's license at home—an uncharacteristic oversight—which gives him a chance to be an observant passenger, noting all the castles and churches, researching them in his Baedeker guide, and calling out obscure facts to the rest of us. One night, on the veranda of the apartment he has rented, Bob sweeps Sheryl up and they dance slowly while the sun sets behind them. He is playful and reckless for the entire trip. As we visit vineyard after vineyard, driving along the narrow roads that wrap themselves around hills and wind their way through valleys, Bob will burst into song, sharing with the countryside the various Italian curse words he has learned, stringing them together in a jubilant, triumphant, nonsensical ballad.

Bob and Sheryl in Italy, summer of 2000, after his cancer returned, and in the midst of a much-anticipated trip that he refused to put off.

In these memories Bob is vivacious and dynamic, handsome and full of false health. The cancer is in his bones, plotting his death, but not yet controlling him.

When we come back from the trip in early August, I head off to a job and Bob starts chemotherapy. A few months later, by Thanksgiving, when he presides over Bear's wedding, it is clear that he is losing the fight. He seems shockingly hollowed out, his scalp shaved, his face smoothed out by the steroids, his eyes gravely self-aware, hinting at a great sadness, capturing the inevitability of his end even in the midst of so much familial joy. Family members who haven't seen him in a few weeks are horrified. Sheryl is protective, and always within sight.

The wedding is in the living room in the new house, in front of the big fireplace. At Bob's request, Mark lights a small fire before the guests arrive, and the room smells lightly of cherry. There are twenty people in the space, including many close relatives, Bear's friends, and the family of the bride. Libby, dark skinned, her hair in braids, wears a white silk dress, and carries herself with all the dignity of a Marine Corps veteran. Her nervous, excited smile is a jubilant contradiction to her disciplined body language and posture.

Bob holds the text of the wedding rite in his hands. When he speaks, there is so much Jersey City on his tongue. Bob grew up at a moment in time when regional accents were smoothed out in movies and on television, replaced by a sort of generic "mid-Atlantic" accent in the nation's soundscape, a reflection of the mid-century unification of whiteness. Now, depleted and less cautious, he has let the Jersey City boy back into the room. His vowels are rounded. Consonants are dropped. Wearing his typical dark suit and tie under his robes, he reads the script carefully, walking the two prospective partners through the ritual of marriage. Eve—Libby's daughter—stands by his side, holding the rings in a small box. Libby dabs tears from the corners of her eyes. Bear, his two-inch Afro neatly picked out, wears a formal, deep blue, Asian-inspired outfit, the sort of thing that Steve James might wear, with two rows of buttons running from his neck to his waist, a high collar, and broad white cuffs, rolled back. His face is serious, even forbidding, as if the fate of the world is at stake.

Libby reads her vows from a piece of paper, a crisply delivered, precise, and very personal revision, but it hews close to the script. While she reads, Eve stands perfectly still, the rings held aloft, staring into the video camera, and matching the formal, stiff mood in the room. But when it's Bear's turn, the mood shifts. He drops theatrically to one knee, takes Libby's hands in his, and offers a brocaded soliloquy, larded with colorful, ornate metaphors. He brings the assembled guests back to his origin point, to Vietnam, where Mae, Peter, and Amy gave him "the gift of love." For the first four years of his life, Bear admits, he prayed for nothing but peace. "When I was five," he continues, "it was love and hope that brought me to America, to my Yahweh-given family." Yahweh. Elohim. Haile Selassie. As he goes deeper, Bear calls out these figures, describing his guiding religious principles, reminding the room of his newfound, heartfelt Rastafarianism. For the previous few years, whenever we returned for Thanksgiving, he would bring along the heavy *Book of Yahweh*, sharing his deep understanding of philosophy and self-help and mysticism over turkey, oyster stuffing, and canned cranberry sauce. He sought no converts, of course, just listeners among his brothers and sisters. Now, kneeling in front of a packed room, his bride trembling with emotion, Bear reminds us of the road he has traveled. He closes by reciting his gifts: his love, and hope, and faith. "These are the only three things that I possess in the world," he concludes, "and I give them to you." Everyone has been holding their breath, and now, at last, they exhale. The room erupts in applause. Bear rises to stand next to Libby, to complete the formal ceremony, to say the words that everyone already knows by heart: "With this ring . . ." He is oblivious to the cheers.

After the ceremonial kiss has been granted, the couple prepares to jump the broom. Libby, acknowledging the diversity of the room, the presence of white people and Black people and brown people all in the same space, explains the meaning of the broom, that Africanist signifier of another future, another stage of life, a new set of relations. Bob kneels down on one side and Sheryl is on the other, each holding an end of the broom, a delicate and decorative thing, stitched together from twigs and decorated with ribbons. The new couple—beaming, but with great intent—hop over. Then they switch roles, and Bear and Libby hold the broom for Bob and Sheryl. "Hold it real low," Bob jokes, eliciting laughter in the room. All of the other couples in the room, no matter their color or combination, follow the tradition, hand in hand stepping over the broom held by Bear and Libby.

The couple are soon ringed by friends and family. Champagne flute in hand, a big grin on his face, Bear jokes that he wanted a small wedding—just an intimate little thing, with only him and Libby, Bob and Sheryl. "My botched elopement," he calls it. What Bear proposed has become a big, ribald family affair, with wisecracking aunts and uncles and cousins and brothers and sisters. "Nothing in my family has ever been done alone." Bear laughs and looks around the room as he says it. "We've always done everything together." The room responds with more laughter. Mark raises his glass to "my brother, who once rubbed my face in his armpit when I called him a 'sweat-hog.'" With a chuckle, Amy remembers that when he was younger, Peter would trick Bear into touching the electrical socket in their home in Saigon. Then Peter, the self-appointed moral conscience of the room, speaks up. "Your dreams are going to come true," he says reassuringly. "I will be here for it. *All of us* will be." The stress on those last words—all of us—is hard to miss. Peter's eyes flick to Bob when he says them.

The circle disbands, and the reception becomes church basement–style kaffeeklatsch. Stevie Wonder and Aretha Franklin play in the background. Larry Graham belts out "One in a Million You." Small groups form, with a dozen different conversations happening at once. Bear, Amy, and Peter take photographs as a trio. Mark finds the three of them in the kitchen talking about Bear's outfit—"custom-made in Vietnam," he tells them. Anna holds court in the family room, in the dining room, in the hallway, in the kitchen. Everyone has a camera out, taking pictures with Bear and Libby. Sheryl pauses to make a connection with "the mothers." The dining room table is full of fresh fruit, shrimp cocktail, sliced ham, and finger sandwiches. A big bucket sits in the middle, filled with forks and knives and bright blue napkins. The coffee pot is out on a side table. Mark teaches Libby how to use the video camera. Bear jokes that the ring on his finger is already weighing him down. A friend asks Bear what he remembers of Vietnam, and he recalls the airplane, a US serviceman standing with a rifle at the door, and the wild flight out of the city. At last, there is a two-layer cake, decorated with autumnal flowers and a white plastic centerpiece. As Bear waits with the knife, Mark runs around turning lights on so that he can take better photographs. Predictably, Libby stuffs the first piece in Bear's mouth and the room cheers.

For a little while afterward, Bob stands in a corner, talking to Libby's mom. Then he moves to the low-slung, red leather couch in the living room. And then, abruptly, he vanishes. Only Sheryl knows that he has retreated to the second floor, lying down on the bed to rest. Despite the company and the roaring fireplace, his dress shirt is too thin, and he's gotten cold and tired. When he returns an hour later, he is wearing a thick, warm sweater and comfortable sneakers. His face is paler, his shoulders stooped. His voice is lower, too, reduced to a half whisper by shortness of breath. Anna asks him how he is feeling. "Washed out," he admits, with a sheepish grin. "Worn." Bob's return to the celebration comes just as people begin to leave, slowly, in ones and twos. Wanting to be gracious, he stands in the small foyer, leaning against the wall, diminished and quiet, but still the host, ready to offer a hug or a handshake.

Bear brings him a marriage certificate for a few final signatures— Peter and Amy serve as the official witnesses. They talk for a minute, and Bob leaves again.

The guests exit quickly, now. Some offer a quiet word of thanks to Bear, discreetly embracing the couple of the hour, and then slipping out the side door. Others call dramatic attention to their departure, lining up in the front hallway to say their goodbyes. Peter, especially, needs a crowd. On his way out the door, he calls everyone together for a big send-off. "I retired for nine years in Colorado," he laughs as he says it, "and now it is time to get back to work." He half-jokingly offers Mark, the day's videographer, a job with I-in-Eye Productions, his aspirational filmmaking company. If Bear is uniformly serious, Peter is warm and friendly, fast with a joke, working the exit line with the smoothness of a salesman. He is halfway out the door, standing on the stoop, drifting toward the gravel driveway when he sees Bob in the front hallway, breathless, pale, and leaning against the wall for support.

He fell asleep again in the living room, with Sheryl holding his hand, and everyone vacated, giving him time and space. He woke up with a start when he heard Peter saying goodbye, when he heard the voice of the child he has known for decades. Now, back in the foyer, the jokes stop and Peter's face drops when he sees Bob is awake. With an urgent suddenness, he reenters the house. They embrace tightly, while the younger man pays a compliment to the "blessed, blessed house," to the spirits of amity and comity that animate the hallways, bedrooms, and kitchen.

Looking Bob in the eye, Peter speaks even more softly, so that no one else can hear him. "You take care of yourself, all right?"

Peter is saying goodbye. Goodbye to the man he met at the farmhouse in 1975. Goodbye to the man who raised his brother. Goodbye to the man who welcomed him into the house as a guest so long ago, and who encouraged the two brothers to stay connected. Goodbye to the man who has treated him kindly, almost like a son, in the decades since.

"You take care of yourself, all right?" A gentle instruction, an imperative ending in a question. As he asks it, Peter reaches up, cradling the back of Bob's head in his hand. An intimate, loving gesture. Bob smiles and puts his hands on Peter's shoulders.

"Take care of yourself." An impossible task, as everyone knows. "I will," Bob replies quietly, accepting the role reversal with some grace. His shaved head bows down. He lowers his eyes and looks at his shoes.

Peter smiles slightly, with eyes only for Bob. He opens his mouth to say something else—perhaps to express the hope that they will see each other again soon—but thinks differently, and instead embraces the older man one last time. Then, with a broad smile and a wave to the rest of the guests, he steps out into the cold. Bob watches him leave, and then heads back to the living room, where the warmth of the fireplace beckons.

34

Bob works a few months longer until he dies.

One Friday in May of 2001, he stops off at a mall in Bridgewater to catch a sale at Lord & Taylor. It is late afternoon, and he buys, as he is wont to do, a set of snazzy new dress shirts wrapped in plastic, putting them in the back of his car to deal with later. The shirts are a steal. Flush with his triumph, he heads home, stopping once to get pizza on Route 202. Pizza is a personal favorite, and he has a preferred joint on the route home—Phil's Pizza, the kind of weathered, working-class place that serves a thin Jersey pie with oil and mozzarella cheese glistening across the top, the kind of slice that you have to fold twice to eat. He eats, showers, watches a little television, and goes to bed early.

He passes away peacefully in his sleep. After years of chemotherapy, his heart suddenly, unexpectedly gives out. Sheryl wakes up in the morning to find him gone.

This is a surprising death, especially given that we are all sure that it will be cancer that ultimately takes him. Or that his ending will be suitably theatrical, with all of us clustered, as if we were in a movie, around a hospital bed. That is how I preemptively imagine it, in the time before his death, when it feels inevitable but still well off in the distance. I dream that there will be an agonizingly long period of time in the hospital—enough time for reflective conversation, for some necessary mending. One of us will always be asleep in some corner chair. We might read to him from a favorite book. We will all attend his final breath. Together, with our hands intertwined, our variegated flesh juxtaposed, a beatific smile on his face and on ours.

A Hollywood ending.

Instead, we are shocked, and immediately plunge into personal and collective chaos. For one thing, we are scattered. Anna, living in Jersey City, and Mark, living in Hoboken, are nearby and get there first. Bear is in North Carolina, roughly a day's drive away. With his usual patience and stolid determination, he wends his way north, one hour at a time. Bug is in the next town over, but never comes, now estranged from Bob, from Sheryl, and from us, a distancing that has grown slowly, inch by inch, in the wake of the incident. Eddie is in jail, having been arrested after assaulting someone with a deadly weapon.

I am on the other side of the planet. So it is and so it feels, in Madrid, where I have traveled for work. I call Sandi that morning to let her know that I've arrived at the hotel safely; she goes to relay the news of my arrival to Sheryl and then returns my call immediately, in tears, to share the terrible news. I crawl into the shower, sit down in the basin, and weep as the water runs down my face until I can weep no more. And then, thinking of us, I get dressed, wearily, and head right back to the airport. It takes me a solid day of travel—I am routed through Paris, Charles de Gaulle, then have to get a car and drive from Queens to New Jersey—to get home. The airlines do their part to get me to the States, but the Belt Parkway is jammed and characteristically slow. Bear beats me home by twelve hours.

When Sandi and I pull up, the house is a hive, buzzing with emotion. Aunts and uncles and cousins have converged on the place, cluttering the driveway with cars parked haphazardly. They've uncorked a full-on Irish wake. I can hear bellowing voices in the backyard and wild, unrestrained laughter. I walk in the front door looking for Sheryl, shuffling past a pile of packages strewn on a nearby bench. A glass of red wine is pressed into my hand almost immediately, and Mark, and Anna, and Bear gather around me. The sounds of music and laughter and sobbing and boastful speechmaking overwhelm my senses in every room.

Arriving a day later than most, I compete for attention with the army of delivery trucks—most of them carrying food from friends and family—that arrive regularly. There is a tower of salami, roast beef, and Italian hoagies stacked on the kitchen counter, and the room smells pleasantly—or nostalgically?—of fresh bread, lunch meats, oil and vinegar. The dining room table is covered in big, square casseroles, all of them dropped off by generous neighbors. Somewhat humorously, the UPS delivery person arrives pretty regularly, jockeying for a position in the driveway, and routinely hands off another set of packages that Bob ordered for himself that same Friday before turning in for the night. Each time, we greet the deliveryman with a rousing cry. The crowd favorite is an oversize box with an elaborate felt fedora. Opening the boxes, we laugh while we weep, wondering what on earth Bob was thinking about in his final days. Inspired by the delivery of each parcel, we drink more, and toast his reckless spending habits. One thing is clear: he would have been surprised by his passing, too.

A souvenir, I know, is a magical thing, a materialization of memory, reminiscence condensed into a single physical object. A touch, a look, a scent evokes a sort of time travel. The very first souvenir I claim in the wake of Bob's passing is that ridiculously garish brown fedora. It sits in the hallway for a week or so in a giant delivery box while we grapple with everyday necessities. And then, when we start trying to clean up, I take it for myself. A mere glance at it reminds me of his indescribably unique fashion sense, his outlandish, implacable personality. His optimism, even when facing death, that the next day would be better, and that the solution was out there somewhere.

My son keeps the fedora in his room, a part of his memorial to a man he never met. It sits on a shelf alongside Bob's navy officer's cap, with its elaborate gold embroidery, and a white construction helmet with the state seal on the front, a memento of another time, when the courthouse was under construction and Bob was asked to survey the work. Occasionally, he brings it down to examine it, running his fingers along the brim and the crown, gently brushing the dust off of the trim.

35

A few days later, we gather at the funeral home in Somerville to wait for the public. We are in a century-old home that has been retrofitted for this sort of thing, just a few blocks down from the county courthouse. It is vast and silent, layered with carpet and full of soft furniture to absorb sound. Looking left or right, you will find rooms of requirement, rooms that can be closed off in an instant with heavy sliding doors. We shuffle around, still in shock, making quiet small talk. The home's director fusses over us and shares his anodyne condolences. He waits for everyone to arrive before he begins to formally lay out the schedule for the next few hours. And then, with no fanfare, he walks us into the viewing room, where Bob lies in an open casket. His hair, I note with no real emotion, is perfect.

Bug shows up after the initial instructions are given.

Eddie is in the county lockup, just down Main Street from the funeral home, jailed for another violent offense, but he is due to arrive at any minute. We appealed for compassion and a temporary release, though I cannot remember to whom. Somehow, arrangements have been made, a small town's accommodation to the passing hero's legacy, so that his youngest son can honor him. In a way, this bending-of-the-rules is the last act of liberal patriarchy, a reminder that the passing of the great white man, the architect of our multiracial ensemble, should extract a performance of grief from each of us. Before the front doors swing open for the public, then, the sheriff's office brings Eddie through the home's back entrance to pay his respects.

We are required, the officiant instructs after a brief conversation with the officer, to stay separated from him. He isn't allowed to see us, to be embraced, to be comforted. A partition door separates us, another reminder of the building's functionally segregated spaces. As he stands before the casket, bookended by uniformed officers, we pull the door open a few inches and peek through it.

He stands solemnly—with a great stillness—wearing a light gray suit that is slightly too large for him, his hair cut close to the scalp. He looks tired and sad, with shoulders that are stooped. His skin is sallow. The homemade teardrop tattoo on his cheek stands out against his paler-than-usual flesh. I exhale, feeling grateful in that moment that he isn't in an orange prison coverall.

That is it. That is the very last time we are all together. That fractal moment, defined by our relation to the lacquered door, those glittering steel handcuffs, the open casket, the looming officers, and our sequestration in another room. We are within ten feet of Eddie, but the entire racial state, with its regime of barbed wire and steel shackles, lies between us. I can still recall the feel of the wood on the partition door, warm and slick with old varnish, as we seek our brother's face, our diverse structural positions encoded in the funeral home's very layout. That glossy door, meant to give bereaved families some privacy, establishing an enclosure around "the good," protecting us from his supposedly corrupting influence. There is a brief, stunning flash of connection—we seeing him, in a suit that we hastily arranged to be delivered, flanked, almost theatrically, by his jailers; and he seeing us, in our consanguinity.

We have all been hoping to make reassuring eye contact of some kind, to give Eddie a wink, an affirming look, anything that will signal our care. He looks over, catches our frantic gestures, and gives a slight smile.

And then, with brisk, clinical precision, he is escorted out and returned to the ordinary custody of the carceral state. We scramble, paralleling his movement to the back door, and through a kitchen window watch him leave. For a time, he sits alone with his thoughts in the rear of the county sheriff's office car. We, in turn, watch through the window until they pull away.

With barely a pause for breath, we are ushered back to the viewing room. The front doors are swept open, and we stand to face our father's admirers, each of us a fixed racial symbol, graciously accepting their condolences. Bob, as a prominent figure and a respected lawyer, is able even in death to command a potent ensemble. There is a long line of mourners outside. "He was a saint," they tell us. Those who once watched us so closely—with a wary, discerning eye—now pause to endorse his most fervent liberal intentions.

"He was a saint."

"Your father was a saint."

"Your parents were saints."

The words come out like a poem. A performance of sincerity and aggrievement, accompanied by a physical touch. A hug. A handshake. Each time those words are spoken, they look us up and down, seeking our acknowledgment of his beatification, seeing in our composed unity proof of our intelligent design. We shake hands, nod, provide level stares and gracious smiles, and play our role. We envelop Sheryl, who is in shock, wordless and blank-faced. My stomach turns. Eddie's absence—and his representation as "the bad son"—ensures that we, in our pleasing multiplicity, are seen as dutiful.

I cannot unsee Eddie, his head bent down over the casket, wearing handcuffs.

36

The *Courier News* runs a front-page story about the funeral.

"Judge Was Devoted to Family, Court," the headline declares right beneath a photo of us. Or, all of us except for Eddie. Reading the black-and-white text, one would discern that Bob was a much-loved state judge, a family man, a veteran of the JAG corps, and a technophile. And that he has left behind a raft of votaries and a vast, sprawling family: six kids of his own, a grandchild, and a larger collection of nieces and nephews. This is a moving journalistic account, rich with adoring quotes from family members, friends, and fellow jurists.

The accompanying photograph includes an iconic representation of a new kind of American family. Three brothers, dressed in somber funeral suits, surround the casket. Bear looks down, as if in prayer, while his stepdaughter, Eve, has her head turned, listening intently to the director of the funeral home, the steward of souls from the previous day. He, in turn, is issuing directions to us all in hushed tones. Mark and I face each other across the flag-draped casket. The casket itself stands out, with its thick red and white stripes running horizontally,

A scene from the funeral in May of 2001, reprinted from the front page of the local newspaper. (© Kathy Johnson – USA TODAY NETWORK)

their brightness at odds with our somber comportment. So, too, does the diversity of the mourning family, our Black and brown and white skin tones, our heads bowed in sorrow, reflecting mutual affection for the dead hero.

The tactile memory of that day lingers in my skin. The air that day is brilliant, cool, and dry, and I feel it on the back of my hands and my face. As we stand together, I run my fingers across the flag, feeling its textures, the hardness of the metal coffin lid beneath. Sheryl, ashen-faced and mute, stands behind us, tightly gripping the hands of Anna and Bug. I can hear her breathing, sobbing.

Inside the church, the front pew is taken up by members of the state judiciary. Stolid, serious-looking men and women soaked in gravitas sit on hard, dark oaken benches, ordinarily reserved for the penitent. The chief justice of the state supreme court is there, the *News* notes, as is an associate justice. As are various other county freeholders, elected officials, court clerks, members of the state bar, colleagues, neighbors, friends, and family.

Mark ascends to the lectern first. Reaching inside his suit jacket, he fumbles with a letter he has written to Bob, straightening the folded paper a few times, biding his time. With a shuddering breath, then, he loosens his shoulders, gathers himself, and looks up at the windows at the far end of the church. Addressing Bob directly, he begins with the simplest declarations of love and admiration before turning to the man's character, his faith in justice. "I know how strongly you believed in the system," he shares. "No matter what the situation was, you had faith the system would work." The letter turns back to the family, back to us. "You were," he continues, "the epitome of a father." "Right now," he emphasizes, tears on his cheeks, "our family is stronger than ever."

Bear—with his dark-brown skin and his deep baritone voice—is next. Taller and broader than Mark, he smiles at the audience, disarming them in an instant. "I stand before you in awe of his ability to love," he confesses, arms outstretched as if delivering a sermon, closing his eyes for effect. "I stand in awe of the love he shared with the world." In conversational tones and with abundant good humor, he goes on to celebrate Bob, reminiscing about his "contagious laughter and warm smile." He tries to evoke, for the listeners, what it was like to live behind the white picket fence with Bob, to be drawn together in relation to this singular, heroic figure. "He had a way of listening that made you feel loved," he stresses, remembering their great epistolary debates, wherein Bob worried about his son's reputation; "whether he agreed with you or disagreed with you, he made you feel loved." And then, at the close, Bear brings the audience together in a chorus of shared laughter, reminding them all that "for the first time, heaven was going to open its gates to a lawyer."

Much like the receiving line at the wake, this is a virtuosic, balletic performance. And it, too, is closely watched and greatly appreciated. The *News*, quoting Bear's remarks extensively, helpfully reminds readers that Bob's eldest son was "adopted at age 5 from an orphanage in Vietnam." Every saint, we all know, needs to have performed a miracle, and then to have that same miracle documented for the public and sanctioned by the Church. That day, Bear is the proof. Bob once saved him. Now, with a smile on their faces, they all know. Or are reminded.

The two brothers on the dais are a touching, camera-ready pair. Bear is the older brother, the engineer, the good son with a new wife and family of his own. Mark is the younger brother, the teacher dedicated to a life of service and working in a small inner-city school in Newark, the embodiment of liberalism's best effort. Their complementarity catches the journalist's eye and ear, as it is meant to. After decades of careful study, we know the power of a black-and-white connection on stage. Bear and Mark, representatives of our politics of integration, are brought to life in front of the altar, their familiar pairing offering additional proof to our public—if any is needed—that the experiment has been a success.

The family escorts the casket to the curb. The photographer stands at a distance, catching us together in the bright sunlight. Tomorrow's headline is already written.

As the crowd disperses, a keening, heartbreaking cry comes from the church. Bug howls like a wild, wounded animal, drawing us back inside. We haven't seen him in many months, despite Bob's effort to reconnect. When a family member delivered the news of our father's death, Bug's initial response was cold and dispassionate: "I'm sorry for your loss." At the wake, he was quiet and detached, a mute, half-hearted participant in the day's events. Now, as we prepare to leave for the burial, he has collapsed.

Fictive, cinematic families fall apart, just like any other kind of assemblage. Repairs take time, dedication. They can take decades. Sometimes families fall back together. Sometimes the repair is impossible.

A few years earlier, after a gradual drift toward independence, Bug simply fails to come to Thanksgiving dinner. Bob decides to just show up at his apartment, hoping that a heartfelt, radical gesture will offer a chance at a much-wanted reconciliation. He brings a beloved uncle, a peaceable third party, to evince the love and care of a family that extends beyond us, beyond the eight of us who once lived together in that white house with the picket fence. It doesn't go well. Bug stands stony-faced on the brick front porch of his apartment complex, refusing to let them inside. Refusing to speak.

Bob comes home dejected. Striving for reconnection, he writes Bug a letter, expressing puzzlement and worry.

"For a long time," he confesses, "I have felt like I am walking on eggshells when I talk to you. Maybe that has been a mistake. I am worried about you. You have seemed alone and isolated. There is no reason for that. You have a large family that loves you and wants you as a part of their lives." He adds, "We missed you at Thanksgiving. Will you be here for Christmas?"

Bug's reply comes a few days later. Hastily written on lined notepaper, tightly folded and heavily creased, it is addressed to the family as if we are strangers. A rejection, at the very start, of the familiar predicate of the entire conversation. Of "us." And a fitting beginning to a lengthy excoriation of our premise. He goes on to request—in prose dripping with sarcasm—an end to the armchair clinical psychiatry. Showing up on Bug's front porch, Bob offered a from-the-hip diagnosis, which is taken as a provocation—and soundly rejected in the letter. Bug blames the misunderstanding on the narrow-mindedness of the American middle class, on the popularity of psychological labels and the valorization of fixed types of good behavior, on Bob's intellectual and moral simplicity.

Even now, I read this as a radical gesture of refusal, a defiant unwillingness to be constrained by conventions of the family as Bob and Sheryl defined them. To demonstrate that he does not wish to be pitied. Or rescued. To assert that there is no reason to be grateful. A determination to make his own way, to eschew labels. An insolence, as the French philosopher Michel Foucault would call it, that reveals the weight of one life coiled and tensed against the overbearing discipline of the white house with the picket fence. It is one of the tragic ironies of this family, this instantiation of us, that a regime of care, of salvage and repair, can also legitimately—righteously—be understood as a cruel disciplining of the racial self.

Bob is indefatigable. He tries, once more, hinting at his illness, using the levers of guilt, shame, and pity. "I'm still fighting the good fight," he confesses at the close, "but it is not clear if I am holding my own or losing the battle with cancer. I'm in the middle of a battery of tests that may shed some light on what is happening. I turned 60 this year and my warranty has run out." He asks if they might have lunch someday. "Life is very unpredictable. Let's not wait too long to get together again."

There is silence, after that letter, until the end.

Before he dies, Bob often speaks to us about this estrangement, emphasizing its tragic, indecipherable plotlines. He is deeply troubled by this exchange of letters and by the texture of Bug's reproach, which he finds to be irrational. But he also lets it be, and stops writing or visiting that front stoop, assuming that he still has time to reach Bug, to bring him back to the family.

In the church, the wailing continues. Wearing all black, and with dark sunglasses that never come off, Bug has curled himself into a ball in a back room, wept, railing against the unresolved disputes, the torn sinew, the desolate truth. His piercing, mournful wail is the most visceral, plaintive sound I have ever heard. Others will remember the pleasing duet of Bear and Mark. But, for me, that howl is the lasting soundscape for the funeral.

37

We find the shirts from Lord & Taylor, the shirts that he bought at the mall on the drive home that Friday, in the back of Bob's car the next day. They are still in their crisp plastic packaging, still stacked neatly in a white bag from the store, their careful organization a sign of Bob's faith that he was going to be around for a while. We see evidence of that faith everywhere. Next to the shirts we find a new pool skimmer. And packages continue to arrive.

That material abundance, though, is a problem. There is so much stuff. Sheryl needs help disposing of it, including his vast wardrobe, his abundant tools and technologies, and his disorganized archive of paperwork. Bob was, we all know, a serial collector and world-class impulse shopper, and the house is filled with stuff he accumulated out of need or want. Cameras. Nail clippers. Gadgets of all kinds. Shoes and shirts and jackets. Enough to fill several closets. She can go through it herself alone, after we have all left. That might take a year. And it might also be emotionally difficult, as every decision will return her to the shock of that morning's discovery, or to the wild sentimentality of the wake. Or she can enlist us in the effort right now, in the moment when everything is already shit. The work is going to be horrible anyhow. Wisely, she decides to do the latter, and so we set out to redistribute what remains of him.

More than anything, though, Sheryl needs help going through his big, dark rolltop desk, that fittingly convoluted monument to his grand and complicated personality. The desk has been with us from the beginning. Tall and imposing, the exterior is a glossy black pine, a match for the furniture they originally purchased for the Green Room so long ago. The interior, hidden away by the rolltop screen, is a maze of small drawers, nooks, and hidden crevices, with mysteries in every tight space. When we were little, we would open the desk to explore his most intimate territories, finding strange, mysterious trinkets everywhere—an old porcelain owl, an impossibly small antique glass milk bottle, a letter opener shaped like a sword, a broken pocket watch.

Somewhere in that desk, Sheryl hopes, is a set of life-insurance policies she needs to help cover the funeral costs. Bob didn't share any emergency plans with her, and his passing was obviously a surprise, so she has only the faintest grasp of where things might be and what she might need to do in order to live independently. On a deeper level, she worries that she will have to take control of—and understand—the clunky, user-unfriendly checkbook software he installed on his computer. And that we might not be there to help her. Once more, the paying of the bills is a source of strain.

Bear, our resident computer expert, takes the lead on the forensic recovery of the laptop while the rest of us explore the desk. It takes a few hours to find the life-insurance policies, largely because they are scattered and strangely located. One of them is in a file labeled "In Transit," and the others are nestled amid the most random assortment of papers and bills and catalogs in other files. We sit with the policies for a bit, struggling to understand why they aren't together, why they aren't just in the empty folder marked "Life Insurance." The desk gives no answer. We find an entire drawer filled with undeveloped rolls of film and drawers stuffed with old bills. There are several nail clippers and an old-school hairbrush, further proof—we joke—that he wasn't expecting to die anytime soon.

Eventually, and despite Bear's best efforts to explain how everything works, Mom gives up on the software and just starts using a blank spiral notebook. Eminently practical, she sits down at the dining room table and draws up a simple list of bills and due dates. Bear, meanwhile, keeps digging. The rest of us try to make sense of the trove of contradictions we have uncovered.

"I think I found something."

It is Bear, diligently and systematically sifting through the laptop, who discovers the goodbye letter.

It is dated a year before his death. By the summer of 2000, Bob knew that his cancer had come back, and he was in pain, but he decided to defer treatment for a little while so he could fulfill his lifelong dream of exploring Tuscany, with its medieval churches and hilltop castles, its olive groves and vineyards. We were all worried about his deferral of treatment, and the trip—two weeks he planned out in great detail—had a melancholy tone to it. Still, there was quite a bit of joy and more than a little reflection. It is unsurprising, in a way, that he returned home from the vast seas of sunflowers to draft a somber goodbye letter to us all.

The note Bear finds is uncharacteristically full of small typos. This suggests, to me, that he wrote it in one sitting and never returned to it for editing. That is, he set out to express himself earnestly, in raw, confessional prose, and probably forgot that the note even existed. Certainly, it is pure luck—amplified by our need to reconstruct his finances so that Mom can get on living—that we even find it. And yet, rereading it now, there is something in the urgency of those last few years, in the need for repair and reconnection, in the frenetic engagement with Eddie's circumstance and Bug's estrangement, that reveals a more determined focus on his decline. On some level, I realize, he always knew his death was imminent, growing nearer and nearer.

Bear reads it aloud.

"I've been reflecting on death somewhat lately," Bob began, "but I don't want to talk about it too much because I'm concerned that it could bring my mood down and probably make Sheryl and the rest of the family more worried. By writing these thoughts down, I get it off my mind and leave something behind to make things a little easier for those I may leave behind."

This all sounds just like Bob, this notion that he might be able to expel his worst thoughts onto the computer screen so that they can't haunt him any longer.

"My body, while never a masterpiece, is in decline. I have begun to think of it as a 1950 Studebaker. Good functional design, durable, relatively inexpensive to run, but not meant to be a functioning antique."

We pause and laugh at the idea that Bob was "relatively inexpensive."

"I want you to remember me—but do not waste time lamenting. Say a prayer for me when you think of me and move on. Feel free to remember and laugh at my many foibles. What was the name of that movie? I pass on the message my father left with me: Keep the family together. God has brought you together. You should draw strength from one another. Don't hold grudges! I love you all so much."

Bob may have loved movies, but he was terrible at remembering their features, and he would routinely get them horribly wrong, scrambling the titles, misnaming the actors. It was a source of great humor. And yet, in a moment when he pondered death, he drew directly from their clichéd dialogue and hokey sentimentality. The letter reads like something from a Frank Capra film—and that, I know, is because he loved those moves, and watched them over and over and over.

"Take care of your mother," he added, sounding again like a Hollywood script. "She is the love of my life. During my teens, I used to pray daily that God would send me a wife and I know my prayers were answered. She is a saint! She has made my life a wonderful thing."

"I am sorry I couldn't hang around any longer."

A few private words addressed directly to Mom close out the letter. At the bottom, he typed, colloquially: "More later . . ." He never returned, though. The file was opened just the one time, on the day he wrote these words, and he never revised it or edited it. There is nothing else on the computer like it.

That is it: an unedited, hastily written note, drafted a year before his death. A self-deprecating, lighthearted paean to the foundational, even generic ideas of family, togetherness, and solidarity, in which he encourages forgiveness and begs us to stay together.

The discovery takes the wind out of us. There is still so much to do. And so little time.

We redistribute Bob's things, the most basic material reminders of his existence, as best we can. Bear takes some suits, of which there are many. So does Mark. Bob has so many tools that we all take whatever we need. I take an old hammer, one I remember from childhood, and a sign with his name on it that I made in wood shop. "Attorney at Law," it reads, mimicking the metal standard he hung at the fence line, that warning to every stranger that something precious lay within. I take some shoes, and some winter jackets, one of which I still wear. Bear takes the rolltop desk. We load it all up in the back of our cars—or, in Bear's case, a U-Haul trailer—hug each other tight, and drive back to Jersey City. Or North Carolina. Or Queens.

38

A year later, we have our first reunion. Eddie is still in jail.

The weekend starts with a quick, comfortable return to the old grooves in our shared life. The weather is sunny, warm, and glorious. We walk through town together, hand in hand, laughing and joking and stopping only to enter some small store or to admire some old house. We eventually come upon an old athletic field and find a small group of white kids playing ball in the sandlot. Boastful and exulting in our togetherness, we challenge them—our platoon against theirs— and they accept, albeit with a knowing smirk, suspecting an easy win.

They are right, of course. We are relatively old and tired, and they are young and nimble, racing around the field like gazelles. For an hour or so, though, some of the old magic is back. We are joyful and familiar with one another's rhythms. We all know where to play Bear and Mark, our two best athletes, and where to hide Anna, so she won't have to do much in the outfield. We jaw at each other relentlessly, and trash-talk those kids, bringing smiles to their faces. We hurl ourselves into the game with an enthusiasm our bodies do not share, an enthusiasm that goes well beyond the game's immediate significance. As I remember it, we revel in that intoxicating sense of togetherness and

camaraderie, once more enthralled to the notion of "us," to our mutu-
ally reinforced star power, to the expansion of our shared public ego.

It is achingly familiar, a reminder to us all of what it used to be like
when we were together, when we were younger, when Bob was alive,
when we could be offstage, and before it all went radically sideways.
Games of inches in church. The sun-tanning competition. Larger
family get-togethers where we entered as a swashbuckling, power-
drinking gang. Those endless days at the lake in New Hampshire.

Despite the loss, then, we walk back to our house from the game
triumphantly, dirty and sweaty and thrilled with our teamwork. We
open some wine and melt into the soft leather furniture of the place.
And then we spend time reminiscing in soft voices, thinking about
Bob, about us, catching up on life's twists, and revisiting every play of
the game against those kids on the old baseball field.

Later that night, the usual racial banter has returned, one of the
comfortable grooves from our past. Anna says something in her
sometimes-imperfect English—a habit when she is speaking fast, or
emotional, and the sort of thing we all made sport of before. I jokingly
correct her, the kind of move I made—we all made—for years without a thought. And that night, when we are all so saturated with feeling and drink, the familiar joke lands all wrong. Anna leans forward,
finger pointing—at me and also at what I signify, at the vast edifice
behind me.

"That is racist, and I can't take it anymore."

The laughter in the room, so long a staple of our family dynamic,
is instantly snuffed out. The room is dark and spacious, but that night
it seems phantasmagorically small, with dark-green walls that suf-
focate the conversation, throbbing with an intensity of correlative
feeling. The euphoria of teamwork is replaced, almost instantly, by
a kind of terrifying sobriety, as if suddenly and without warning we
have found ourselves locked into a roller coaster, with no way out but
to go forward.

Having named the thing she is struggling against, Anna goes on, indexing my failings, the failings of the racial state, and the failures, in so many ways, of us. Of the idea of us, that is. There is a terrifying, heartbreaking asymmetry in the room, Anna explains. She moves through the world in a racialized body—a Korean "half-breed" living in Jersey City. She reminds us of the snide remarks, dark looks, and material wounds she has suffered everywhere, from bodegas to the workplace. Gesturing to our massive backdrop, she notes that I represent the same atmospherics of power and authority she so regularly confronts. I am treating her like a sibling, making a joke of something intimate, poking fun at her, but I am also ignoring in that moment the yawning racial context, the larger world that surrounds us, that envelops her, that ridicules her, that demeans her on a daily basis. With brutal efficiency, she cuts through the last few strands of our carefully manufactured bonds of affection. There never was an us, she implies, or at least not in the way I have imagined.

The narrative she spins that night captures, in high relief, the rapid unraveling of our plot, as much a consequence of Bob's passage as it is the decades that preceded it. As children in a family meant to undo racism, we were asked to learn—and to unlearn—race. To see one another as siblings—to see beyond our skin—but also, dissonantly, to see one another as color-coded, as representatives of different histories and different potentialities. Those parallel lessons are, in the end, impossible to suture together, perhaps especially when we are out and about in the world, separated from one another, once our experiences with race are no longer collected at night and shared over dinner, no longer disarmed by our community.

I lie awake for hours that night, sorting through everything, trying to bind the facts to a narrative that makes sense. A narrative that exonerates me of that terrible charge—and that also restores our logic. But I cannot do both at once. My imagination fails me, and that failure is troublesome and unnerving. The dark walls close in.

39

Eddie gets out of jail later that summer. After visiting the wake in handcuffs, he was returned to the county lockup to serve out the rest of his time. Now, he is paroled He wants to turn a corner, he says, and needs financial support to get back on his feet.

We are ready. And hesitant. Narratives of rebirth are powerful in a family full of new beginnings, and it would never occur to us to do nothing. Still, given the challenges of the past several years, we refuse a simple handover of cash. More than cheerleading, we know that what he needs is money. From experience, though, we just can't trust that he will spend it on food, or clothing, or rent. After some conversation, a meeting is called to lay out the terms. Sheryl and I are dispatched as emissaries in a hastily improvised effort to provide aid and comfort in a moment of need and potential transformation. The others are simply too far away.

The idea is that he has one more chance to get right with the law. We will throw everything we have behind him and hope for the best. Like many previous efforts, this laughably simple approach shows our limits and our blind spots, our trust that we can devise a system that will protect Eddie—and us—and, simultaneously, our incomplete understanding of the unevenness of the world for those marked as Black. This plan is also the final, clearest lesson for us—or perhaps for me—about what we are up against, revealing structures and systems that are bigger than any one of us—and bigger than all of us combined, even in those increasingly rare cases when we all pull in the same direction.

We meet Eddie at an old diner over a tall stack of pancakes. The layout is classic New Jersey, with worn laminate countertops, pie under glass, a long service counter with chromed details for single patrons, and deep booths with red vinyl bench seats for larger parties. None of this is styled as "vintage" or "retro"—all of it merely shopworn, looking old because it is old, not because it appeals to middle-class sensibilities or to nostalgia. Duct tape covers a gash in one of the benches.

Eddie seems upbeat and ready for anything, smiling gently and awkwardly at us. He greets us outside with a hug, and is wearing a gray oversize sweat suit, clean and smelling faintly of laundry detergent, a detail I find reassuring, because it suggests that things are going well with his girlfriend and in life. He has a big appetite, he says.

Two things are true in that moment:

First, we know there isn't much state support available to help felons out on parole. No real job training, no real social safety net, no meaningful support of any kind. Not even in "liberal" New Jersey, which often congratulates itself on being progressive. You leave prison or jail through a guarded metal door. You materialize in real life on a curb, dropped off by a bus. From that moment onward, everything you have ever done follows you like a shadow, a shadow that can be seen in the black-and-white disclosures required on every job application, in the unnatural paleness of your sun-deprived skin, and in the handmade tattoos on your arms and your face. All you have is that shadow—and your family. But the shadow is bigger and heavier. Even then, we know this is true—know that it will be difficult for Eddie to do much beyond trying his best, and that it will be nearly impossible given the representational weight on him as a Black felon with a history of violence. There is power in the notion of personal responsibility, but people are returned to prison because of the pernicious weight of that shadow, because of the resulting stagger on an uneven landscape where some kinds of people—those with the shadow pressing down upon them, Black, brown, poor—are presumed to require inhumane isolation so that everyone else can feel "safe."

Eddie understands all of this, and so do we.

Second, Sheryl and I have not a single clue as to what, exactly, we should do. She certainly doesn't feel like he can move back in with her, given that he repeatedly stole cash and blank checks and other valuables when Dad was alive. She also doesn't feel like she can just pay for his rent for an apartment. She worries that if he stays with an old girlfriend, it won't end well, but there really isn't another option. Eddie is the first person in my generation to have been incarcerated, and there is no body of knowledge that he—or we—can tap, no reservoir of experience with the carceral state. Except, of course, for our powerful connections to the legal system, which aren't helpful. With Bob gone, we have lost all connection to the county and to the criminal justice establishment. We feel terrifyingly alone.

This is the kind of thing that Bob often "handled" by himself.

In Bob's files, there are a dozen copies of a letter from an earlier effort to find Eddie a better job, all of them written by a former boss at a local bagel shop who testified to his maturity and timeliness. "If you decide to hire Eddie," the letter confides, "you will find him to be extremely reliable and honest. He has excellent customer relations skills and is always trying to satisfy every customer." The letters are all addressed to the same place—a chain video store on the main drag in Somerville. But this leaves me puzzled. Did Bob make the copies at work? Why make so many copies of the same letter addressed to the same person? Is the letter a forgery? Did the copy machine malfunction? Did they send the letter to multiple video stores? The thick stack in the files reflects unrealized ambition and hope, either from Eddie, from Bob, or from both. But it is also a mystery to me, further evidence of the dense, dynamic, symbiotic relationship Bob found with Eddie, a sign of the long tail of family history that lies behind our meeting at the diner that day.

In the booth, Eddie sits across from us and we make sad small talk, at first. The scene surely catches the eye of other patrons. An integrated group, with two white folks talking to a younger Black man— sometimes reaching out to touch his hands. A trio speaking in hushed tones and without much laughter.

The rules we lay out are simple. We will provide Eddie with all of the financial support he needs to get a job. All of it. We will buy and drop off all the new clothes he needs. We will hustle out and get gift cards redeemable only at a grocery store for food. If he needs a ride somewhere we will supply it—though he is living with his girlfriend, and within easy walking distance of Somerville's downtown—so we hope he will be able to get a job near enough that he can do without a car. If he needs a cell phone, we will provide one for him and pay for it. There are no time limits on the offer. No expiration date on this commitment of eternal support.

Over lunch, we make sure that the high stakes of this patronage are clear and brightly drawn. He has a young daughter at home. He invokes her, refers to his obligations and responsibilities, now that he is out. To ensure their relationship survives and has a chance at prosperity, he now has substantial financial support, well beyond what might be ordinary or typical. And he has a lot of soft skills—he is charming and easygoing. Perhaps most of all, in the logic of the family, he is one of us, raised behind the white picket fence in that small town.

You have one strike already, we say. You get one more. One more chance with full support. One more opportunity to draw upon the family as a resource and to get straight.

This sounds great, he replies earnestly between bites. I really appreciate it.

Trauma allows the brain to record memories with greater, more vivid detail. Such memories are just as often fragmentary and incomplete, disorderly, and difficult to set aside. For me, this meal is one such memory. I can recall the smell of the meal, the feel of my fingers around the coffee cup, the look on Eddie's face as we lay out the plan, the sound of the silverware on the plate as he scrapes up the last syrupy bits of pancake. The stakes of the meal are enormous. This is my brother. He is in crisis. If he can't figure this out, I'm not sure what will happen next.

We spend the rest of the meal talking about strategies for the job hunt and for time management. We've brought him a prepaid cell phone so it will be easier to stay in touch, and we fiddle with that for a little while, making sure it is set up right. Our focus on the quotidian details of that moment—adding minutes to the phone so it can be used, programming our numbers into it so he can reach us—distracts us from the overwhelming weight of everything else, from the incipient sensation of impending tragedy. And the contrasting surges of hope.

Looking back on it, this bootstrapping discourse of self-improvement, offered with an adoptive twist, repeats the very first articulations of salvage and repair, way back when we brought Eddie into the family. It echoes Sheryl's plaintive communiqués to him when he was out in Colorado. And it is tinctured with regret, because the repetition of the discourse signals that something isn't working.

I drive him home to his girlfriend's apartment afterward, give him a long hug, tell him we'll be in touch. I text him that night.

"Great to see you, man. Let me know what you need."

"Love you, man," he writes back.

For a couple of weeks, we deliver grocery bags of food and carefully folded stacks of new clothing. We hand over gift cards redeemable only at the local grocery store, stacked with enough credit for Eddie to provide for himself and for his daughter and her mother. Enough, that is, for a family. We routinely refresh the minutes on his cell phone, so that he can contact us—and so that he can have a reliable number for potential employers to contact. We send him uplifting aphorisms, tender declarations of support. We do everything we can conceive of— within the constraints of the troubling rhetoric of safety and distance we all embraced so long ago, pushing together, one last time, against the racialized slope of the ground beneath us all.

One day, Eddie simply stops responding to texts. His girlfriend tells us he is missing. Then, once more, he is back in jail. Visiting his daughter that week, we find the clothing we purchased on the ground outside the house, much of it still folded, and some of it still in the brown grocery bags we used to deliver it, scattered across the ground, like fresh colorful confetti on top of the dirt. We leave it all there.

He has returned to jail, closing a loop that seems predestined—to him and to us.

Is it even possible for anyone to escape the snare of representation? To shed the discourse—the images, the stereotypes, the rumors attached to your body by the larger world? There is a recursive quality to this brief narrative, as it repeats in slow-drip fashion, without much change.

Years later, Mom doesn't remember any of it. Not the lunch at the diner. Not the two-strikes plan. Not the tattered bags of clothes on the front lawn of Eddie's place. "I was such a mess," she says. What is for me the moment of our most profound failure—and one we could not avoid, meaning that it was built into us, and inevitable given the world's commitment to anti-Blackness—can't be recalled at all. She was grieving for Bob and was adrift in her own sadness.

I cannot forget it, though. At night, sometimes I dream of the enormity of the systems and structures and fields of gravity aligned against

Eddie's taking of each breath. The dream takes place on a sailboat, much larger than any we once had on Haunted Lake in Francestown. We're caught up in a storm and an ocean surrounds us. Eddie is overboard. The dark, surging waters drag him underwater, make it nearly impossible to see him, and threaten his body with a drowning. We throw him a life preserver—the round, donut-shaped ones you see in the movies—and he floats back to the surface. And then, after a few minutes, the life preserver disintegrates and the currents drag him back under again. Over and over again, everything around him wants him dead, locked up, left to shrivel away. It is up to us to keep throwing the life preserver into the water. If we miss, he dies. The danger, once more, is the water, the dangerous context of the mere fact of his life. If we don't believe in the life preserver, though, it will fail. It won't keep him afloat. Our doubts are dangerous, too.

And Eddie, for his part, is not a passive actor here. He has a determined will of his own, and is driven by his own interests, his own sense of what is good, or necessary, or urgent, his own demons and angels. Sometimes, in the dream, he smiles and refuses the life preserver and swims away.

With every willful choice that he makes, with every consequence that accrues to those marked as "bad," and with every catastrophic failure of the social safety net, we lurch once more into action.

Bob's final words haunt us: "Keep the family together. Draw strength from one another."

Coda

"Before I start," Bear writes reassuringly in the family group chat, "I want you to know I am well and mostly unharmed. I got assaulted by two young racists this morning." His message goes on for a while, and my eye picks up a few key details. "Baseball bat." "Screwdriver." "Police."

I ignore the rest of the text and call him instead.

"Welcome to America!" he announces, laughing, upon answering.

Bear has lived in the United States for almost five decades, and yet those are his first words that afternoon, "Welcome to America," as if he is suddenly estranged from this place again, once more a new arrival, a foreigner, an outcast. There is frustration in his voice, but there is also the wry humor that has often gotten us through the worst. He is at the hospital in his home state of North Carolina, impatiently waiting to be CT-scanned. He tells me that someone chased him on the highway that morning, called him "n——," and tried to brain him with a bat.

Only a few months earlier, I'd called him to ask a few questions. I was writing a memoir, I explained. About us. Bear confessed to me that he had only experienced racism in its most abstract, "indirect" manifestations. Like every other large Black man, he can recite examples of awkward conversations, cultural malapropisms, and troubling or even disturbing encounters, but he has always contrasted them with his childhood in Vietnam, where his mixed background and out-of-place darkness drew what he called "death stares," saturated with murderous intent, in the midst of a bloody imperial war. Bear wasn't blind to the realities of American racism. He didn't imagine that racism was worse in Saigon. He just hadn't felt the worst of it on the flesh *here*, hadn't been stung or scraped or burned by someone who wanted him dead *in this place* because of his dark-brown skin. Now, he mourns the end of this good fortune.

"I have lived a charmed life," he writes. "I knew it couldn't last forever."

We saw each other just two days earlier, at the close of the latest family reunion, in the summer of 2021. Mom has been organizing these get-togethers for the past decade, up and down the eastern seaboard. Typically, they are at the Jersey Shore, where we have many fond memories. We are, as ever, a family of six, each of us resonating at a different racial pitch. Some of us are in mixed marriages. Others are not. Many of us now have children and partners of our own, and the little ones who assemble with us resonate at odd angles, too. Some are mixed and some are not. Some identify as white, some as different kinds of biracial, some as Asian, and some as Black. There is little abstract theorization of identity at these events—that would be considered rude in a family where most of these issues were largely settled decades ago—and quite a lot of shared, uninterrogated intimacies. A tangled mass of grandchildren on the couch, with various skin tones and hair textures. Big, hearty hugs shared by the adults, along with boastful drinking and rapid-fire catching up, and a dizzying mixture of food and music and culture brought together from around the world. The easygoing practice of a mixture that is fifty years old, rather than its explicit consideration. For us, this is all normal.

Bear arrives at this year's reunion late and leaves early, having driven the farthest, all the way up to Maine from North Carolina. He is Black and Asian, the son of a US serviceman in Vietnam, and a refugee entrusted to adoptive white American parents. For a long time, he has worn these intertwined identities thoughtfully and comfortably. For most of the weekend, he wears a shirt with Vietnamese script on it—and when it is his turn to cook dinner, he makes us a feast of spring rolls and BBQ. A mixed child himself, he jokingly muses with my daughter throughout the weekend about whether her personal genealogy is enough for her to be called Black, or only to be mixed, and she in turn wonders with a grin why it is that everyone seems to think that she is Mexican or Latina, genealogies she cannot reasonably or responsibly claim. They talk about hair and skin. This terrain—this complicated mélange—is comfortable for us all.

We are in Kennebunkport, Maine, home to the Bush family, summer vacation spot of the WASP elite. We are in a big house tucked away on a cul-de-sac near the end of a long road. This is an especially intimate and somewhat jubilant year because the pandemic has pushed off the reunion. Much has changed, but we are all still alive, still relatively healthy, still expanding. Bear, now a mechanical engineer, has brought his new daughter, nicknamed Nugget, to meet us all. A bright, smiling three-year-old with colorful beads in her hair, she gives us all big hugs when she gets there—and we all get hugs again when she leaves to go back home. The embraces confirm it: she is now one of us. Bear's notion of what makes a family, I can't help but notice with a smile, is bigger and more ambitious than ours ever was, including radical improvisations of gender and biology. Nugget isn't his biological daughter; she is a child he cares for.

Despite the camaraderie of the reunion, everyone is on edge. Not for the first time, I note that the idyllic, integrated, multicultural utopia we were supposed to herald has never come. We were a symbol, or a weapon, for a future that has never been won. When we part ways, we all survey the uneven landscape outside, the way the ground is sloped against some of us, depending on skin tone and hair texture, and on the prejudicial eye of strangers. The "goodbye" I whisper to Bear also means "good luck" and "be safe."

"I want you to know I am well and mostly unharmed," Bear's text reads two days later. "I got assaulted by two young racists this morning." The cheery tone is typical. Bear is still the can-do optimist. The story he tells us, though, is grim.

At the end of the reunion on Sunday, Bear returns home to Durham, a trip that takes almost a full day on the interstates. The next morning, he drives to work in nearby Hillsborough. It is early—7:30 a.m.—and the roads are nearly empty. He enters the fast lane to pass a slow-moving car, and an old brown pickup suddenly roars up behind him. He moves over to allow it to pass, but the truck changes lanes, too, and trails him menacingly off the highway. At the first traffic light, two white men jump out of the car and taunt him, promising to *kick his ass*. He pretends to ignore them, and drives through the light to get away, but they continue their menacing pursuit. At another light, one of them rolls down the passenger window and extends his upper body out, gesturing wildly and revealing his sandy-colored hair, his colorful tattoos, and his pale white skin. All in all, they follow him for three miles, right onto the main drag in the town where he works, and at each stoplight, they deliver the same percussive enticement: a challenge to get out of the car. He makes a left turn, and they turn with him. A right turn, and they do the same. And after each drumbeat, Bear finds a way to keep moving forward, hoping to get away from them, to return to a reality he might recognize.

Bear's workplace is across the street from the local police station. He is headed there, assuming that the location of the parking lot might scare them off. He believes, that is, that once he arrives at work his pursuers will see the row of shiny police cars and slink off.

They don't, though.

Instead, the men in the truck are bold. And he is unnerved by that. I can see it in the details of his story as he shares them. Bear is ordinarily cool and unflappable, but he doesn't think to call the police, to call his wife, or to call a friend, which might be a normal response. As a sign of his nervousness, after he eventually pulls the car into the parking lot, he also inadvertently leaves it in neutral—a reflection, he tells me, of his tight, strained focus on other things. Looking up, his eyes widen as he sees in the mirror that they have followed him into the lot and are getting out. He forgets what he is doing and fumbles for the door latch. His failure to put the vehicle in park means that his car rolls backward slowly until it bumps into the rear quarter panel of their pickup, grinding into it with a low-pitched shriek.

Later, when the story's villains hustle to get out of there, the weight of Bear's car will slow their escape. Their truck will have to scrape its way out, forcibly disentangling itself from the encounter, showering the asphalt with tiny red and white and orange fragments of a shattered taillight.

Something in this parallelism strikes me—this image of the physical conflict between two white men and my brother in a parking lot, and the slow-moving material clash of their vehicles in the background. When I try to imagine the scene, I hear the sound of the baseball bat against the side of Bear's head as dramatically crumpling metal and shattering plastic, instead of the flatter tones of hollow aluminum against Black flesh. I hear the furtive, desperate shuffle of shoes on asphalt as if it were rubber tires rolling slowly. Instead of a body falling to the ground, I see the bits and pieces of the broken taillight twinkling like confetti, scattered around and darting left and right.

In the parking lot, the young men—tatted up, Bear recalls—now leap out of the pickup. "Let's get that n——!" they yell, one carrying a bat and the other holding a screwdriver. Bear is relieved, he confesses, to see that neither man carries a gun. Nevertheless, this is serious, an echo of Klan-style aggression against the everyday life of Black folks.

The first one out of the truck hits Bear upside the head with the bat while the other circles warily with the screwdriver. Stumbling forward and desperately shrugging off the first blow, Bear—the broad-shouldered black belt and former linebacker—wrestles the bat away and knocks the truck's passenger down. He turns with the bat in his hand to face the man holding the screwdriver. The two white men finally think better of it, scramble back into the truck, and take off, leaving a short trail of broken plastic in their wake, the air pierced by the sound of the two cars decoupling. If Bear were not so athletic—if he was not deserving of the nickname Bear, that is—he would have been killed.

Bear brushes himself off, shakes his head clear, and walks across the street to the police station to file a report. Walks past that row of police cars, which failed to protect him. He hands the bat to the officer who takes his report.

"He is lucky," I say to myself, "that the police didn't shoot him, a bloody, oversize Black man carrying a bat in broad daylight."

"This stuff is happening everywhere," the cop explains to him with a verbal shrug. The devastating, obvious implication, as Bear sees it, is that this is not a big deal, that it is rather ordinary these days for white people to chase Black people, to call them "n——," and to assault them with deadly weapons.

North Carolina is on fire in the summer of 2021. And in Hillsborough, the fires are most intense. Just two years earlier, I brought a student up to my campus who was protesting a memorial honoring Confederate soldiers on the nearby Chapel Hill campus of UNC by wearing a noose around his neck. He described a hellish state of perpetual war, with armed men and women campaigning for the statue's survival on-site every day. Since then, local reporters have covered the meteoric rise of organized white supremacists, including the taking over of a local bar as a new headquarters for the Proud Boys. Bear recognizes the boldness of those two young men, their refusal to curb their tongues or guard their actions. He sees this all around him. Racists are out in the light and determined to stay there. He understands what is happening in North Carolina in the aftermath of Trump's political desolation. The deeper subtext, he recognizes, is that so much of this—the dismantling of any concern for the common good, any respect for the life of any Black person—can be traced back to the election of 2016. This is the new American terrain. "These people used to live in the shadows," Bear puts it to me later, "and Trump gave them permission to come out. And now they are here with us and they aren't going back into the dark without a fight."

"Death stares."

The phone call hollows me out. I measure the breathtaking precarity of Bear's life against the certainty of my own, comfortable in my whiteness, safe in a deep-blue city and state, and the gap is visible from space. I think back to Peterborough, to my encirclement by those young white boys, by the realization that day—a realization that was at once terrifying and reassuring—that they weren't really interested in hurting me. They chased me through the woods, surrounded me, heckled me. But they wanted to hurt Bear, to scare him away from their town, to jump him in the woods. They wanted to hurt him. They dared not hurt me.

"I'm lucky they didn't have a gun," Bear says, and this is true. Still, I remind him, they had the forethought to keep a baseball bat and a screwdriver handy. And the malice to follow him while he was on his way to work. To trail him for three miles. To harangue him at every stoplight. And the hunger for violence that propelled them to stay in the fast lane, to hurl that old pickup down the highway, to pin themselves to his bumper as he moved through town, all toward some inevitable racialized conflict. Something woke them up that morning and pushed them out into the early morning light to seek out some random Black person and pick a fight. It is, indeed, just plain luck that he is alive. That he wasn't the next Medgar Evers. This sense of fortune or providence extends to their strange improvisations, including their repeated failure to extract him from the car, their doomed effort to provoke a fight far from the flat, suburban street grid of Hillsborough, their wrongheaded decision to go after someone big and dangerous in his own right, someone who could fight back. A different swing of the bat, I know, might have left him paralyzed. A different set of antagonists might have brought a gun. On another day, Bear would be dead. Or, if they found someone else to terrorize, that person would be dead instead. For some other family a similar story surely ended in tragedy. Someone else was beaten, or chased, or worse. Someone else wasn't lucky. Somewhere else, another cell phone pinged with a text, and the first words weren't "I am well and mostly unharmed." Or maybe the phone didn't ping at all, and the family went on about their business, not realizing that a brother, or son, or aunt lay bleeding in a hospital bed, or a jail cell, or a ditch.

I ask Bear if he wants to go to the press. "Baby racists tend to have big brother racists," he responds. "I'd rather not have a target on my back for the big ones." He has to make that same drive every morning, that same grim run through white supremacist country. He has a young daughter, an older stepdaughter, and a wife. He wants to live. He is concerned about preparing for the next time, for the white supremacists with a gun who come for him. I hear something in him that I have never heard before: the diminishment of hope. There is now a sense of inevitability in his voice, the sense that somewhere out there, there is another pickup truck gassed up and loaded with weapons, all prepped to cruise the highways in search of someone Black. Someday, he knows, the grill of that truck will roar into his rearview mirror. Someday he won't be lucky. In preparation for the day his luck runs out, he considers applying for a permit to carry a concealed weapon.

There is a pause in our phone call. Bear is tired and sore. His head is throbbing. He has told this story all day long and relived the chase repeatedly and just wants to lie down and rest. His voice is scratchy.

He begins to repeat himself. We shift gears to bring the conversation to an end.

"Love you, brother," he says. I know he means it.

The next morning, Bear drives his wife's car to work and parks in a different spot, just in case. He sends us texts from the road to let us know that he gets in safely. He keeps us updated about the progress of the investigation. The CT scan comes back clean, and what remains— we all know—is the longer-term, agonizingly slow and uneven recovery from psychological trauma. He will be looking over his shoulder, or hearing footsteps, and watching in the rearview mirror for the rest of his life.

A reporter for the *News & Observer* calls me. I wrote to a friend in Chapel Hill to connect Bear with some resources, and he encouraged the reporter to call me. "They were from out of state," she says. "The police think they were drug runners headed to Florida." Maybe even serial users, she adds. They might have been high. She exhales, hesitating for a second. "These guys won't be caught," she confesses. Another pause. And then: "We should keep your brother's name out of the press." I thought that maybe having press coverage would help ensure that the police would take it seriously. The reporter, though, is worried about blowback from drug traffickers. She says that she is also worried about other, more locally rooted white supremacists reading the story and getting angry and seeking Bear out. "He has such an interesting story," she says. "I hope I can find another way to tell it." I understand what is not spoken aloud: "Let's try to keep your brother alive until that can happen."

It is early evening, so I make a drink. A double. I contemplate heading down to North Carolina, to provide comfort and support. My thoughts turn to Florida. "How hard would it be, really, to find them? And what would I do if I did?" My finger circles the rim of the glass. I look inside for answers and find none.

Within days, Bear's life in North Carolina settles—slowly and imperfectly—back into its old, well-worn pattern. He is urgently needed, he knows. He is our sentinel, our watcher on the walls, in another regard. He has no time to waste on himself.

"I've been out of order for a long time," Eddie wrote to me, just a few weeks earlier. "It's a daily struggle but I'm still here pushing forward." He is still living in North Carolina, still in Durham. And out of prison now. He didn't make it up to Maine for the reunion.

We've had occasional contact over the past few years, and there is always a theme of repentance. He apologizes for his past and asks me for a little help. "I need," he writes, "some things that would help me in my journey." Assuming my lack of interest, he admits that "I'm not asking for the family to send me money personally because I've been known to make bad decisions." "Whatever you can spare," he adds, disarmingly. "I need clothes shoes and boots/work clothes etc. Money can be sent to Bear and he will help me get everything I need."

"Always your brother," he closes.

"Of course," I tell him.

"Don't listen to the words," he writes back, "watch the actions. Thanks."

I send the money to Bear.

For the past decade, Eddie has always trusted Bear to watch out for him. So, too, have we.

Beyond their shared residency in the state, there are good reasons for this delegation. Bear never doubts that Eddie is going to make it— that he is going to dig himself out of a deep hole and rejoin us, return us to some normal, prelapsarian steady state that never was. Eddie has now spent more years in prison than he has spent out of it. When he is out, he needs help just to survive. And despite the early articulation of the bootstrapping, tough-love "two-strikes plan," every month, and in part because of Bear's enduring faith, we still send monthly remittances, proving distant support in those all-too-brief instances of freedom. Bear provides on-location assistance, the pat on the back, and organizes the gift cards, doles out clothing and supplies. He is the designated steward of our youngest brother's half-life, one Black adopted child taking care of another.

"He's back in jail," Bear texts me, just after I dispatch another hundred dollars. Eddie was out for a few months but ran into the wrong people—or rather, as Bear puts it, "stole from the wrong people." Only a few days after his encounter with the racists in the pickup truck, Bear finds himself providing triage for our younger brother.

"He is ready to stop living in the streets," Bear continues.

"I think he is really going to make a go of it."

"This time it is different."

"It isn't up to him," I think to myself.

Beyond the white picket fence, there are only monsters. Bear and Eddie are exposed, and dangerously so.

Bear's capacity for hope is, to me, astonishing. "I think he is going to get on the straight and narrow," Bear writes to me. Eddie was beaten by what Bear describes as "some bad dudes." "He doesn't want that to happen again," Bear says, as if a bright line has finally been crossed, as if the scales have fallen—at last—from Eddie's eyes. He tells me that Eddie has been to a therapist, who has diagnosed him as bipolar and prescribed some medication. This is a new diagnosis, I think, and maybe it is the source of the renewed optimism. Bear tells me that he drives our brother to get his meds, and he sees a real difference. This is Bear's personality. He hopes and he hopes. He is Herculean. He extends himself until he comes close to breaking, believing that he has the strength of thousands.

I recall the long list of the Black dead in the movies we once watched. I can see Bear as a young man, leaning in, inching closer to the television, holding his breath. Jefferson. Nestor. All of them. Sitting with Bear now. Apparitions from the long history of the United States, all of them leaning in, holding their breath with Bear. Hoping with him.

"He is going to survive."

From my great distance, though, I am less sanguine. To me, it feels like the rest of us are all watching a family death that unfolds beyond our line of sight, just over the horizon, where the curvature of the earth obscures. A death in slow motion, where we cannot see it, where we have only historical abstractions to guide our precognitions. I have less hope. But I want to have more. I want to be like Bear.

And then:

Another text.

It is Bear again—still searching the rearview mirror, still struggling with sleep, still circumnavigating the back roads to work—now writing with more bad news. In nearby Durham, Eddie went off his meds and walked out into traffic, possibly seeking to end his life. He was hit by a truck driving forty-five miles per hour. His femur snapped in half, his head was scraped up, and his ribs were broken. The driver stopped and called the police and an ambulance immediately. Eddie lived, but will be hospitalized for months, the doctor says. The recovery will be agony.

"He is going to make it," Bear assures us, by phone and by text.

Despite his eternal optimism, Bear suspects suicide right away. He tells me this privately, offline, and then shares another confidence: Eddie tried to kill himself months earlier in the same fashion, walking out into the street and lying down in front of a speeding car. The car avoided him then, and he was hospitalized and visited by a staff psychologist. The new diagnosis—and the new meds—flowed from that still-too-recent event.

At the hospital, though, Eddie doesn't remember what happened. His skull is covered in scar tissue. His legs are braced. His face is pale. His voice is a whisper. He doesn't recall stepping out into traffic. Bear, who is there when the breathing tube is removed, seems relieved, and hopes that it wasn't what he feared. That it wasn't a suicide attempt. He brings Eddie home, sets him up on the couch, and sits patiently as our younger brother makes his way through a lengthy set of instructions and warnings the hospital has printed up.

Bear sends me a slightly out-of-focus photograph—proof of life, one might call it—but what I see is well-nigh unrecognizable. Half of Eddie's head has been shaved for recent surgeries and his brown skin has been replaced by red-and-pink scar tissue across the bulk of his face. He is hunched over, reading pages of instructions from the hospital, surrounded by bottles of prescription pain medication, some of the most addictive medicines around. I see our youngest brother, shattered into a thousand pieces. I see Bear's perspective in the organization of the photo, in the small bottle of juice within reach, in the hastily taken snapshot, which he meant, surely, to be read with a sigh of relief. There is only a flicker of real life in the frame, though; most of it is proof of Eddie's terrible desolation, and of Bear's inspiring practice of care and hope.

"Why didn't you tell us?" I am curious about Eddie's first attempt at suicide. Or concerned. And hurt. Sometimes, the "fear of a breakdown" in your past, as Maggie Nelson suggests, might well be what causes it in the future. The thing you fear will someday happen is actually a thing you've already experienced. The nightmare of what you initially envision as some undiscovered country is actually the terror of yesterday, a terror you barely remember, if at all. What seems like a prognostication is actually a memory.

"It was a secret," he responds. This is a flat, descriptive fact. Not an answer.

A secret between the Black brothers in the family. Between two Black brothers living in the same town in the American South, the hypsometric curve putting them beyond our sight lines. Skinfolk *and* kinfolk. What a burden for Bear to shoulder alone, I think. Another burden I cannot share. If, that is, it is a burden. Perhaps Bear relies on Eddie for comfort and solace. Perhaps their connection sustains him. Just at the edge of perception, I discern a meaningful Black interiority shared between them, away from the spotlight, offstage, in a place where my eyes cannot—and should not—easily see. I remember that my eyes are not mine alone, and that I bring whiteness with me wherever I go, and to whatever I see.

"A secret."

Maybe, I think, it should be.

We grew up enveloped in protections. I recall the fence at the property's edge, and the gate that closed off the driveway. I remember our old backyard, that green and leafy enclosure where we felt safe and unwatched, walled away from the world by a tall privet hedge on one side, the back of a two-story barn on the other, and our house blocking the street. I can feel the sun on my face as it moves across this private garden. I know how scrupulously we maintained our privacy, our sense of security, our intimacies. And how innocently we engaged, as children, with one another, how carelessly we played with the toxic material of race, in a moment when it seemed like we all might live forever, learn and laugh forever, and be together forever. That is where our story began, in that backyard, guarded by a white picket fence, hidden by nature, in that ark, where we were arranged two by two, in a small town where we were an experiment. Our sense of public mission—troubling, but not fatally so—required a private retreat, a place of respite and recovery.

I imagine Eddie's body, propelled into the street after a concussive, shattering impact, pulpy and nearly unrecognizable. How far we are now from the newspaper photographers, the sanctimonious headlines about saintly parents. His near death didn't merit a mention in the police blotter. An attempted suicide by a Black homeless man with a long felony record, his body etched with prison tattoos, ending up in the emergency room. Just another Black body, denied humanity, struggling to live and breathe, striving for the surface but pinned underwater. Clutching for a life preserver that might not sustain his weight. Not a relic of some grand dream, not a symbol of the nation's idealized self-image as an integrated orchestra, or a melting pot, or a noble venture.

Alone and exposed, in the street and dying, whether this time or next time.

Alone, that is, except for Bear, whose life hangs every day by a different thread.

Alone until Bear brings him home, where he can attempt another heroic restoration.

Acknowledgments

The first debt is to Rama.

I was in the basement of a university library when the haunting memories of my family story first crawled out of an old green folder, gripped me by the shoulders, and shook me down. I was there to write a book about Josephine Baker, the extraordinary African American performer who once conjured up a global family out of thin air, serially adopting children from around the world in the middle of the twentieth century, both to make room for a better future and to attempt to break the modern world. Celebrity is a powerful thing. Ordinary people, I discovered in my research, were caught up in Baker's revolutionary magic. Some of them were charmed forever; others were collateral damage.

Rama was one of those ordinary people, a "Hindu girl" adopted from Belgium on a whim while Baker was on tour. Though the superstar intended the child to be her own, when Baker arrived back at her estate in the Dordogne, she decided to hand off Rama as a gift to her sister, Margaret, who ran a bakery in the buildings adjacent to Les Milandes, Baker's famous sixteenth-century chateau. Tucked away in that green folder in the basement of that library was a small photograph of a slim, chic teenager taken a few years after Josephine's death. Rama. I studied it for a long, long time. And, in a way that is hard to describe, it moved me.

I was writing about someone else's radical, earth-shaking family, when I started to think critically—or carefully—about my own. About its consequential assembly, its political provenance, its willful architects, its collateral percussion. Sitting in the reading room, I was transfixed by the photograph, by the recollections, which were shocking. I leaned in to see the outline of "us"—my brothers and sister. I started to think about JFK airport in 1972, about the white house with the white picket fence, and about so much more. Rama, unflinching, held my gaze. As I remember it now, under her instruction, I started to remember, to think, and to write, privately at first and against my better judgment, about something I have long kept private.

There are many more debts, for sure. Ally La Forge diligently sought out the truth behind some family folklore about William Pratt. In the midst of finishing her own work on Japanese internment, Nicole Sintetos read the whole manuscript and provided an imaginative mapping of its major themes. Kathryn Lofton once encouraged the composition of a few early pieces; if she reads this, she might even recognize a word or two she suggested back in Bloomington. My surrogate father, David Levering Lewis, took time away from his own historical memoirs to ask me, indelicately and yet with tenderness: "What was the point of the whole enterprise?" Harilaos Stecopoulos, then the editor of the *Iowa Review*, published one piece of creative nonfiction about Jean-Claude Baker and encouraged me to go deeper but in a different direction. Khaled Mattawa and Aaron Stone at *Michigan Quarterly Review* stewarded a short chapter draft to publication with great sensitivity. Anonymous readers at *MQR* were candid when it mattered most, giving me the straight facts on skin, the haptic, and touch. Peggy Cooper Davis graciously read the opening chapters and nailed the takeaways. Leticia Alvarado, Denise Cruz, Jacques Khalip, and Hugh Hamilton scrutinized every word and idea, responded to every text and every midnight email, and enthusiastically encouraged me to keep writing, keep going, keep revising. In the last stages of drafting, Leti and Denise also supplied intense, one-on-one conversations about the vexing intimacies of this work. Lisa Redd, another surrogate parent, volunteered to talk adoption. Maud Mandel read a draft of the preface and reminded me that sharing a difficult story is one way to make a new friend. Loc Truong shared a cocktail or two, performed some translation, cracked a few jokes, and rolled the ice cubes in his glass with typical elegance. Mark Simpson-Vos set aside his long-term interest in a book on racial passing to discuss the contract, and to check in on my brother Bear in a moment of truly life-threatening crisis. Eric Estes, our erstwhile dog co-parent, tolerated my cryptic questions over drinks around the pandemic firepit, even in the coldest winter months. The warm virtual community of the Grafton Line endorsed the idea of this book right away. I owe you all, for sure.

I am grateful, as well, to several people I've never (or just barely) met. Maggie Nelson doesn't know me from a can of paint, but *The Red Parts*, which I read in the midst of composing this memoir, inspired me as a would-be memoirist and moved me as a human being. Arissa Oh's historical work on Korean adoption should be required reading for anyone who wants to understand how families are broken and rebuilt, made and remade by war, and I've returned to it regularly as I try to make sense of so many things. Long ago, Julia Scheeres talked to me briefly about the subject of this book, and though she might not remember any of it, her words were decisive. *Jesus Land*, her own memoir, almost broke me. Brought together by Faulkner, Hortense Spillers and I once had a magical dinner in Oxford, Mississippi, and shared some improbable big laughs about Reese Bobby, the neo-Confederate antihero of *Talladega Nights*. The night closed with me standing on the curb, offering thanks for her theoretical work on the hieroglyphics of the flesh—work that, obviously, shakes me still.

Skinfolk would not exist in any form without my unfailingly supportive agent, Faith Childs. It was Faith who phoned me up after reading the brief piece I published in *MQR*, convinced me to set aside another project. And it was Faith who championed the project to Bob Weil, whose demanding intellect, humane curiosity, and insistence that every line of prose should "evoke" haunt me still. Bob, I hope these pages are evocative in all the right ways. Through Bob, I met Haley Bracken, the best assistant editor in the business. Haley got me here, for sure, with her deft sequencing maneuvers and her patience with my imperfect grasp of English grammar, especially the simple comma. Sarah Johnson, my copyeditor at Liveright, can fix my prose any day. Thanks so much, Faith, for making these wonderful introductions to Bob, Haley, Sarah, and so many others at the press. And for believing.

Family is another matter. Our mom has been a widow for over twenty years now. We spoke almost every day while I was writing this book, and she answered every question I asked—no matter how obscure, how banal, how painful, or how difficult—with typical midwestern practicality and fearlessness. My brothers and our sister were involved in very different ways, some insisting on the preservation of their privacy, some laughing about the preposterousness of the idea, and others sharing deeper, previously hidden intimacies. Knowing no other way to be in the world, I am—and always have been—eternally grateful for our shared history and for the history we don't share. I'm so glad we're all still alive, still in conversation, still figuring out together what "we" mean. It could easily have been otherwise.

Robert and Maya, my children, never met Bob. They know my siblings unevenly, because they grew up in Indiana and Rhode Island, far beyond the white picket fence. When I started writing *Skinfolk* they were stuck at home on Zoom. Our summer family reunion had been postponed by COVID. Everything had been canceled. And I was in the attic, writing every day and looking through dusty old bins. Still, I paid attention. They should know how proud it has made me to watch them grow up as the world burns and to hear them take on the uncertain future with determined courage. I hope they find themselves in the pages. I hope we make good trouble together.

Sandra Latcha, my beloved for almost thirty years, read the book in draft, marked it up, insisted that it not vilify anyone unnecessarily, and asked me—asked herself, really—one particularly damning question over and over again. A question that appears herein. "Would I have married you if you hadn't grown up in that family?" I have tried to answer that question, Sandi. Feel free, of course, to disagree.